The Role of Ethics
in Social Theory

ETHICAL THEORY

Robert B. Louden, Series Editor, University of Southern Maine

Recent years have seen a proliferation of work in applied and professional ethics. At the same time, however, serious questions have been raised concerning the very status of morality in contemporary culture and the future of moral theory efforts. Volumes within the SUNY Press Ethical Theory series address the present need for sustained investigations into basic philosophical questions about ethics.

The Role of Ethics
in Social Theory

Essays From a Habermasian Perspective

Tony Smith

State University of New York Press

Published by
State University of New York Press, Albany

© 1991   State University of New York

For information, address State University of New York Press,
State University Plaza, Albany, N.Y., 12246

Production by Marilyn Semerad
Marketing by Theresa A. Swierzowski

Library of Congress Cataloging-in-Publication Data

Smith, Tony, 1951–
    The role of ethics in social theory : essays from a Habermasian
perspective / Tony Smith.
        p.   cm.–(SUNY series in ethical theory)
    Includes bibliographical references and index.
    ISBN 0–7914–0652–0.–ISBN 0–7914–0653–9 (pbk.)
    1. Ethics. 2. Social ethics. 3. Habermas, Jürgen. I. Title.
II. Series.
BJ1012.S53   1991
170–dc20   90-40194
                                                                CIP

10 9 8 7 6 5 4 3 2 1

Contents

Contents

Preface

The essays that make up this book[1] cover a variety of topics yet form a coherent whole. They are all contributions to the same fundamental project: the exploration of the role of ethics in social theory.

Before examining the role of ethics in social theory, we should first consider what exactly social theory is. This is the topic of Chapter I. The overview of social theory presented here articulates the book's unifying framework. I divide social theory into three general areas: social science, social ethics, and social policy.[2] Under these areas there are a number of distinct branches of social theory. The three branches of social science are *empirical research*, the accumulation of both quantitative and qualitative data regarding the social realm (econometric studies in economics, surveys in sociology, etc.); *empirical theories*, that is, hypotheses formed to account for this data; and the construction of *empirical models* (e.g., Weberian ideal types). Social ethics consists of the articulation of the logical structure of different value systems (*value analysis*); the *selection* of one or another of these systems of values; and the *normative evaluation* of general social systems or of specific practices within social systems. Finally, theoretical work falling under the heading of social policy consists in the construction of *normative models* to serve as the ultimate end of our practical activity; and the formulation of *strategies* and *tactics* that set our medium and short term goals, respectively.

I believe that Jürgen Habermas's greatest contribution to social theory can be located in the selection of normative principles.[3] He has provided compelling reasons for accepting the principle of universalizability. The remaining chapters of this book attempt to think through some of the implications of this for various branches of social theory.

Part Two discusses themes that arise in social science. In Chapter II, I first present Habermas's derivation of the universalizability principle, contrasting it with Weber's decisionism. I then argue that Habermas's defense of "critical social science" can be sustained against Weber's insistence on value-free social science. Chapter III examines a number of mechanisms operating in the thought of social scientists studying the agricultural sector, mechanisms that I believe operate in other areas of social science as well. These mechanisms systematically distort what Habermas would term the anticipation of an ideal speech situation. For this reason we may properly term such instances of social science "ideological." Chapter IV has to do with a debate that can be located on the third branch of social theory. It concerns both the construction of an ideal type of historical development, and the role of ethical consciousness in this development. I contrast the model of historical advance presented in Cohen (1978) with Habermas's theory of social evolution. I argue that the technologism of the former must be rejected, and that Habermas's position is more plausible. Habermas sees developments in the structures of moral-practical consciousness as a crucial factor in social evolution, with the principle of universalizability as the most advanced stage in this development.

Part Three of the book deals with normative evaluations. More specifically, both of the chapters in this part engage a recent attempt to argue for a positive evaluation of capitalist markets. Chapter V discusses some of the standard ethical defenses of capitalism found in business ethics texts. Chapter VI replies to an important article by Arnold (1987) on this topic. My arguments in these chapters are once again ultimately based on an appeal to the universalizability principle.

Part Four offers contributions to the construction of a normative model serving as the ultimate end of social policy. Kant, Rawls, and Habermas all defend quite similar versions of the ethical principle of universalizability. They also all construct normative models of the just society within which that principle is supposedly institutionalized. My position is that the normative models these philosophers have constructed are all flawed, and that the model of council democracy that we find in the anti-Stalinist tradition of socialism would better institutionalize this ethical principle. This thesis is defended at length in Chapters VII–IX.

The final two chapters concern the strategies and tactics that make up the remainder of social policy. One of the most profound philosophical issues here is the "dirty hands" problem. The effective actualization of ethical ideals often requires exercises of power that may lead us to compromise precisely those ideals. Habermas's work, discussed in Chapter X, provides a great deal of help in thinking through this tension. In Chapter XI, I discuss the social policy calling for a much closer interrelationship of university research and private industry. I ask: To what extent is this policy compatible with universalizable interests?

I would like to dedicate this book to the people who first taught me the importance of values, Ann Burns, Mary McBurney, and, especially, Alice and Arthur Smith, my parents.

PART ONE
THE FRAMEWORK

Social theory as a whole can be divided into nine branches, each with its own specific tasks. In the following chapter I describe these branches and the complex role played by philosophy within them. I also sketch various connections among the different areas of social theory. Special note should be taken of how ethical considerations permeate the entire enterprise of social theory. It is possible to approach social theory as a whole from a number of different perspectives. Social ethics and social policy could be examined in light of some central notion taken from social science.[1] Likewise, it could be very illuminating to consider social science and social ethics from the perspective of a demand raised within some social policy. In the present work, however, social ethics will form the pivot around which our consideration of social theory as a whole will turn.

I

The Role of Philosophical Discourse in Social Theory

Introduction

Philosophical Discourse in General

At the dawn of history there were but two forms of discourse, the sacred and the profane, myth and ordinary speech. With Greek philosophy theoretical discourse (*logos*) broke off from *mythos*. And so with Aristotle all theoretical inquiry fits under the heading "philosophy." Since then one branch of theoretical discourse after another has split from philosophy. Natural philosophy gave way to the various natural sciences, political philosophy begat political science, economics, and sociology, and in our own day linguistics has arisen from the philosophy of language. It would seem that these inquiries have divided up the world among themselves, each discipline selecting some particular area to investigate. What, if anything, does this leave as a subject matter for philosophical discourse?

After all the other disciplines have completed dividing up the world among themselves there remain four types of questions not yet considered. Philosophical discourse is that form of speech in which such questions are considered and answers to them are proposed. First, each of the other forms of theoretical inquiry are directed towards a particular realm of objects in the world. But besides the objects thought, there is the thinking itself. This thinking can be treated as just another object in the world to be investigated, in which case it is psychology that undertakes the investigation. But

1

this thinking can also be considered as providing an ultimate framework within which all objects (including thought processes *qua* objects) appear. At the most fundamental level one could attempt to articulate the set of basic categories that makes experience coherent and intelligible (e.g., Kant and, more thoroughly, Hegel). Or one could restrict oneself to a particular discipline and investigate the ultimate categories used in that discipline. A physicist, for example, employs the category "time" with reference to specific physical processes; a philosopher of science (who, of course, may also be a physicist) considers the category "time" in its most general significance. Because the ultimate categories we employ determine what sorts of entities are manifest in the world, we may term this first form of philosophical speech *categorial-ontological* discourse.

One category deserves special mention. In both ordinary speech and theoretical discourse the category "truth" is used. Usually this is done in an unreflective fashion. What are the different meanings of this word? How are they related? When—if ever—is it legitimate to employ it? These questions are discussed in a second form of philosophical discourse, *epistemological* discourse.

A third area of investigation that remains after the other disciplines have divided up the world is that of normative questions. Norms are, of course, present in the world in the form of beliefs held by individuals and cultural standards regulating the life of communities. As such they are objects investigated by disciplines such as psychology and anthropology. But the question of whether norms are valid or not cannot be answered by any empirical discipline. To raise and attempt to answer this question is to engage in a third form of philosophical speech, *normative* discourse.

Lastly, other theoretical concerns focus on a particular realm of the world. It is, of course, possible from the perspective of one discipline to consider the relevance of another discipline to its own concerns. In doing so one is still engaged in the first discipline. But it is also possible to ask how a set of diciplines fit together. For example, both neurophysiology and literary studies teach us about human activity. If we ask how the results of these two investigations can be put together, we are doing neither neurophysiology nor literary studies. From Aristotle through Aquinas to Hegel and beyond, philosophy has claimed this meta level for itself. Here the task is to take the results of other investigations and synthesize them into a single coherent perspective to the greatest degree possible. We may term this final form of philosophical speech *systematic* discourse.

Philosophical Discourse within Social Theory

The concern of the present chapter is the role of philosophical discourse within social theory.[1] Social theorists who are also philosophers must regularly confront the question of the nature of philosophical discourse. They must do so in debate with two opposing camps. On one side there are those who feel that philosophy has nothing but obfuscating abstractions to contribute to social theory and that social theorists should concentrate exclusively on empirical inquiries and practical actions. On the other side there are those who feel that merely engaging in philosophical investigations gives philosophers a warrant to pronounce on the social issues of the day. By considering the role of philosophical discussion within social theory I hope to cast some light on the nature of philosophical speech in general. But I also wish to argue against the above two views. Against those who would limit social theory to empirical investigations and practical actions I hope to show the necessity of philosophical discourse within social theory. And against those philosophers who feel competent to pronounce on social issues without a deep and critical appropriation of the relevant facts I hope to show the limitations of philosophical discussion within social theory.

What, then, is social theory? Like other forms of theorizing, social theory can be fixed in terms of the sorts of questions it attempts to answer. Initially we can include under this heading all those disciplines that attempt to answer two questions: How are we to grasp social reality? How are we to transform social reality? All those inquiries concerned with the first question are termed *social science*. All those disciplines concerned with the second question are termed *social policy*. Further reflection establishes the need for a third heading. A divine intellect could grasp all reality at once. But our finite intellects must proceed discursively. A precondition for social science, then, is that we select some limited portion of actuality to investigate. Likewise a divine will could create a totally perfect world at once. But our finite wills must proceed in a more limited fashion.

A precondition for social policy, then, is that we select some limited goals to attain. Interests and values come into play as preconditions for both social science and social policy, as it is interests and values that determine what portions of reality are to be selected for our investigation and what goals are to be chosen for our action. A third branch of social theory deals with these matters, which we may term *social ethics*.

In the remainder of this chapter I shall consider social science, social ethics, and social policy in turn. Each of these headings will be further subdivided; there are altogether nine branches of social theory (see Table 1.1). For each branch I shall consider the role played by the various forms of philosophical discourse, categorial-ontological, epistemological, normative, and systematic. Various positions in philosophical debates that have arisen within social theory will be mentioned as illustrations. No attempt will be made at this point to prove the correctness of one or another position. My goal here is not to resolve any philosophical issue. My goal here is to outline a complete system of social theory and to derive from this outline a systematic account of all the places where philosophical discourse contributes to social theory. Thus this chapter is itself a proof writ large of the contribution philosophical discourse can make to social theory. *Only* philosophical discourse can show the systematic connections among the different branches and thereby make the whole intelligible.

Table 1.1 The Branches of Social Theory

A. SOCIAL SCIENCE
　　1. empirical research
　　2. empirical theories
　　3. empirical models

B. SOCIAL ETHICS
　　4. value analysis
　　5. selection of normative principles
　　6. evaluations

C. SOCIAL POLICY
　　7. normative models
　　8. strategies
　　9. tactics

Social Science

It is customary to divide up "social science" according to the various familiar empirical disciplines, each of which has a distinct object of investigation (e.g., political science for political institutions, economics for the production and distribution of goods and services, etc.). For our purposes however, it is more helpful to make the principle of division the different questions posed in the course of investigations in the social sciences. In the course of answering the general question, "How is social reality to be grasped?" three more specific questions arise: What are the particular facts regarding social reality? How can we account for these particular facts? What can we know of social structures in general? The three branches of social science answer these questions. They are, respectively, *empirical research, empirical theory,* and *empirical model construction*.

1. Empirical Research

All attempts to collect information regarding what the facts are in society fit under this branch of social theory. Examples range from public opinion surveys to estimates of tonnage of steel production in a given year, from researching diaries left by communities of the distant past to the latest unemployment figures. Here, where social theory is the closest to concrete social reality, a number of philosophical questions arise. While we cannot yet talk of systematic issues, categorial-ontological, epistemological, and normative issues are posed.

Categorial-ontological. The most basic categorial-ontological issue is where, if anywhere, the line between "nature" and "society" is to be drawn, a distinction which involves that between "person" and "non-person." Because this issue determines the possible scope of any empirical research in social theory, it must be resolved prior (in a logical sense) to any specific research. Once made, this decision is not without further implications for the research. There is a direct correlation between different views on the distinction and the methodologies deemed appropriate for empirical research in social theory. On one end of the spectrum there are those who insist on an extremely sharp distinction between persons and non-persons, society and nature. For them qualitative methods of research alone are legitimate, quantitative ones being restricted to the investigation of non-persons (ethnomethodology, Garfinkel, Goffman, etc.) On the other end of the spectrum are those for whom the distinction between persons and nonpersons is virtually nonexistent. For them the quantitative research methods that have proven so effective in research in the natural sciences are the only reliable tools for social research as well (e.g., behaviorism). For those who hold an in-between position, a combination of quantitative and qualitative research methods is appropriate.

Once the division between the natural and the social realms has been fixed, a second categorial-ontological issue arises: What are to count as entities within the social realm? No one would deny that individual social agents are to count as entities. But empirical research in social theory would be pointless and blind if it were restricted to inquiring into randomly selected individuals. For empirical research to proceed intelligently the social world must already have been divided up into various groups. To know, for example, how many individuals belong to a certain class or race is a matter for empirical research. But in order to undertake this research the social realm must already have been divided up according to classes and races. This is a matter of social ontology. A socal ontology must be accepted at least implicitly before empirical research can begin. Likewise the lines separating one class from another or one race from another are not simply given empirically. These too are categorial-ontological matters that must be settled prior (logically) to undertaking specific research (although subsequent research may lead the researcher to modify where the lines are drawn).

Epistemological. What is the cognitive status of a social ontology? Are all social ontologies simply socially determined, that is, relative to a particular culture? Or are they relative to the interests of particular researchers? Or can some ways of dividing up the social world claim a validity beyond this? If so, how can such validity be established? Then there are the familiar epistemological questions regarding the research itself, as opposed to the framework within which the research is conducted. What is to count as evidence? What effect does the presence of the researcher have upon the subjects of the research? How and to what extent can these effects be controlled? And so on.

Normative. It is quite obvious that value commitments shape to a considerable degree the way the results of the empirical research are presented. For example, a defender of the capitalist order will point to the quite sharp rise in living standards for U.S. workers since the recession of the early 1980s. In contrast, a critic of that order will point out that real gross weekly wages after the recession remained lower than those attained in 1972. Two other ways in which values operate in research are more hidden. First, values shape the very categories used in empirical research. The U.S. government, for example, does not include under the category "unemployed" those who, knowing they have no chance to find employment, have ceased to look for work. Those holding a more negative evaluation of the capitalist order than the federal government no doubt would consider unemployed discouraged workers as unemployed. Second, the values of the researcher determine the questions asked in the research – and those that are not asked. For decades considerable resources have been spent in the U.S. researching fluctuations in the money supply. But until quite recently no statistics were collected regarding how many firms have engaged in large layoffs of a hundred or more. Clearly the only way we can explain why the first sort of research was undertaken and the second not is by noting that certain value commitments were made prior (logically) to undertaking the research.

Another area where normative issues arise involves the results to which the research is to be applied. Few ethical theorists would dispute that we are morally responsible for the rationally foreseeable results of our acts. Many of the applications of a researcher's work may not be rationally foreseeable to her or him. But many applications are foreseeable, and for these the researcher can be held morally accountable. Market research devoted exclusively toward learning how best to manipulate subjects to purchase unsafe products presupposes the value judgment that such manipulation is acceptable. This is so even when the researcher never reflects on the connection between his or her research and the subsequent manipulation.

We have seen that social theorists engaged in empirical research must take positions on philosophical issues regarding social ontology, the question of truth, and normative commitments, prior (logically) to undertaking their research. For the most part, however, they are not aware of having done this. Philosophical discourse makes the implicit explicit. It articulates in speech the categorial-ontological, epistemological, and normative decisions that have been made. By doing so, it now is possible for the first time to consider the validity of these decisions in a discourse involving a community of speakers. This points to the profound necessity for philosophical discourse. Philosophy brings to light what otherwise would remain hidden, and it allows views to be discussed which otherwise would be simply presupposed.

The limitations of philosophical discourse here are twofold. First, answering the philosophical issues does no more than make explicit the framework for empirical research. The research itself, of course, remains to be done. Second, the philosopher ought always to be open to the possibility that the results of the research may suggest the desirability of revising this framework. Research in the sociology of knowledge, for example, may suggest that a social ontology defended by philosophers as universal and necessary may be conditioned by the class position of intellectuals within a given social order. This in itself does not refute the philosophical claim. Nonetheless it should set off a process of critical self-reflection on the part of philosophers. It is surely as important that philosophers be open to the possibility of revising philosophical views due to empirical research, as that empirical researchers be open to the necessity of reflecting upon the philosophical views implicit in their research.

2. *Empirical Theories*

How can we account for the results of empirical research? All the answers to this question given by the various social sciences fit under this second branch of social theory. Such accounts are concrete in the sense that they are concerned with individual events or processes, or with recurrent patterns of events or processes. Our discussion of the relevance of philosophical discourse to this branch of social theory can be brief, since philosophy's role here is parallel to that in empirical research.

Categorial-ontological. The categorial-ontological question concerning how to delineate the social realm arises in this second branch of social theory no less than in the first. It affects not only the method of collecting data but also the methodology of theory construction.

Here too there is a direct correlation between one's answer to this problem and the methodology that one can consistently employ, and here too it is the former that has logical priority. If a sharp gap between the natural and the social is accepted, then the social sciences must construct theories that are radically distinct from the natural sciences. They will, for example, be seen as being concerned with the interpretation of meanings (hermeneutics). If the line between nature and society is seen as being thin to nonexistent, then the model of natural science will be transposed to social inquiry. The goal of empirical accounts will then be to formulate explanatory laws with predictive powers (positivism). If one's way of categorizing the social world is somewhere in between these two poles, then some sort of combination of explanatory and interpretive methods will be seen as appropriate (Marx, Weber). Thus the philosophical issue must be resolved prior (logically) to the actual construction of empirical theories. Usually the philosophical commitments are made without conscious reflection. Here too the role of philosophical discourse is to bring these choices out into the open, where they can be discussed and evaluated.

Epistemological. Another sort of philosophical issue here concerns the cognitive status of the empirical theories of social science. How are we to consider the truth claims made for these theories? Are they to be taken in a realist sense? Or are they purely instrumental? How are the truth claims to be verified or falsified? Here too the social scientist makes claims whose soundness can only be tested in philosophical speech.

Normative. Just as with empirical research, the ways empirical theories are organized and the sorts of questions they answer or ignore are a function of the value commitments of the social scientists. Likewise social scientists share in the moral responsibility for the rationally foreseeable uses to which their theories are put. Even as staunch a defender of "value-free" social science as Max Weber recognized that values play these sorts of roles in social science (1949, passim).

More controversial is the claim that the very categories employed in constructing a theory involve value judgments (Habermas 1970b). Consider the attempt to account for wage contracts in a given capitalist society. In most writings from bourgeois labor economists the theories

9

that attempt to account for these events employ the category "choice." Marxist economists point out that wage laborers must as a class sell their labor power to one or another member of the class that privately owns/controls the society's productive resources if they wish to guarantee their subsistence. Marxists therefore use the category "coercion" rather than "choice" in their theories. Here it is fairly clear that the very categories used in the construction of an empirical theory suggest value judgments. And there are few, if any, cases of social science theories in other areas where this is not the case as well. In this sense there are grounds to doubt whether there is any value-free social science. But in another sense Weber was right; social science may be value-free in the following sense. Even if the categories social scientists employ suggest certain value judgments, they are never committed to those value judgments even while they employ these categories. More precisely, they may be committed to the values implicit in the categories they use prima facie. But it is always possible for other factors to outweigh this commitment when it comes time for the social scientists to take a value stand.

Weber himself is the best example of the above. Practically alone among bourgeois social scientists, he insisted that the category to be used in accounting for wage contracts in capitalism be "coercion,"[2] a category as evaluative as it is descriptive. But while this category suggests a negative evaluation of capitalism, in his own social ethics Weber nonetheless defended this sort of system on other grounds. In principle this is fully legitimate. No matter how value-laden the categories used in the construction of theories may be, the social scientist who employs these categories is not ultimately committed to any specific set of value judgments. However, few social scientists are as sophisticated in this regard as Weber. So here we have another role for philosophical discourse. It is the task of philosophy both to explicate the values implicit in the categories used in social science, and to insist on the distinction between employing value-laden concepts and making value commitments.

Systematic. We have considered two branches of social theory thus far: empirical research and empirical theories. When one inquires into the systematic connection between them, one is doing neither research nor empirical theory. Such metalevel inquiry is an instance of philosophical discourse. Here the main issue involves the notion of "theory-free observation." To what extent, if any, does empirical research provide access to a reality "independent" of the theoretical framework of the researcher? This question, of course, is directly connected to the question of the cognitive status of both the results of empirical research and the results of empirical theory.

It take it as fairly accepted that while there may be a dumb staring that is not informed by theory, such is not true of observation, or at least not of that observation relevant to questions of verifying theories. This premise implies that in a strict sense one cannot consider research independently from theory construction and leads to a systematic point regarding social theory in general. We shall see that no branch of social theory can fulfill its task without being informed by work done in all the other branches. It is important to recognize the distinct problematics defining each branch, the distinct methods each branch employs, and so forth. Fundamental category mistakes result when these distinctions are not kept clear. Nonetheless, it is also true that these branches form a unity. To treat any one branch as if it could be pursued independently from the rest would be most misleading.

3. Empirical Models

Empirical research and empirical theories are concerned with the investigation and accounting for specific events, structures, and processes in the social world. But scientific assertions can also be made at a more general level. Some examples may help here. Social scientists may research and attempt to explain unemployment levels in specific capitalist countries, say in Brazil in 1920s, the United States in the 1950s, etc. But they may also consider what general tendencies regarding employment follow as a general rule given the set of basic institutions that defines a capitalist social structure. The defender of a "free market" will derive an immanent tendency to an equilibrium at which full employment is attained, while a Marxist will derive a structural tendency for a reserve army of the unemployed to be formed. Social scientists who make assertions of this sort cannot limit themselves to empirical research and empirical theories. They must construct empirical models of social systems (or

11

parts thereof) and deduce immanent structural tendencies from those models.

Similarily it is possible to consider the particular social transformations that occurred in France or Peru during a specific historical period. But it is also possible to ask to what extent there are general patterns of development in social history. This question too demands a distinct theoretical activity, one concerned with the construction of abstract models. In both cases philosophical issues arise.

Categorial-ontological. The main ontological issue here is that of the status to be assigned to the constructed models. For Weber these models are mere thought entities ("ideal types") made up by the social scientist to aid in the construction of empirical theories. They have no independent existence of their own. Marx, in contrast, makes a much stronger ontological claim. Much of *Capital* is devoted to working out a model of the capitalist mode of production and its general tendencies. In his view this model fixes the essence of capitalist societies, the depth level of the capitalist system that underlies surface level appearances. The speech within which this sort of issue is discussed is philosophical.

Epistemological. In this branch of social science models of social systems and processes are constructed that somehow relate to the historical societies more concretely investigated in empirical research and empirical theories. But if no empirical theory is ever directly refuted or verified by any bit of empirical research, so much more is it the case that no construction of a model of a social system or process can ever be directly refuted or verified by any bit of empirical theory or empirical research. To what degree, then, do empirical theories and empirical research provide a check on the construction of these models? This question is connected with one's views on the ontological status of the models. If one believes with Weber that ideal types are simply tools, the models will be subject to the single criterion relevant to any tool, usefulness. If a model proves helpful in any way for constructing empirical hypotheses and orienting research, then it has been "verified." If, however, one believes that a model of a social system or process ought to grasp the essence of historically existing societies, then more stringent criteria for the adequacy of the model are demanded. It must, for instance, be able to give an adequate account of the appearances in those societies. The question of the criteria by which the epistemological validity of models is to be measured is another example of a specifically philosophical issue.

Normative. In constructing models of social systems and processes the social scientist must always abstract from some of the information presented in empirical research and empirical theories. Any principle for deciding how to do this will involve the values of the social scientist. A libertarian, for example, in constructing a model of a capitalist social system will stress those features which make it plausible to assert that an "invisible hand" behind market transactions ensures the common good, and assert that everything else is contingent and nonessential to the system. In contrast, a Marxist will stress those features which ensure the recurrence of class struggle, and assert that everything else is contingent and nonessential. Such differences are inevitable; no models can be constructed without values coming into play in this manner. But it is not inevitable that the social scientist is aware that value judgments are operating here. For this awareness the social scientist must be willing to engage in philosophical discourse regarding normative matters.

Systematic. We have already referred to the feedback relationship between model construction on the one side and empirical theories and empirical research on the other. The materials for constructing a model of a social system or process are taken from empirical research and empirical theories, and the usefulness/truth of a model is somehow measured by the results of empirical research and empirical theories. Conversely, the investigations of researchers and empirical theorists must be oriented by models in order to select what sorts of questions theories should answer and where among the infinite manifold of reality researchers should investigate. To point out that (to coin a phrase) empirical theories and research without models are blind, while models without empirical theories and research are empty, is to engage in neither research, nor theory, nor model construction. It is to take a metalevel stance and engage in philosophical discourse. As we proceed we shall see from this metalevel perspective that model construction is extremely significant in other branches of social theory yet to be considered, especially normative models.

Social Ethics

We have noted that normative issues arise in empirical research, empirical theories, and the construction of empirical models. We shall see below that they arise in social policy no less than in social science. In a fully worked-out social theory these issues are explicitly confronted. For the first time philosophical discourse is not a mere servant to other sorts of inquiry, as was the case in the first three branches of social science. Instead, philosophical discourse now takes center stage (although, as will be seen, it must share the stage somewhat). The main issues to be discussed under the heading of social ethics can be divided up into three questions: What are the various possible value systems? Out of the various possible systems of values, which should be selected? What specific evaluations of social phenomena can be justified in terms of the selected value system? Accordingly, three further branches of social theory are to be discussed here: *value analysis, selection of normative principles,* and *evaluations.* All are examples of philosophical discourse in the normative mode.

4. Value Analysis

The task of social theorists engaged in value analysis is a complex one. They must (1) articulate the various ultimate principles used in normative argumentation; (2) derive the secondary principles that follow logically from each of those first principles; (3) enumerate the values which, while not logically deducible from any given ultimate principle, are logically compatible with it; and (4) list those values which are not logically compaptible with a given ultimate normative principle. In this way the plurality of different value systems is brought to light, along with the inner logical structure of these systems. These value systems can be differentiated according to the scope to which they apply. Ethical principles can have a scope extending to the individual alone, or can be limited to a group, or can extend to a universal moral community.

Categorial-ontological. Two sorts of categorial-ontological questions arise in all the branches of social ethics. While not themselves normative issues, taking a position on them (whether explicitly or implicitly) is a condition of the possibility for engaging in normative discourse. First, how should the ultimate categories employed in normative discourse be fixed? In formulating the various value systems certain basic terms will be used, such as "obligation," "right," "good," etc. These categories must be defined prior (logically) to constructing the plurality of different value systems with their aid. Second, what is the ontological status of these value systems? Some philosophers (e.g., N. Hartmann and Max Scheler) have argued that these value systems form an ontological realm of their own. Other branches of philosophy (hermeneutics, Marxism, etc.) deny this.

Epistemological. In constructing value systems no special epistemological issues seem to arise. The procedures employed in deriving value systems from basic normative principles and in testing the logical compatibility/incompatibility of other values with a given value system do not differ in essentials from familiar logical tools. But epistemological questions do arise regarding how we come into contact with values in the first place. Answers here range from the naturalism of pragmatists to the transcendental intuitionism defended by certain phenomenologists. Different answers to this question will lead to different views on the epistemological criteria for coming to know values.

Systematic. Value analysis is connected to the other branches of social theory considered thus far in a number of ways. First, philosophers who attempt to explore the plurality of possible value systems would be well advised to include in their studies intensive work in areas such as the sociology of religion. Most philosophers are familiar with but a handful of ultimate normative principles. The sociology of religion makes one sensitive to just how vast the number of ultimate principles people have lived by is, thereby helping the philosopher avoid ethnocentrism.

Second, value analysis has an important role to contribute to the theorizing that attempts to account for the behavior of individuals and groups. Such behavior is often motivated by the belief that the behavior is consistent with ultimate values held by the individual or group. These motivations can serve as causes of the behavior. Any theory that attempts to account for this behavior must acknowledge this causal role. It therefore must incorporate reference to the underlying value systems. Of course, people are not always rational. And so the actual behavior will often diverge from that which is logically demanded by adherence to a given value system. Nonetheless, people often enough do act in a fairly rational manner, in which case knowledge of the value system that motivates the action can be extremely helpful in accounting for their actions. And in cases of something less than fully consistent action, knowledge of value systems can help measure the divergence between a person or group's conscious intention and the actual behavior. This is surely relevant to any attempt to propose theories to account for that behavior.

Third, constructing a full model of a social system in the third branch of social theory requires constructing an ideal type of the cultural subsystem. An ideal type of the system of normative principles defining a culture will also rarely have the logical coherence possessed by a value system worked out in value analaysis. Weber, for instance, stressed that the ideal type "Protestant Ethic" includes cultural values that are *not* consistent with the ultimate first principle of the ethic, unconditioned faith in a God who has predestined all. Nonetheless, working out logically consistent value systems can aid in the construction of models of systems of cultural beliefs in that (a) the latter will always have *some* degree of internal coherence; and (b) to the extent they are not fully coherent, the results of value analysis allow the social theorist to measure this divergence.

Finally, value analysis is important for allowing social scientists to reflect on the value stances orienting their own research, empirical theorizing, and model construction. Confronting the plurality of different possible value systems will lead reflective social scientists to greater insights regarding how the specific value systems to which they adhere affect the questions they ask, the categories they use, their acceptance of the foreseeable ways in which their work will be used, and so forth.

5. *Selection of Principles*

Once the plurality of different possible value systems has been presented, the next task is to select one for the orientation of both social science and social policy. No new categorial-ontological issues arise here.

Epistemological. Perhaps the central issue in social ethics is that of the cognitive status of a selected normative principle. Can we know that one normative principle has validity and another doesn't? And if so, how? There are three general types of grounds for selecting a normative principle. The selection could be based either on a decision by the individual theorist, or derived from one or another cultural tradition. Both of these views involve epistemological scepticism, as ultimately no cognitive grounds for defending the validity of a normative principle can be given. The third approach asserts that there are cognitive grounds for establishing the validity of a normative principle.

Systematic. Once a set of principles has been selected, it forms the horizon within which social science (and, as we shall see, social policy) take place. The necessity of philosophical discourse in social theory is perhaps nowhere more clear. More hidden from view, however, is the limitation of this philosophical discourse. Social theorists do not act within a social vacuum. They have been socialized within the dominant world views of their day. It is inevitable, then, that their search for ultimate first principles will often initially conclude with the first principles of these world views. Further, their professional lives revolve around employment, promotion, grants and publications, each of which provides rewards and punishments that serve as filtering devices. It is not necessarily the case that these devices simply filter out views that fail to meet sufficiently rigourous academic standards. It is at least possible that they also tend to filter out views incompatible with the world-views dominant in the society. In this case social theorists may tend to select certain normative principles without noticing that the system of rewards and punishments in their field has preselected that choice. To guard against this, the social theorist must make every effort to become informed of relevant social science investigations. This means investigating matters such as how given socioeconomic interests tend to be compatible with some values and incompatible with others; how the organizations within which social theory is pursued can be structured so as to reward those with value perspectives compatible with certain socioeconomic interests and not others; how intellectuals as a class tend to take on a world-view reflecting their position in the social system, and so forth. Even when social theorists take into account all the relevant findings on these issues, they still may not ever be totally sure their pronouncements are not ideological in nature. But if these findings are not taken into account, it is quite likely that the line between philosophical discourse and ideological discourse will be imperceptible.

6. Evaluations

Having selected a specific value system, the next task for the social theorist is to apply it. This is a twofold task. First, the normative principles are to be applied to the ethical evaluation of the general models of the various social systems and processes. This task is central to political philosophy. For instance, models of slave, feudal, laissez-faire capitalist, welfare-state capitalist, bureaucratic socialist, and democratic socialist social systems can be evaluated from a utilitarian, Rawlsian, libertarian, or Habermasian ethical standpoint. Second, the normative principles are to be applied to the evaluation of specific structures or practices that occur within a given social system. This inquiry is termed *applied ethics*.

Our discussion of this branch of social theory can be brief. No new categorial-ontoloical issues arise. But one systematic point must be stressed. Philosophers engaged in this branch of social theory cannot adequately evaluate either specific practices or general models prior to having attained a detailed knowledge of those practices and models. This requires that social ethicists work closely with social scientists.

Another point involves both systematic and epistemological considerations. I have already acknowledged above that there is a sense in which some work in social science may be said to be "value-free." From a systematic perspective it is possible to combine work in different branches of social theory. More specifically, it is possible to combine work in social science with normative evaluations. (This sort of social science is termed "critical social science," and will be the topic of Chapter II.) What is the epistemological status of the resulting synthesis? Can it also claim scientific standing? Or must it be dismissed as mere ideology? Might the answer vary from case to case? If so, what criteria can be used to distinguish one case from another?

Social Policy

We have traced a systematic progression in social theory from social science to social ethics. Once the question "What can be known about social reality?" has been answered, the question "How are we to evaluate this social reality?" inevitably arises. Likewise, once the latter question has been considered, a third question emerges: "What ought we to do about this social reality?" There is thus an immanent transition from the realm of social ethics to that of social policy. There is a systematic unity to social theory, a unity grounded in the systematic connections among these three questions. While each branch of social theory has its own problematic, its own methods of inquiry, its own standards of verification, and so on, it would be arbitrary to cut off any one branch from the others. To engage in social science, or to proclaim certain value judgments, *is* to effect the social world. The repercussions of a social scientist's research, or of the promulgation of the social ethicist's normative beliefs, are part of a social policy, whether the scientist or the ethicist happens to intend this or not. Engaging in social policy allows the social theorist to become conscious of these implications and to connect her scientific or ethical concerns with a social practice going beyond herself.

From the general question "Wht is to be done?" three more specific questions can be derived, that fix the three branches of social policy. When we take a long-term perspective we must ask, "What ought to be the ultimate end of our actions?" In a medium-term perspective the question arises, "What ought to be the proximate end of our action?" And in a short-term time-frame we must ask, "What ought we to do here and now to attain our proximate end and to move closer to our ultimate end?" The three branches that answer these questions may be termed "normative models," "strategies," and "tactics," respectively.

7. Normative Models

All social action is at least implicitly oriented towards an ultimate end, namely, a model of a social system that the agent accepts as desirable. Social theory has the task of explicating this implicit model. The normative principles selected in the fifth branch of social theory can be used not only in the evaluations of branch six, but also to ground a model of fundamental institutions to be advocated as an ultimate goal for policy. The seventh branch, then, provides a utopian element in social theory, utopian in a positive sense. This utopian element cannot be removed without impoverishing social theory as a whole. Political philosophers have been constructing normative models of social systems at least since Plato's *Republic*.

Categorial-ontological. In constructing normative models philosophers employ terms such as "private," "public," "legitimation," "authority," etc. Conceptual clarification of these terms is not an end in itself. But it is surely an important aid in proposing a normative model of institutions. In the course of such clarification, questions regarding the ontological commitments implied by the categories being used can arise.

Systematic. Obviously there can be a close connection between the empirical models described in branch three and the normative models presently under discussion. The very same model might be involved in both cases. For example, consider the model of a laissez-faire capitalist economic system conjoined with a minimal state. In branch three this model may be presented by economists, political scientists, and others as an ideal type from which empirical assertions regarding the immanent structural tendencies of a capitalist social system can be derived. They may also use the model as a guide for research into and accounts of specific occurrences and processes. For example, they may explain an economic event in terms of how it diverges from what the pure model would lead one to expect, as when "burdensome government regulation" allegedly prevents the market from functioning efficiently. Here the model is an aid in the construction of an explanation. The very same model may now be defended by libertarians in this seventh branch. But the same model is not being considered in the same manner. It is now considered as an ideal, to which reality ought to be made to conform through social policy. Here a normative commitment to the model comes into play that is in principle lacking in the first three branches.

This commitment suggests a close connection between the present branch and the normative evaluation of fundamental institutional frameworks in the sixth branch of social theory. How close is the connection? In branch six normative principles were employed to ground normative evaluations of basic institutional frameworks and processes. When Nozick justifies a laissez-faire economy and a minimal state from the libertarian principle, or when Rawls defends liberal welfare-state capitalism in terms of his difference principle, is this not the same as proposing the ultimate end for social policy? If so, there does not seem to be any good reason for introducing a seventh branch of social theory distinct from branch six.

There are, however, two reasons for introducing a distinct seventh branch. First, when models of social systems are evaluated in the sixth branch these models are viewed either as the essence or an ideal type of past or present social phenomena. But the ultimate end of our social policy may be to bring about a type of social system that has not ever existed. Second, a model of basic institutions that is compatible with our normative principles has met only a necessary condition for being the ultimate end of our social policy, not a sufficient condition. Before even a normatively grounded model can be accepted as the end of social policy, we must be reasonably assured that it (a) can indeed function, and (b) could continue to function over time in a manner consistent with our normative principles.[3] Even models of social systems not yet in existence must meet this condition, given our general knowledge of psychology, sociology, etc. Otherwise we are indulging in utopian speculation, "utopian" in the negative sense of the term. These sorts of empirical matters go beyond what is relevant to the normative evaluations worked out in branch six.

This point can also be made in terms of a difference between "ethics" and "politics." A model of social institutions that is to serve as the ultimate end of social policy, that is, to have practical political relevance, has to take into account more than ethical considerations. As Kant (1970, 112–13) stressed in his *Rechtslehre*, the model must function in a manner compatible with ultimate normative principles *without* being based on the assumption that people will be motivated by a pure duty to obey those principles. Because of this, normative models claiming political relevance must involve features that models constructed with purely ethical considerations in mind may lack (e.g., resort to material incentives, the institution of coercive legal mechanisms, etc.)

While the seventh branch has its own subject matter, it is dependent on the other branches of social theory to a degree perhaps greater than that of any other branch. Fixing a model to serve as the ultimate goal for social policy is entirely a matter of synthesizing the normative principles we have selected, the normative evaluations of social systems based on those principles, and our general empirical knowledge of structural tendencies in various social systems.

8. Strategies

In branches four through seven philosophy has played the dominant role. In the final two branches of social theory we return to a situation analogous to that in the first three branches. Philosophy's role is once again strictly limited. After all, philosophers themselves (or intellectuals as a class) have rarely been the major agents of social change.

The branch of social policy concerned with strategy has the tasks of studying (a) the sorts of alliances among groups that in principle could bring about the ultimate end of the social policy; (b) organizational frameworks that would make these alliances effective; and (c) the strategies that can best form an alliance within one of these organizational frameworks. The empirical information gathered in the social sciences regarding what groups constitute society, their perceived and nonperceived interests, the strengths and weaknesses of various organizational structures, and so forth, are all obviously relevant here. Likewise, so is the normative model that explicates the long-term goal of social policy.

One example of work in this branch is provided by Leon Trotsky (1973). In Trotsky's estimation of the relevant data from the social sciences, wage laborers and small-scale farmers share a basic interest against the system of monopoly capitalism and for worker control of production and distribution. Yet these groups at present do not take a model of worker control as the ultimate end of their social action. Trotsky proposed a medium-term strategy, which he termed a *transitional program*. This program consisted of medium-term goals for social policy designed to fulfill two criteria. First, they must appear plausible to workers and farmers as they are by appealing to their own perceived interests. Second, these medium-term goals must be designed so that in struggling to institute them workers and farmers undergo a learning process culminating in a new understanding of their fundamental interests. For example, workers and farmers today believe that their interests and the interests of the capitalist class can in principle ultimately be reconciled. Hence any attempt to convince them to take on the long-term task of instituting a socialist system of institutions is bound to fail. Thus in his transitional program Trotsky advocated such strategies as demanding complete disclosure of all corporate records. This demand is a reasonable one to workers and farmers as they are. But in Trotsky's view it is one that business cannot fulfill without revealing the extent to which workers and farmers have been exploited. Business can be expected to resist this demand tooth and nail. Trotsky reasoned that workers and farmers, confronting this resistance, would ultimately be led to question their belief in the possibility of harmonizing their interests with the interests of those who own/control capital. They will then be more prepared to form an alliance against this class. Thus the medium-term strategy of instituting a transitional program leads us closer to attaining the ultimate long-term goal.

What role does philosophical discourse have to play here? A very modest one. We have already mentioned systematic connections between this and earlier branches of social theory, connections articulated within a philosophical discourse. Normative issues are clearly involved in that the ultimate end must be clearly kept in mind when formulating medium-term strategies. No new categorial-ontological issues arise; the social ontology coming into play here would be the same as that employed in previous branches of social theory.

This branch does pose a new issue for epistemological discourse. This issue goes back to Aristotle's distinction between *episteme* and *phronesis*. Proposing strategies requires a different sort of insight than that considered thus far in the other branches of social theory. It requires insight into unique historical situations, which Aristotle termed *practical wisdom*. The contrast between this and the knowledge of general laws (and other forms of knowing as well) must be worked out within a general theory of human knowledge. This leads to a further systematic point connecting the eighth with the first and second branches of social theory. If the hermeneutical interpretation of meanings is at the least an important part of social science, and if—as

23

Gadamer (1975) insists – meanings cannot be hermeneutically appropriated without applying them within the theorist's own historical horizon, then there is a systematic connection between hermeneutical social science (concerned with the appropriation of meanings) and strategies (and tactics) in social policy (concerned with applications).

Of course engaging in the various forms of philosophical discourse stemming from this branch does not bring us any closer to being able to formulate correct strategies. Here the philosopher has no special competence. Indeed philosophical training may be a liability. Most ethical philosophers, for example, tend to be idealists in the sense that they believe that transforming shared moral beliefs is a sufficient condition for a fundamental change in social structures. They tend, therefore, to restrict social policy to this. In reality, this is at best one necessary condition among a great many others, such as political organization, mass mobilization of the community, powerful slogans, strategic manipulation of events, and so on.

9. Tactics

The final branch of social theory attempts to offer theoretically defensible answers to the question What is to be done in the short term, here and now? Answering this question involves practical wisdom, *phronesis*, even more than formulating strategies does. Here, too, then, the philosopher can claim no special competence.

No new categorial-ontological, epistemological, or systematic issues arise here. However there is one significant philosophical problem that arises in normative discourse connected with both strategy and tactics: the problem of "dirty hands," a second place where a tension arises between "ethics" and "politics." Let us suppose we are formulating tactics to move towards our medium- and long-term goals. We shall want to select efficient means to attain those ends. But it may very well be that what appears as the only effective means either directly involves activity that contradicts our values and/or has foreseeable secondary consequences that could do so. It would seem that we cannot act effectively in this circumstance without "dirtying our hands." However if in the wish to avoid this we refrain from action, the dirty hands problem comes into play no less. For by supposition we are now acquiescing to a status quo whose continuance also contradicts our values. Hands that do nothing can also become dirty. (For a discussion of these and related issues, see Merleau-Ponty 1969; and Chapter X, this book.)

Conclusion

A number of points regarding the role of philosophical discourse in social theory have been made throughout this discussion. These can be summarized as follows. First, philosophical discourse is autonomous. Discussion of categorial-ontological, epistemological, normative, and systematic matters cannot be reduced to the speech of the empirical scientist or that of the policymaker (or to ordinary language speakers either, for that matter). Our discussion has shown that those who believe philosophy can be ignored in social theory are mistaken. Consider the claim made by some Marxists that concern with questions of ultimate normative principles has no place in social theory. On this view there are simply different classes in struggle against each other, and ultimate ethical judgments are simply a function of which side one is on. These theorists have a point insofar as ultimate principles of justice do not often provide the main *practical* motivation for social change. But from a *theoretical* perspective that is irrelevant. We wish to know what sorts of reasons could be given for one sort of stance rather than another, whether some reasons are more compelling than others, and so on. Once these questions are posed, there is no way around engaging in a specifically philosophical form of discourse.

Second, philosophical discourse has a legitimate claim to being "prior" to other forms of speech: (a) in the speech of the empirical scientist and the policymaker fundamental categories are employed, which define an ontological framework within which science is done and policies are made; (b) in the course of these types of speech, claims to epistemic validity are continually being made; (c) theory and practice in both spheres are oriented by certain normative commitments; and (d) any specific type of theory and practice has systematic connections with other forms of theorizing and practice. Some sort of stand on these categorial-ontological, epistemological, normative, and systematic matters must at least implicitly be made *before* empirical science or policymaking can begin. But in most cases scientists and policymakers do not explicitly consider these issues. Instead they simply take over the dominate assumptions of their milieu without question. Philosophical discourse brings to speech these previously unquestioned assumptions, thereby making them open to investigation. In so doing, philosophical discourse widens the range of human rationality.

Third, despite this "priority" of philosophical discourse, it is also true that philosophy is not fully autonomous. For one thing, it is parasitical on other forms of speech. It is only in the course of attempting to know the world and of deciding how we should act in the world that categorial-ontological, normative, epistemological, and systematic issues arise. Without scientific and policy-making speech philosophical discourse would be empty. An example of this point is the philosophical speech concerned with applying normative principles and constructing normative models. Here it is absolutely imperative that the philosopher critically appropriate the results of the empirical social sciences. In this sense empirical discourse is "prior" to philosophical discourse. This limitation of philosophy shows that by its nature philosophy must be fully open to interdisciplinary cooperation.

An even more striking limitation of philosophical discourse has also been referred to: that philosophical discourse is always historically situated. This means it is situated within a field of power struggles. There are economic struggles over the control of production and distribution. There are political struggles over the control of the state apparatus. There are also struggles on the microlevel. Foucault (1980) has taught us to recognize power struggles in the asylum, the prison, the hospital. He has also taught us to recognize how forms of discourse are situated within these struggles; the discourse of the psychiatrist, the criminologist, the doctor has become dominant because the discourse of the madperson, the prisoner, the patient has been suppressed. The psychiatrist, the criminologist, the doctor may not be aware that their discourse is so situated, and may not intend that this discourse play any sort of role in power struggles. They may think that their speech is simply "rational" and "objective." This misjudgment merely shows the limits of their subjective awareness and private intentions in the face of structural forces. Some philosophers too may be naive enough to believe that their discourse is not situated within a field of power relations and to insist that they too have not intended that their discourse play a role in power struggles. They may also think that their speech is simply "rational" and "objective." But this misjudgment only shows the limitation of their subjective awareness and private intentions in the face of structural forces. Philosophers who truly wish to fulfill the Delphic injunction "Know Thyself" must give up claiming for philosophical discourse a purity it does not have. They must learn to ask of every dominant form of philosophical discourse, no matter how neutral it may appear, what forms of discourses does it suppress, and whose power interests are furthered by that suppression.

In the course of this survey a great number of specific questions have been formulated, far more than can be examined in a single book. It is now time to attempt to answer at least some of the questions that concern the topic of the present work, the role of values in the different branches of social theory.

PART TWO

SOME ETHICAL ISSUES
IN THE SOCIAL SCIENCES

The chapters that make up the remainder of this book all explore
the role of ethics in social theory. Part Two consists of three chapters concerning the role of values in social science. Before we turn
to social science, however, it makes sense to consider branch five,
the selection of normative principles; after all, one's position on the
role of values in social science depends on the normative principles
selected and the cognitive status granted those principles.

One of the central theses of this work is that the *principle of universalizability* is the normative standard that ought to be selected in
the fifth branch of social theory. There are a number of ways to derive this principle, associated with philosophers such as Hare, Singer,
and, originally, Kant. In my view an especially cogent derivation has
been made by Jürgen Habermas within what he terms a *communicative
ethic*. In Chapter II, I defend Habermas's attempt to place the derivation of this principle upon a rational foundation against Weber's
decisionism.[1] As a result the normative evaluation of social systems
and processes (branch six) can in principle be synthesized with empirical social science, a synthesis that may itself claim scientific objectivity. I argue that Habermas is thus warranted in claiming that value
judgments have a legitimate place in social science, as opposed to
Weber's insistence on value-free social science.

Chapter III is a case-study illustrating the connection between
value commitments and social science. In this piece I examine how
unexamined value commitments of sociologists and economists studying the agricultural sector often do not allow generalizable interests

29

to be articulated. As a result their work can be more ideological than scientific.

Chapter IV has to do with an example taken from the third branch of social science, the construction of empirical models. More specifically, the topic concerns the construction of an abstract model of historical development, and the role of ethical consciousness in this developmental model. I contrast Cohen's (1978) model of historical advance with Habermas's theory of social evolution. I argue that the (very sophisticated) technological determinism of the former must be rejected in favor of Habermas's position, which sees developments in the structures of moral-practical consciousness as a crucial factor in social evolution. The connections between these two abstract models of development and more concrete issues of social policy are also explored.

II

The Scope of the Social Sciences in Weber and Habermas

One important difference between "critical social science" and "noncritical social science" can be stated in terms of the branches of social theory outlined in Chapter I. Defenders of critical social science such as Jürgen Habermas hold that when the sixth branch, dedicated to normative evaluations of social processes and structures, is combined with empirical research, theory building, and model construction, the synthesis that results may in principle claim scientific validity. The critics of critical social science, such as Max Weber, deny this. They hold that only value-free propositions may claim such validity. The root of this disagreement lies in their contrasting views of activity within the fifth branch, the selection of the normative principles employed in the evaluation of social phenomena. In this chapter I contrast Weber's and Habermas's views on these issues, and argue that the latter defends the more compelling position.

Weber

Often Weber seems to eliminate assertions that imply value judgments from the scope of the social sciences by definition. For example, he writes of the intrinsically simple demand that "the investigator . . . should keep unconditionally separate the establishment of empirical facts (including the "value-oriented" conduct of the empirical individual whom he is investigating) and his own practical evaluations, i.e. his evaluation of these facts as satisfactory or unsatisfactory (including among these facts evaluations made by the empirical persons who are the objects of investigation). These two things are logically different and to deal with them as though they were the same represents a confusion of entirely heterogeneous problems" (Weber 1949, 11).

Weber often seems to suggest that this logical heterogeneity is sufficient to establish his thesis that the social sciences are restricted to a value-free appropriation of facts. But it is not; one can affirm with consistency that statements of fact are logically distinct from value judgments, that empirical research, theory building, and model construction form branches of social theory distinct from that devoted to normative evaluations, without concluding that a synthesis of the two pursuits necessarily lacks scientific validity.[1]

If it is not the mere logical heterogeneity between assertions of fact and judgments of value that can serve as the philosophical foundation for Weber's position on the scope of the social sciences, what then might that foundation be? It is not "the empirically demonstrable fact that . . . ultimate ends undergo historical changes and are debatable" that removes value judgments from the scope of science, "for even the knowledge of the most certain proposition of our theoretical sciences—e.g., the exact natural sciences or mathematics, is, like the cultivation and refinement of the conscience, a product of culture" (Weber 1949, 55). An argument for value freedom from the fact of the cultural diversity of values thus would prove too much.

Weber's position rests upon certain arguments regarding the cognitive status of value judgments. Whatever else might be the case about statements which fall within the scope of the social sciences, it is clear that they must involve a claim of transsubjective validity. "Transsubjective validity" here has its meaning defined in terms of the notion of "warranted assertibility." A statement can involve a claim to transsubjective validity if and only if its assertion can be defended with good reasons (warrants) in argumentation. If it in principle cannot be so defended, then the statement can still be asserted, but the assertion does not involve a claim to transsubjective validity.

At this point it might seem as if the extremely difficult task of working out criteria for what are to count as "good reasons" must be faced. But this is not the case; the philosophical foundation for Weber's exclusion of value judgments from the scope of the social sciences is that it is not possible even in principle for value judgments ultimately to be defended in rational argumentation, no matter what criteria for "good reasons" are eventually accepted. And if, because of this, it is not possible in principle for value judgments to involve a claim to transsubjective validity, then it is not possible in principle for them to claim scientific validity.

I have just asserted that for Weber values cannot be defended in rational argumentation, and that this is the basis for his exclusion of value judgments from the scope of the social sciences. The following passage, however, seems to call this assertion into doubt: "The statement 'the protection of the weak is the duty of the state' is—if we here first abstract from the vagueness of the concepts 'protection' and 'weak'—a general practical maxim whose truth-content in the sense of ought-to-be-valid obviously also is capable of discussion" (Weber 1922, 311. The translations of all passages from German texts are my own). Weber immediately adds that this is so "in an absolutely different sense from that of the fixing of an empirical fact or 'law of nature.'" Nonetheless, here he takes it as "obvious" that the validity or "truth content" (*Wahrheitsgehalt*) of a value ("practical maxim") can be tested in discussion. If this is indeed Weber's position then his postulate of value freedom is contradictory. There is no reason it would not be possible in principle for a rationally tested practical maxim to serve as the normative basis for a critique of historical processes and structures claiming transsubjective validity. But before Weber is accused of inconsistency, we must take a look at the "discussion" that is to test the validity of practical maxims. What is its structure and where are its limits?

Let us suppose that the relative merits of two practical maxims are to be considered. Weber writes, "The two maxims struggling against each other are ultimately themselves values which eventually must be 'weighed' against each other and between which eventually a choice must be made" (1922, 312). Weber then continues, "But this choice certainly cannot be grounded in the manner of a 'generalization' from 'observation', but rather only in the manner of the 'dialectical' determination of their 'inner consistency', i.e., of the 'ultimate' practical 'axioms' to which these maxims can be traced back (1922, 312–13). Practical discussion in this sense places the value embodied in a given imperative within the context of an internally consistent system of values. At the "summit" of this system lies the ultimate practical axiom from which the value in question can be derived. If two values are being discussed they will prove either to be compatible (if both fall within the same value-system) or not. In either case, the choice for or against a given practical maxim concludes the discussion, and that choice is grounded in an acceptance or rejection of highest practical axiom of the value system within which the maxim falls.

The next question which arises is, of course, what justifies the choice of the ultimate practical axiom itself? Weber's answer is simply that the "ultimate possible attitudes towards life are irreconcilable, and hence their struggle can never be brought to a final conclusion. Thus it is necessary to make a decisive choice" (1969, 152).

Weber, then, allowed for and encouraged the open discussion of practical maxims.[2] This activity was termed "value analysis" (the fourth branch of social theory) in Chapter I. The goal of such discussion is "to lay out the decisive, not further reducible axioms, upon which conflicting standpoints rest, so that one can choose" (Baumgarten 1964, 103). The limits of rational discussion are reached with the uncovering of these decisive axioms. But when we turn to the selection of normative principles (branch five), decision based solely on subjective belief takes over. Now, as Robert Alexy (1978) points out, "This has the consequence that the correctness or truth of the statement to be grounded [a given value judgment grounded in terms of the ultimate practical axiom from which it can be derived] can be spoken of only in a very limited sense. The arbitrariness of this decision would be carried over to the whole grounding which is based on it." If the taking of an option for or against a system of values is based ultimately on a simple choice, then in principle no evaluation based on that value may claim to be transsubjectively valid and in principle defensible in rational argumentation.

It is extremely important to be clear on this point. This does not mean that values play no role in scientific activity.[3] Further, the principle of value freedom does not mean that values cannot be made the object of scientific inquiry. Also, the principle of value freedom does not mean that scientists must refrain from making value judgments in their writings or lectures. While Weber himself chose to refrain from this, he did not see this as a matter of principle; scientists may interpose value judgments in their writings and lectures without contradicting the principle of value freedom as long as they make clear where scientific assertions end and value judgments begin. But for Weber "critical social science," the attempt to claim scientific validity for a synthesis of empirical and normative propositions, is a contradiction in terms. This is so for the simple reason that "critical social science" invokes subjective beliefs that have no cognitive claim to being rationally defensible.

The value freedom of Weberian social science can be made clear through examining the concept of "legitimation." In Weber's social science, "legitimation" refers to the belief of the members of a social order that an institutional arrangement is legitimate. For social science, "It is only the probability of orientation to the subjective belief in the validity of an order which constitutes the valid [i.e., the legitimate] order itself (Weber 1964, 126). Thus from this perspective any social order is "legitimate" if the belief systems of its members result in their action being oriented in a certain direction. And it is impossible to criticize the legitimacy of any social system by reference to some normative principle without overstepping the boundary of social science.

Habermas

From the perspective of the present work Habermas's most significant contribution to social theory falls within branch five, the selection of normative principles. Habermas claims to have established that there is an "ultimate value axiom" the acceptance of which does not rest on a subjective and ultimately irrational decision, the principle of universalizability. Because this principle is built into the structure of communication, he claims, the normative force of this principle is no more a matter of personal choice than is the necessity of engaging in speech.

Habermas explicates conceptual connections among the following notions: "communicative action," "validity claims," "discourse," "ideal speech situation," and "principle of universalizability." In communicative social action[4] validity claims are made. The acceptance of these claims (to truth, truthfulness, and normative correctness) forms a "background consensus" without which the language game in question would cease to function. These claims are accepted only so long as the participants find it plausible to assume that they could be shown to be worthy of recognition were they to be called into question. When this assumption is no longer present, then either the communication breaks down or an immanent transition is made to a discourse situation in which the validity of the claims is tested through argumentation. If this argumentation is to proceed without coercion, then an ideal speech situation must be anticipated. In an uncoerced discourse within which an ideal speech situation is anticipated, only those claims that embody generalizable interests would be agreed upon. Hence there is a nonarbitrary link between "communicative action," on the one hand, and the "principle of universalizability" on the other, a link mediated by the immanent connection between the validity claims necessarily made in communication and the testing of those claims in discourse. Thus "universalizability" is not a principle itself in need of justification. It is not a principle opposed to other principles, chosen as a result of a merely subjective decision. It is derived rather from the very structure of communication itself:

> The problematic that arises with the introduction of a moral principle is disposed of as soon as one sees that the expectation of discursive redemption of normative validity claims is already contained in the structure of intersubjectivity and makes specially introduced maxims of universalization superfluous. In taking up a practical discourse, we unavoidably suppose an ideal speech situation that, on the strength of its formal properties, allows consensus only through generalizable interests. It is based only on fundamental norms of rational speech that we must always presuppose if we discourse at all. (Habermas 1975, 110)

With this we are not only at the heart of Habermas's theory of practical discourse, but at the cornerstone of his social theory as a whole. He has written, "The fundamental norms of possible speech built into universal pragmatics contain . . . a practical hypothesis.

From this hypothesis . . . the critical theory of society takes its starting point."[5] What this means is that the principle of universalizability, an ultimate value axiom whose acceptance does not rest on an arbitrary personal decision, provides a normative standard that may serve as the basis for a critical evaluation of social phenomena claiming objective (transsubjective) validity. Thus the philosophical foundation has been provided for a critical social science, that is, a type of social science that goes beyond Weber's restriction of social science to a value-free appropriation of facts. When confronted with a plurality of conflicting values a choice among them can be based on rational argumentation, as long as the value system chosen embodies universalizable interests (as determined within a practical discourse which anticipates an ideal speech situation). As Habermas writes, "It is not the fact of [value] pluralism which is disputed, but the assertion that it is impossible to separate by argument generalizable interests from those that are and remain particular" (1975, 108).

Has Habermas adequately answered the Weberian position? A Weberian might very well agree that a nonarbitrary resolution of value pluralism is indeed possible once a principle of universalizability has been accepted. Nonetheless, our Weberian might continue to insist, the acceptance of this (or any other) value principle itself rests on a mere decision.

For Habermas to answer Weber fully two propositions must be established: (1) The anticipation of an ideal speech situation is not based on a merely arbitrary decision; and (2) The principle of universalizability is "built into" speech which anticipates an ideal speech situation.

Proposition 2 is unproblematic. In a discourse without coercion the participants would agree only to proposals and evaluations in their interest. Any consensus reached would be thus an expression of generalizable interests. It is proposition 1, then, upon which Habermas's attempt to construct an alternative to Weber rests.

Habermas's efforts to establish proposition 1 rest on a unique sort of argument, with a unique structure and, most importantly, with conclusions that claim a unique status. We can term this argument a tu quoque ("you also") argument.[6] This argument can be reconstructed as follows. Let us suppose that someone is attempting to refute Habermas's thesis by imagining some more or less involved counterexamples (a typical pastime of philosophers!) in which the ideal speech situation is *not* presupposed. Habermas would claim that his thesis that an ideal speech situation is anticipated in all communicative speech can be defended and rationally affirmed prior to hearing the results of these counterexamples. This can be done simply by considering the process whereby the philosopher who had imagined the counterexamples would attempt to convince her colleagues that she has indeed provided a refutation of Habermas's notion of the ideal speech situation.

A refutation can be undertaken only through the presentation of arguments. It is, of course, always possible for a speaker to bring about a change in the attitude of an audience through the threat of force. Ordinary usage, however, quite correctly refuses to term such a process of manipulation a "refutation." An argument that is to count as a refutation brings with it a claim to be rationally compelling. In other words, it is implicitly supposed that the force of the better argument, and not argument by force, prevails. It is precisely this situation that reference to the anticipation of an ideal speech situation attempts to explicate. Thus any attempt at refuting the notion of an anticipation of an ideal speech situation—which, *qua* refutation, must be presented as an argument—itself *presupposes* that anticipation. Of course, this does not mean that Habermas's theory of the ideal speech situation cannot be revised in the sense of being open to proposals for clearer formulations, conceptualizations that bring out aspects neglected in Habermas's account, and so on. But it does mean that the general point of Habermas's thesis cannot be revised or refuted because any attempt to do so itself presupposes precisely that which it set out to question.

So far, all that has been established through Habermas's tu quoque argument is that presenting an argument rationally presupposes the anticipation of an ideal speech situation. Could one not grant that on the level of argumentation the ideal speech situation indeed is anticipated, while insisting that the move to the level of argumentation itself involves a nonrational decision? In other words, a new Weberian objection might be formulated stating that if one is in the language game of argumentation, then the ideal speech situation may indeed be anticipated, but in presupposing that we are in this language game Habermas has begged the question. Argumentation, after all, is surely not the only language game. And so the *tu quoque* argument has at best a restricted significance; it does not establish the relevance of the ideal speech situation to any other language game besides that of argumentation.

We are already familiar with Habermas's reply to this objection from the above discussion. Any functioning language game, that is, any language game within which an exchange of speech acts takes place such that communication occurs, presupposes a background consensus. That background consensus is not part of an immutable order; for any number of reasons it may break down. When it does break down, that which was taken for granted before must now be made a subject for discussion and argument if the communication is to be reestablished. Thus any functioning language game always has an immanent connection to the language game of argumentation. The ideal speech situation, and the principle of universalization built into its structure, does not rest upon any arbitrary choice that we make, beyond the "choice" that always has already been made for us to be communicating beings:

> Anyone who does not participate, or is not ready to participate in argumentation stands nevertheless "already" in contexts of communicative action. In doing so, he has already naively recognized the validity claims – however counterfactually raised – that are contained in speech acts and that can be redeemed only discursively. Otherwise he would have had to detach himself from the communicatively established language game of everyday practice. The socio-cultural form of life of communicatively socialized individuals structurally refers every interaction context to the possibility of an ideal speech situation in which the validity claims accepted in action can be tested discursively. (Habermas 1975, 159. See also Beatty 1979)

Habermas, then, has successfully presented an alternative to Weberian value analysis. If the anticipation of an ideal speech situation is not based upon an arbitrary decision, but is rather built into the structure of all communication; and if a principle of universalizability is built into the communication that anticipates an ideal speech situation (since in an uncoerced speech situation participants would agree only to what was in their interest, so that any consensus reached would be an expression of generalizable interests); then it follows that the acceptance of a principle of universalizability is no more arbitrary and based on mere decision than is the fact of human communication. What implications does this have for the social sciences?

Critical Social Science

The goal of the present section is to show how Habermas, armed with the critical standard of "universalizability," proposes to fulfill the project of formulating a critical social science. I shall limit my discussion of this topic to the notion of legitimation critique.

In his discussion of the fundamental concepts of sociology, Weber defines "legitimation" in terms of the empirical probability that the behavior of the members of an order is oriented by a belief in the legitimacy of that order. It has been shown that this value-free conceptualization is a function of Weberian value analysis. Habermas proposes an alternative conceptualization. Referring to the political order he writes, "Legitimation means that the claim to be recognized as correct and just which is bound to a political order has good arguments for itself: a legitimate order deserves recognition" (1976, 271). Referring to the speech acts through which an order is manifested, he continues, "I would like to proceed from the fact that the statement 'recommendation x is legitimate' is equivalent in meaning to the statement 'recommendation x is in the general (or public) interest,' whereby x can be as well an action as a norm of action or also a system or norms of action (in our case: a system of authority)" (1976, 298). The key terms in these passages are "good argument" and "general interests," respectively; the latter specifies the content of the former. Given the connection between these two notions, which Habermas would claim is established in the theory of practical discourse, the scope of an empirical theory of legitimation is broadened considerably from Weber's formulation.

Given sufficient factual knowledge of a given social framework, it is in principle possible to reconstruct the social processes that would have resulted had disputes been resolved through practical discourse. In other words, we can answer the question,

> How would the members of a social system, at a given stage in the development of productive forces, have collectively and bindingly

interpreted their needs (and which norms would they have accepted as justified) if they could and would have decided on organization of social intercourse through discursive will-formation, with adequate knowledge of the limiting conditions and functional imperatives of their society? (Habermas 1975, 113)

This can then be used as a basis for a critique of the legitimation of that society if the following assumptions are made:

I make the empirical assumption that the interest constellations of the parties involved, which are revealed in the cases of conflict, coincide sufficiently with interests which would have to find expression among those involved if they were to enter into practical discourse. Furthermore, I make the methodological assumption that it is meaningful and possible to reconstruct (even for the normal case of norms recognized without conflict) the hidden interest positions of involved individuals or groups by counterfactually imagining the limit case of a conflict between the involved parties in which they would be forced to consciously perceive their interests and strategically assert them, instead of satisfying basic interests simply by actualizing institutional values as is normally the case. (Habermas 1975, 114)

If these points are granted, then we can construct and compare the following columns:

1) validity claim to legitimation	1) validity claim to legitimation
2) overt or hidden conflict	2) discursive testing of claim
3) particular interests retained	3) norms of ideal speech situation
4) resolution based on overt or hidden power ("argument of force")	4) true consensus/justified compromise' ("force of better argument")

Both frameworks begin with the usually unproblematic validity claims of everyday interaction. But the process on the right brackets out these validity claims in order to test them through seeing whether they embody universal interests. This process and its results then can be compared with the conflict and power struggle to resolve it—either latent and in need of theoretical reconstruction or else given historically—within the given society. To the extent that these processes differ, the former can be used as a basis for the critique of the legitimacy of the latter. This critique does not refer to the subjective psychological belief systems of the members of the society, but to rationally established normative claims. Thus the Marxian tradition of social science with a critical intention is secured and continued.[8] This is, of course, quite vague. Perhaps an explication of the methodology Habermas would employ in the legitimation critique might be useful. As I understand it, there are a number of steps to be performed by the social theorist. I shall now consider these in order.

(a) Some central event of the historical and cultural order in question is selected out.

(b) If this central event is a series of nonlinguistic social actions of some sort, then its meaning content must be transformed into speech utterances. ("All meaning contents which are presented in expressions and actions in principle also must be able to be transformed into speech utterances, while the semantic contents of speech in no way are all capable of translation into action and expressions" ["Theorie der Gesellschaft," in Habermas and Luhmann 1972, 195].)

(c) The speech utterances of the test case in question next must be translated into the standard form of speech acts; that is, the illocutionary force of the speech art ("I assert to you . . .") must be clearly distinguished from its propositional content (". . . that the cat is on the mat.").

(d) Each speech act (better, the person through the speech act) reveals something of the intentions and attitude of its speaker, involves an assertion regarding the objectified world in its propositional content, and constitutes an interaction with its hearers through its illocutionary force.[9] The structure of the event in question thus can be traced in terms of a conversational analysis. Each speech act is considered relative to the manner in which the cospeakers are opened to the realms of "inner nature," "outer nature," and "society," respectively.

(e) Each speech act in a functioning language game not only has the three pragmatic functions of opening cospeakers to the realms of inner nature, outer nature, and society, but also involves claims to truthfulness, truth, and normative correctness, respectively. Therefore, through conversational analysis we also can trace the structure of the event in question in terms of the validity claims that are made, implicitly if not explicitly, by the various participants. Because our concern is with the question of legitimation, the first two types of validity claims can be neglected in this analysis. This brings us to stage 1 in the columns of the previous page.

(f) Conversational analysis can then proceed to uncover whatever manifestations of power determine the course of the event. From this perspective the Weberian (1964, 152) definition of power ("Power is the probability that one actor within a social relationship will be in a position to carry out his own will despite resistance, regardless of the basis on which this probability rests") seems too restricted. Even if there is no "resistance," we can still say there is "power" if a speaker or group of speakers "carries out their own will" in cases where the validity claim to normative correctness made in their speech and action could not be discursively redeemed, that is, is not universalizable (stages 2, 3, and 4 of the lefthand column).

(g) Discovering whether or not the claims uncovered in (e) can be redeemed discursively requires that the social theorists simulate a discourse within which the arguments that could be presented for and against these claims, are reconstructed. Through such reconstruction it should be possible, in principle at least, to distinguish arguments that could be defended in a practical discourse anticipating an ideal speech situation from those that do not (stages 2, 3, and 4 of the righthand column).

(h) Steps (a) through (g) next must be repeated with other "test cases" from the sociopolitical order in question.

(i) If at a certain point it becomes clear that interests established as universalizable are systematically ignored in the institutional order in question (i.e., if there is a systematic divergence between steps (f) and (g), then the judgment that the given order is not legitimate (in a strong, non–value-free sense) can be made rationally.[10]

In all this neither the possibility nor the importance of Weberian value-free social science, which for the most part fits under the column on the left, is denied by Habermas. For example, empirical studies concerning the subjective belief systems of the members of an order are both possible and important from Habermas's perspective (otherwise step (f) would be impossible to carry out). But for Habermas the state of affairs that a given order cannot be justified rationally in a practical discourse which anticipates an ideal speech situation (i.e., that an order does not embody universal interests) is itself an objective fact about that order: the order is not legitimate whatever the beliefs of its members might be. Particular empirical studies may choose to abstract from this, but social science as a whole cannot do so. On Habermasian principles, derived from his analysis of values, such "critical" facts also fall within its scope. Given Habermas's point of view, Weber's limitation of the scope of scientific claims is a mistake.

In this chapter I hope to have established two theses. The first regards the fifth branch of social theory, the selection of normative principles. Following Habermas, I hold that there are compelling reasons to accept the ethical principle of universalizability. The second thesis is that when normative evaluations based on that principle are combined with empirical studies in social science, the result in principle may also claim scientific standing. Chapter III will discuss an issue somewhat related to the latter thesis. Chapter III, and all the remaining chapters in this book, explore the implications of the former thesis for the different branches of social theory.

III

Agricultural Science and Ideology

In the previous chapter I discussed the cognitive status of critical social science, that is, social science that explicitly includes evaluations of empirical processes and structures based on an acceptance of the normative principle that social processes and structures should be consistent with the universalizable interests of the community. In this chapter I turn to a related problem. What status should be assigned to the work of social scientists when that work includes implicit normative evaluations based on principles that are not consistent with universalizable interests? In agricultural science, as elsewhere, academic experts confidently claim "objectivity" and "impartiality," and unhesitatingly assume that they are fully capable of separating scientific assertions from value judgements. However I believe that many social scientists studying agriculture implicitly presuppose the normative principle that corporate interests ought to be served first and foremost, and implicitly include normative evaluations of agriculture-related phenomena based on that principle in their work. In social theory "ideology" is a technical term used to describe assertions that claim to be objective, impartial, and scientific, but that actually serve the interests of ruling groups. In this chapter I shall explore some of the ways agricultural science is ideological.

This chapter has two parts. In the first, I discuss some examples of ideological thinking taken from agricultural science in general. In the second, I shall specifically discuss the family farm. The general examples discussed will be taken from a workshop I attended funded by the Kellogg Foundation. For two weeks a dozen faculty members from liberal arts departments at Iowa State University listened to presentations from a variety of academic experts connected with agriculture. Again and again these men (only one woman speaker) shifted back and forth from relatively straightforward, empirical assertions to more or less crass apologetics for the corporate system of agriculture. These shifts took place within the course of a page, a paragraph, a single sentence, or even a single clause. It became evident to many of us attending the workshop that the aura of scientific objectivity often masked a style of thinking where ideological considerations so interpenetrated scientific considerations that one could not say with confidence where one began and the other ended.

This sort of speech is not innate. It must be learned. But neither is it, as far as I could tell, something consciously taken on. The vast majority of the speakers, at least, sincerely felt that their talks met strict canons of objectivity and would be offended at any accusation of partiality. And yet an unexamined partiality and objectivity were somehow fused. In the course of academic training (if not before) scientists are somehow socialized in this strange style of speech and they come to accept it as second nature. This discourse has its own rules, its own patterns, its own logic. I would now like to list some of the discourse mechanisms that were used at the workshop, mechanisms that ensured that the presentations reinforced the powers that be in agriculture although (in most cases at least) this was not the conscious intention of the speakers. Many of these mechanisms are rather obvious, and no claim for the completeness of this list is being made. Nonetheless, it is hoped that this catalogue, provisional as it is, can illuminate some of the forms of ideological speech within agriculture in specific and social science in general. The ideological mechanisms I shall discuss are the exclusion of relevant questions, the omission of known facts, the retreat to abstract models, and the failure to consider relevant power relations. In the second part of my paper I shall argue that the same mechanisms regularly operate when agricultural scientists discuss the family farm. In the terms of the previous chapter, these mechanisms can all be critiqued from the standpoint of a discourse that anticipates an ideal speech situation. These are mechanisms that cut off speech before the point where the universalizable interests of the community can be articulated. It is this, and not the inclusion of normative evaluations, that makes this type of social science ideological.

Ideological Mechanisms in Agricultural Science

Exclusion of relevant questions. An agricultural scientist involved with a consortium that coordinates the transfer of agricultural technology from land-grant colleges to the Third World gave a lecture on the economics of world hunger. The central thesis of the lecture was that however important a factor the unequal distribution of income and power may be, the most significant issue in the hunger problem is the lack of advanced technology in the Third World. As the crucial evidence for this thesis the speaker referred to the fact that even if one totaled all the food presently grown in Africa with Africa's entire food imports and then divided this sum equally, there still would not be enough food to provide the African population with sufficient nutrition. But before we conclude that the problem is primarily a technical one, we should ask what sorts of crops are being produced in Africa. Specifically, suppose that an ever-greater proportion of African cropland is devoted to crops with low nutritional content. Then it could very well be that the problem lies first and foremost with the social relations of economic power that lead to this sort of production, and only secondarily with technical matters. In fact, over the last twenty years in Africa coffee production has increased by 400 percent, tea production increased sixfold, sugar production went up by 300 percent, cocoa and cotton production doubled, and so forth (Dinham and Hines 1981, 187). These increases occured because the native African population, lacking disposable income, offers a poor market for agricultural products. So production controlled by giant transnationals shifts from the production of foodstuffs for local nutritional needs to luxury items of low nutritional level for the export market. The speaker was an expert on the topic of world hunger in general, and of hunger in Africa in specific. His

47

talk made use of a vast array of statistical information. Yet not only did he not incorporate this shift to export production in his talk, he did not seem to be familiar with how massive this shift has been.[1]

Of course no one can know everything. But that a specialist in this area would not know basic relevant facts reveals more than a simple gap in his knowledge. It reveals, I believe, how ideological factors have permeated agricultural science. Somehow something like a filtering device is operating here that tends to filter out from consideration obviously relevant issues when these issues threaten the implicit normative acceptance of the status quo. Such a filtering device operates as the scientist is doing science, so that the very act of doing science is at one and the same time ideological.

Omission of known facts. A specialist in agricultural economics spoke at the workshop on the factors that contribute to the price of food. He especially stressed what a large component of final prices was made up by labor costs. It soon became clear that what he termed "labor costs" included the salaries of agribusiness executives as well as that of workers in the food industry, the $339,000 the head of Hormel receives alongside the Hormel workers who had a wage cut of 23 percent imposed upon them despite the firm's profitability. When pressed, the speaker did not know how to divide up these "labor costs" in a more accurate fashion. Here we have another case of a filtering device at work, filtering out a clearly relevant question. But another omission, even more striking, points to a different sort of ideological mechanism.

In the course of an hour-long presentation on food prices not once did the speaker mention oligopolistic concentration as a factor in the price of food. When pressed, he admitted that economists do accept a correlation between concentration in a sector and higher prices. When further pressed, he agreed that in every major food group (bakery, dairy, canned fruits and vegetables, processed meats, sugar, etc.) four firms or fewer control more than half the market. He eventually admitted that the USDA did a study which asserts that as a result of these quasi-monopoly conditions consumers suffer overcharges amounting to 10 percent of their total food bill (in the breakfast industry alone these overcharges are estimated at more than $200 million a year.) Yet he did not see fit to mention any of this in what was otherwise a quite exhaustive discussion of the factors affecting food prices. Subsequent informal discussion with him convinced me that he had sincerely tried to present the relevant facts regarding food prices as he saw them. How then could he have omitted factors that he himself knew and that he himself later admitted to be relevant? Once again we must have recourse to the idea that somehow or other in the course of being socialized into an academic discipline, one undergoes more than the transmission of scientific information and procedures. One may be simultaneously socialized into a world-view determined as much by what it excludes as by what it includes. Besides filtering devices that screen out relevant questions that could call into question the established state of affairs, apprentice scientists somehow also may internalize ways to filter out known relevant facts that could have the same effect. As a result, each individual assertion made by a given scientist could be fully warranted by the strictest standards of scientific reasoning, and yet her reasoning as a whole could nonetheless be thoroughly ideological in character due to what was systematically omitted.

Retreat to abstract models. When the shift to cash crops was introduced by participants as a possible factor creating hunger in the Third World, a number of agricultural economists introduced the concept of "comparative advantage." According to this notion, initially formulated by David Ricardo (1953), if each country specializes in what it can produce most efficiently, and then trades with other nations that have comparative advantages in other areas, all nations will be better off than if each country attempted to produce all it required itself. According to this reasoning it makes good economic sense for Third World countries to specialize in the export crops they can produce efficiently, sell these crops to First World countries, and then use the money they receive from these sales to import grain and industrial products more efficiently produced in the First World.

In the abstract this reasoning has some cogency. But it ignores the concrete context of world trade. Third World producers are in tremendously competitive sectors of the world economy. Yet when they purchase the inputs they require they must turn to a handful of transnationals based in the First World. Likewise when they sell their output they must turn to a handful of First World firms. A competitive sector sandwiched between two oligopolistic sectors will inevitably experience disadvantageous terms of trade. And in fact, the prices of the crops sold predominately by industrial countries (grains, soybeans, etc.) have risen much faster than the prices of the commodities exported by the underdeveloped countries. So have the prices of manufactured goods imported from the First World. In 1960, three tons of bananas could buy a tractor. In 1970 the same tractor cost the equivalent of eleven tons of bananas and in 1980 the figure stood at twenty tons. And Third World countries receive back very little of the final price of their agricultural products. For every dollar spent on an agricultural product from the Third World, only about fifteen cents goes back to the producing country (George 1984, 10). A full year of Africa's exports can pay for only twenty-seven days' worth of imports.

In light of all this, to refer to the *abstract* model of comparative advantage when discussing the *concrete* impact in the Third World of export crops on local nutritional needs is simply not to be doing science, whatever the scientific rigor used in constructing that abstract model. It is a way of using science to provide an ideological legitimation for existing patterns of trade.

Failure to consider relevant power relations. Many within the academic community have come, somewhat belatedly, to the realization that the current use of agricultural chemicals cannot continue (in the United States alone, for example, over 1.1 billion pounds of pesticides are used each year). The financial burden this places on the farmer and the environmental burden placed on nature can no longer be ignored. Few agricultural extension scientists, however, are prepared to call for a major shift to organic farming. More are slowly beginning to advocate Integrated Pest Management (IPM), where the selective use of chemicals is combined with biological defenses against predators, and the development of environmentally safe forms of biotechnology.

This development is progressive. Nonetheless, claims were made for IPM that cannot be justified. The claim was made by agricultural scientists at the workshop that with the move to IPM, along with recent developments in biotechnology, the trend has been already set in motion away from the heavy reliance on agricultural chemicals. This claim grossly understates the power of agricultural chemical companies, which enjoy immense profits. Today they spend twice as much on market development as they did a decade ago. And today the agricultural chemical companies, who control most of the biotechnological research being done, are not giving priority to research developing plants that are resistent to pests. Such plants would be ecologically beneficial, but not especially profitable for companies that sell products to get rid of pests chemically. So instead, as Congress's Office of Technology Assessment has stated, "It should be kept in mind . . . that much of the agricultural research effort is being made by the agricultural chemical industry, and this industry may see the early opportunity of developing pesticide-resistant plants rather than undertaking the longer-term effort of developing pest-resistant plants" (quoted in the *Nation*, July 7–14, 1984, 13). Ciba-Geigy, CalGene, Monsanto, Du Pont, and other chemical companies are presently developing strains of plants able to withstand potent herbicides. This hardly counts as the abandonment of chemical farming.

The predictions made by agricultural specialists that we are well on our way to solving the problem of environmental damage from chemicals ignore the interests of the chemical companies in a future world of bioengineered crops that grow well only in combination with chemicals; they also ignore the power of these companies to bring about such a world. Power relations within the agricultural system are not taken into account, power relations that make it likely that the problem of agricultural chemicals will remain serious despite the best efforts of a few extension scientists. Predictions that fail to take into account power relations are, in short, more ideological than scientific in character, whatever the private intentions of those making the predictions might be. They systematically exclude consideration of the extent to which the present social order is compatible with generalizable interests.

Ideology in the Family Farm Debate

In the remainder of this chapter I shall argue that the standard academic discussions of the family farm betray the same sorts of ideological mechanisms as those just discussed. The structural position of the family farmer in the United States is quite similar to the fate of Third World agricultural producers. Family farmers are also caught in a competitive sector sandwiched between sectors of extremely concentrated economic power.

Family farmers are independent and dispersed producers. Because of this structural fact they are incapable of influencing the prices they must pay for necessary agricultural inputs or the prices they receive for their agricultural output. On the input side of the equation the family farmer confronts a tractor attachments industry where the four largest companies accounted for 80 percent of sales; a harvesting machinery industry where the top four firms had 79 percent of sales; an industry producing nitrogenous and phosphatic fertilizers where the eight largest firms had 64 percent of total agricultural chemical sales; and the pesticides industry where the top four firms had a 60 percent market share (These and the following statistics are found in Wessel 1983, passim). When dispersed producers confront concentrated suppliers, the terms of exchange always favor the latter. The Federal Trade Commission (FTC) found monopoly overcharges of 5.784 percent for farm machinery and 4.2 percent for the feed industry. If these percentages are applied to sales revenues in these industries, farmers were overcharged $827 million for farm machinery and $775 million for feeds in 1980. Taken together, the overcharges accounted for over 8 percent of net farm income that year. If similiar rates of overcharge existed in the other major farm supply industries that year, the total loss to farmers amounted to at least $2.8 billion, or one-seventh of their total net income (See *Antitrust Law and Economics Review* 5 [3]: 33, table 1). Another manifestation of the structural weakness of the farmer in confronting this concentrated economic power is that between 1973 and 1980 the cost of production outpaced the price increases farmers received by more than 40 percent. With terms of trade this unfavorable it is no wonder that the family farmer fell into deep debt; in 1970 the interest on farm debt equaled about 24 percent of total net farm income; a decade later, 80 percent.

It is true that as this debt accumulated and farmers cut back their purchases, farm suppliers eventually became squeezed too. But this is not likely to bring much relief to farmers over the medium to long term. Instead, farmers will confront an even greater concentration in the farm supply industries. John Deere, for instance, is expected to increase its market share from 35–40 percent to around 50–60 percent. This increase will allow farm suppliers to demand even more favorable terms of trade from farmers.

On the output side of the economic equation the same situation holds. Dispersed farmers must sell their grain on a market where about 85 percent of the world's trade in grain is handled by just six companies. These companies, by the size of their transactions and their access to information the family farmer lacks, are able to influence the market to their advantage and at cost to the independent producer. Similar conditions prevail in food processing and distributing: .25 percent of food companies now control two-thirds of the industry's assets. Here too there is a direct correlation between market power and higher prices. An internal FTC report noted that "if highly concentrated industries were deconcentrated to a point where the four largest firms control 40% or less of an industry's sales, prices would fall by 25% or more (1969)."

The situation is serious indeed. Thirty-five years ago the farmer received about half the consumer's food dollar. Today the farmer gets much less as a result of the structural features I have sketched. In 1979, for instance, about 69 cents of every dollar spent on food went to firms that transport, process or retail domestically grown food commodities. Of the remaining 31 cents, 17 cents went to the farm supply industries, and 10 cents went to pay farm expenses such as rent, interest, capital depreciation, and taxes. This left the farmer with about 4 cents to pocket. In 1980 even this small sliver of the domestic food dollar received by the farmer declined by nearly 40 percent to only 2.5 cents, and the situation has not significantly turned around since. This should come as no surprise given the extremely concentrated economic power that confronts the farmer with respect to both input and output factors.

Such is the underlying structural logic of the farm crisis. Yet throughout the farm crisis how often have speakers from the agricultural scientific community mentioned it? Very, very rarely. Can this be an accident? Or might it be because relevant questions have not been asked, because known facts have been omitted, because agricultural scientists think in terms of an abstract model of markets as neutral mechanisms for allocation and ignore the concrete reality of markets as places where economic power is exercised? Whatever the reason, whenever agricultural scientists ignore the structural power held by agribuşiness corporations over the family farm, their discussion is more ideological than scientific, whatever their intentions might be. Their scientific work is permeated by an implicit normative acceptance of this power of agribusiness, the validity of which is not subjected to testing in a discourse anticipating an ideal speech situation.

My topic here is the connection between social ethics and social science. However a brief digression connecting the above to social policy is warranted, for if the diagnosis of social scientists studying agriculture is ideological, their policy recommendations will be no less so. Many proposals, for instance, those advocating that credit be eased or that the government bail out agricultural bankers in danger of going under, leave the underlying structural factors that caused the problem in the first place completely untouched. They are Band-Aids for a gaping wound. Conservative "compete or die" policies (for example, vast reductions in grain price supports) would in the short term lead to massive windfall profits for food processors, who today continue to raise prices despite using ever cheaper grain. In the short to medium term these policies will eliminate vast numbers of farmers. The result will be a tremendous increase of huge corporate farms, which already account for more than 50 percent of agricultural cash receipts although they represent only 5 percent of all farms. In the long term farming itself might well become almost as concentrated as the farm supply and food processing industries. At that point the few farmers that remained would not suffer from the disadvantageous terms of trade today's family farmer faces. But then *every* link of the food stream leading to the consumer would be controlled by oligopolies. The inevitable result: a tremendous increase in food prices for consumers.

I am afraid that many liberal solutions would lead to exactly the same results. One proposal attempts to save family farms through mandating by law that they act as if they were oligopolies and undertake a drastic reduction of production in order to raise prices. But then food processors would simply pass on these higher costs to consumers. According to some studies, this should amount to no more than an extra one cent per loaf of bread. But given that food processors raise prices significantly even when they use cheaper grain, I am afraid that without strict price controls—which are not a feature of the proposal—we must expect that they would use any rise in their grain prices as an excuse to gorge consumers and that they would then shift the blame onto farmers. Who benefits when food prices are raised at a time when millions of people in the United States remain out of work? Who benefits when food prices are raised at a time when, according to a study done by the Harvard School of Public Health, approximately one-quarter of all United States children are malnourished? A proposal like this simply plays off one group of troubled Americans against another, while leaving the interests of agribusiness untouched. To talk of cutting the production of food while hunger remains a major social problem strikes me as morally questionable.

If the problem of the family farm is to be resolved in a manner that addresses the roots of the problem, a new social movement must arise, one that is not afraid to attack the underlying structural problem, one that is not afraid to challenge the concentrated economic power of the Cargills and the Beatrices. That you will not hear agricultural scientists talking this way has everything to do with ideology and very little to do with science. Consider an argument actually presented to us at the Kellogg workshop by an economist: "Farmers trusted the bankers who lent them money. They have since discovered that bankers will put their own interests far above the interests of farmers. Therefore, farmers should accept the process presently reducing many of them to tenancy and should align with their prospective landlords." In itself, this is simply a bad argument, an extremely bad argument. From an assertion regarding the relationship between Group A (farmers) and Group B (bankers), one logically cannot conclude anything regarding a relationship between Group A and Group C (landlords). Yet, once again, more is going on here than a simple mistake by a given individual. This argument *would* work if we could presuppose that the only groups farmers can work with are bankers and landlords. If the farmer has given up on the former, it would indeed be valid to conclude that the only alternative is to cooperate with the latter. Precisely this assumption was silently presupposed not just by this speaker, but by almost all the agricul-

55

tural experts who spoke to us. The very possibility of other forms of alliance was systematically repressed in a process of which few if any of the speakers were conscious.

But of course there are many other groups with whom family farmers can ally in a new social movement. For every farmer in the United States there are five farm laborers, slaving for low pay under dangerous conditions, harassed by immigration officers and outside the protection of national labor laws. There are tens of thousands of truck drivers getting the produce to market. There are tens of thousands who work in packing plants and supermarkets, most of whom have had huge wage cuts imposed upon them these past years. There are black farmers, who have been losing their land at a rate twice that of white farmers, while the federal government has pursued a deliberate policy of driving them out of business (between 1979 and 1983 federal farm loans to black farmers fell by 71 percent). There are tens of thousands of rural women getting ready to take on leadership roles. And there are, of course, the tens of millions of food consumers whose nutritional levels will be threatened by any rise in food prices resulting from concentrated economic power. All of these groups, who together constitute a vast majority of our nation, have a common interest against corporate agriculture. If these groups could somehow be united within a common organization, say, a labor/farmer/consumer party, then the social processes that agricultural economists assure us are "inevitable" and "irreversible" would lose that appearance at once. Such a movement could demand strict interpretation and enforcement of existing antitrust laws, and the legislation of new ones. Such a movement could demand full and public disclosure of all corporate records in the farm supply and food processing and distribution industries. Such a movement could demand that family farms receive parity for their products while simultaneously demanding strict price controls to prevent oligopolies in food processing industries from passing on those higher prices. Such a social movement could demand that any processor who went on an investment strike to protest its loss of profits from these price controls would have its assets seized and handed over to its workers. Such a social movement could assert that basic nutrition is a fundamental right of all humans, and not something for only those with sufficient disposable income. These policies can be defended within a discourse anticipating an ideal speech situation. They represent generalizable interests and therefore have a firm normative basis. Today in this country our political imagination is so stunted that we cannot even conceive of such radical solutions. But the demise of the family farmer and the eradication of our rural communities will continue unless the underlying structural forces behind that demise and that eradication are removed. Attaining this goal will require a massive social struggle. It is my hope that the community of social scientists will participate in that struggle. It is my fear that on the whole this community is part of what must be struggled against.

IV

Two Models of Historical Materialism

Besides research and the formulation of theories directly accounting for the results of that research, there is a third branch of social science, the construction of empirical models. In this chapter I shall examine a debate within Marxist social theory that occurs within this third branch. Besides empirical research regarding specific transitions in history, and besides theories attempting to account for those transitions, Marxists have proposed general models of historical development. This part of the Marxian project is termed "historical materialism." There are a variety of versions of historical materialism. Two of the most significant recent versions will be discussed here. For G. A. Cohen technological advance is the "motor" of history, pushing forward changes in the political, legal, and cultural spheres. Habermas, however, asserts that changes in the structure of moral-practical consciousness are at the center of historical development, and that these changes cannot be reduced to mere functions of technological growth.

In the previous chapter I have argued that Habermas's derivation of the ethical principle of universalizability provides both a normative foundation for critical social science and an aid in uncovering ideological components in social science. The conclusion of the present chapter is that this principle, which stems from the most advanced stage in the development of moral-practical consciousness, must play a central role in an adequate model of the stages in social evolution. Before making this case, however, we shall first turn to the quite different perspective defended by G. A. Cohen. The strength of Habermas's position can be better estimated when we see how it can resolve difficulties that beset Cohen's view.

Four points should be made at the outset. First, the following discussion for the most part stays on an abstract level. A more complete comparison of the two positions would show how the abstract models of historical development proposed by the two thinkers could illuminate concrete historical research and theory building. This chapter, however, is limited to a consideration of the internal coherence of the abstract models and their practical implications. Second, although I periodically shall refer to the founder of historical materialism, I shall not address the exegetical question whether one or the other theorist has better captured Marx's own position. In his excellent review article, Richard W. Miller (1981) already has shown that Cohen cannot make good his claim that the version of historical materialism he defended is "Marx's theory of history." And Habermas (1979a 130–177) stresses that his theory is a "reconstruction" of Marx's position and not an attempt to reformulate it. Third, this chapter is restricted to a comparison of Cohen and Habermas's models of historical advance. Metatheoretical issues are introduced only when necessary for this task.[1] Finally, certain criteria for testing the adequacy of versions of historical materialism will be assumed here. These criteria will be taken from the position the construction of models of historical development holds vis-à-vis the other branches of social science, on the one hand, and social policy on the other. For a position to count as being an adequate formulation of historical materialism it must be theoretically adequate and have an immanent relation to emancipatory praxis. The main theoretical tasks are to account for past social development in a coherent fashion and to provide plausible reasons for positing a stage of future development after capitalism. The main practical task is to provide a theory capable of orienting emancipatory struggles for socialism, the stage that is to succeed capitalism.

Cohen

Historical materialism often has been identified with a defense of what can be termed the "monocausality thesis." This thesis asserts that technological development (the development of the "productive forces" of society) ultimately is the sole cause of world history. Cohen's position attempts to resolve the following difficulty. He is quite obviously attracted to the monocausality view of historical materialism as articulated by Plekhanov.[2] As opposed to those who defend what Cohen (1978) disparagingly terms a "zig-zag 'dialectic'" (138) of multicausality, Plekhanov and others who defend the monocausality thesis have made a strong claim with admirable clarity. However, theorists like Weber have shown the causal influence political, legal, and cultural phenomena often have on the production relations of society, and the causal influence these in turn have upon the development of the productive forces. In response to this problem Cohen replaces the monocausality thesis with a functional explanation of history. As we shall see below, with this move Cohen (1978) feels that he can defend a "'technological' interpretation of historical materialism" (29) a la Plekhanov without leaving himself open to objections from the Weberian camp. This belief poses three tasks for our discussions. First, Cohen's general theory of functional explanation must be presented. Next the arguments with which Cohen defends his interpretation of historical materialism as a functional explanation must be examined. Finally, the congency of these arguments must be evaluated.

Functional Explanations in General

Since the concern here is not with metatheoretical issues, I shall not attempt to assess Cohen's theory of functional explanation on its own terms. Here his views on the nature of functional explanation are of interest only so far as they illuminate his theory of historical materialism. Cohen (1978) characterizes functional explanation as "a special type of causal explanation . . . deriving its peculiarity from generalizations of distinctive logical form" (250). He terms this unique type of generalization a "consequence law," defined as a "universal conditional statement whose antecedent is a hypothetical causal statement" (1978, 259). That is to say, "If it is the case that if an event of Type E were to occur at t_1, then it would bring about an event of type F at t_2, THEN an event of type E occurs at t_3" (1978, 260). Cohen (1978) insists that this type of explanation is distinct and not a mere mirror image of ordinary causal explanation. It asserts that the explanation of the occurrence of an event (or property, etc.) is that were an event of this type to occur it would have a specific effect: "The character of what is explained is determined by its effect on what explains it"(278).

Not all consequence explanations are functional explanations. A consequence explanation could articulate a dysfunctionality if the effect in question leads to the dissolution of the relevant organism, social system, and so forth. Functional explanations are only those consequence explanations in which "the occurrence of the explanandum event (possession of the explanandum property, etc.) is functional for something or other, whatever 'functional' turns out to mean" (Cohen 1978, 263). For example, the explanation of a religion could invoke the fact that this religion is functional for the stability of a given society.

One other feature of functional explanation must be noted. Not all identifications of function provide functional explanations. Staying with the above example of a religion, Cohen (1978) writes:

> The society may indeed require a religion, but it is a further question whether it has one because it requires one. It may have one not at all because it needs one, but for other reasons. Imagine ten godless communities, each, because it lacks a religion, teetering on the brink of disintegration. A prophet visits all ten, but only one of them accepts his teaching. The other nine subsequently perish, and the single believing society survives. But they took up religion because they liked the prophet's looks, and not because they needed a religion (though they did need a religion). So the fact that there is a religion, and it is needed, does not show that there is a religion because it is needed. That demands further argument. (281–82)

This "further argument" must establish that it was a *dispositional fact* in that which is to be explained (the society's acceptance of religion) that led to the functional effect (stability), and not any merely accidental happenstance (such as attraction to the prophet's looks). More formally, in all functional explanations "a dispositional fact explains the incidence of the property (or event-type) mentioned in the antecedent of the hypothetical specifying the disposition" (Cohen 1978, 263).

Historical Materialism as Functional Explanation

In the beginning chapters of his work Cohen (1978) combines a careful study of certain texts from Marx and Engels with rigorous conceptual analysis to distinguish sharply the following spheres: (1) the productive forces, (all the constituents of the production processes considered as "material," that is, solely as processes of transforming nature; for example, machines, raw materials, technically employable scientific knowledge); (2) the productive relations, the economic structure or basis of society (the relationships of de facto control that fix the social roles within which production occurs); and (3) the superstructure, (the legal system that mainly fixes relationships of de jure ownership/nonownership, the state, and so on.) The central questions for any general model of history, Cohen supposes, are (1) Why is the base, the economic structure, the way that it is?, and (2) Why are the parts of the superstructure the way they are? In Cohen's interpretation, historical materialism answers these questions with functional explanations. To the latter question Cohen's answer is that "superstructures are as they are because, being so, they consolidate economic structures." His response to the former question is exactly parallel: "The economic structures are as they are because being so, they enable productive power to expand" (xi).

On the above view the ultimate explanation of history is the expansion of productive power. Cohen therefore feels that he remains true to the technological interpretation of historical materialism. But within this framework he also is able to reject the monocausality thesis. Cohen (1978) can accept, for example, Weber's hypothesis that the Protestant Ethic (a superstructural phenomenon) affected the development of the productive forces; he insists nonetheless that it arose precisely because (i.e., is functionally explained by the fact that) it was suited for the development of new productive capacity: "Protestantism arose when it did because it was a religion suited to stimulating capitalist enterprise and enforcing labour discipline at a time when the capital/labour relation was pre-eminently apt to develop new productive potentials of society" (279).

Generalizing from this example, he asserts: "Production relations profoundly affect productive forces, and superstructures strongly condition foundations. What Marx claims to explain has momentous impact on what he says explains it. Construing his explanations as functional makes for compatibility between the causal power of the explained phenomena and their secondary status in the order of explanation" (1978, 278). Cohen does not offer any argument in support of his view that superstructures evolve in order to consolidate economic structures.[3] As Cohen presents no argument in favor of this view we shall not examine the claim here. Instead we shall focus upon the heart of Cohen's position, his view that the economic structure is as it is because of the productive forces.

Cohen presents two arguments in favor of this position. The first argument establishes what he terms the *development thesis* (1978, 150ff.). The first premise of this argument asserts the rationality of human agents. Rationality is taken to be a fact of human nature. The second premise introduces a fact of the human situation: it asserts that humans inhabit a world indifferent to their survival, a world in which there is a scarcity of the goods necessary to satisfy human needs. The final premise asserts that as intelligent beings humans will act in such a manner as to improve the situation mentioned in the second premise. From these premises Cohen derives the conclusion that there is a tendency for the productive forces to develop. He writes, "Rational beings who know how to satisfy compelling wants they have will be disposed to seize and employ the means of satisfaction of those wants" (1978, 152), these means being the productive forces.

Cohen himself points out two weaknesses of this argument. In many circumstances people do not behave rationally. And even when they do, it is possible that material scarcity is not recognized as the most important problem facing a given society. If different concerns are viewed as more pressing, human rationality may be devoted toward them and not toward development of the productive forces. In Cohen's opinion neither of these difficulties outweighs the fact that societies have rarely replaced a given set of productive forces with inferior ones. He feels that his argument can account for this lack of regression. Hence, while it may not be conclusive, it is nonetheless "substantive."

Cohen's second central argument employs the thesis of the tendency of the productive forces to develop as its first premise. To this he adds as a second premise the historical fact that not all economic structures are compatible with given productive forces. From these two premises Cohen (1978) draws the *primacy thesis* as conclusion, which asserts that the production relations will change to avoid impeding further productive development, that the productive forces are "primary" vis-à-vis the production relations (158). In other words, the productive forces select production relations according to their capacity to promote the development of productive capacity (1978, 162). The argument is meant to establish a functional explanation of the production relations in terms of the productive forces: "The nature of the production relations of a society is explained by the level of development of its productive forces" (1978, 158).

Evaluation of Cohen's Position

For a position to be an adequate formulation of historical materialism it must fulfill two theoretical tasks. It must account for past social development in a coherent fashion, and it must provide plausible reasons for asserting that there is a stage of development after capitalism. It also must fulfill the practical task of orienting emancipatory struggles for socialism. In this section I shall examine Cohen's position on these points.

Theoretical issues. Although Cohen doesn't mention it when he presents his argument, the gaps in the argument for the primacy thesis are just as significant as in the argument for the development thesis. Quite simply, his conclusion does not follow from the two premises. From the premises one legitimately can derive the conclusion that changes in production relations can be functional for productive development. But, as Cohen himself stresses in his chapter on functional explanation, not all identifications of function provide functional explanations. And so his conclusion, formulated as a functional explanation of the production relations, is not warranted as the argument stands. That conclusion could only be drawn if Cohen provided an analysis that uncovered "dispositional facts" within the production relations that lead to productive development as an effect. Cohen later mentions certain facts about production relations that suggest how he would fill this gap.

In class societies production relations fix a structure that leads to latent or overt class struggle. Cohen argues that there exist certain dispositional facts regarding production relations that specify which of the participants in class struggles are likely to emerge victorious. The class whose interests are most compatible with the development of the productive forces, he asserts, will tend to be successful in class struggles:

> Classes are permanently pointed against one another, and that class tends to prevail whose rule would best meet the demands of production. But how does the fact that production would prosper under a certain class ensure its dominion? Part of the answer is that there is a general stake in stable and thriving production, so that the class best placed to deliver it attracts allies from other strata in society. (1978, 292)

If one grants that this is a defining dispositional fact regarding the production relations and employs this as a third premise in the argument for the primacy thesis, then Cohen's conclusion would follow. An argument, of course, can be logically valid without its conclusion being true. Considerations internal to Cohen's own position suggest a serious difficulty with this argument. Consider two economic structures S and R, with S a "kind of economic structure just higher than R," that is, S allows more productive capacity than does R and there is no third set of production relations that allows more productive development than R but less than S. When considering whether the proposition, "If an economic structure of kind R actualized its maximum productive potential, then an economic structure of kind R perishes," is true, Cohen answers, "No. An economic structure may persist even though it has reached its productivity maximum. We called this fossilization." When considering whether the proposition, "If productivity sufficient for the emergence of an economic structure of kind S developed within an economic structure of kind R, then an economic structure of kind S appears," is true, Cohen answers, "No. Productivity sufficient for structure S does not guarantee its emergence. We called this miscarriage." Finally, when considering whether the proposition, "If an economic structure of kind R perishes, then an economic structure of kind S appears" is true, Cohen once again replies, "No. An economic structure can perish without being replaced by a superior one. What we called regression illustrates this, as does the possibly more drastic outcome envisaged in the phrase 'the common ruin of the contending classes'" (1978, 173). Further productive growth is thus only one of four possible outcomes of occurrences in the production relations. It would appear from this that there are other sorts of "dispositional facts" in the production relations besides the one Cohen mentions, dispositions that lead to fossilization, miscarriage, and regression rather than to productive advances. If these dispositional facts are kept in mind, the argument for the primacy thesis would seem to break down, and with it Cohen's entire theory of history.

Cohen has one remaining move open. He could admit that the possibility of fossilization, miscarriage, and regression reveal different sorts of dispositional facts in the production relations than the one mentioned in his argument. But he once again could appeal to the brute fact brought in to prop up the argument for the development thesis. He could argue that the fact that regression in productive capacity has been rare in human history shows that the dispositional facts in the production relations tending to cause regression are relatively insignificant and therefore can be ignored in an explanation of the role of the productive forces in history.

There are two problems with this move. The first is, it makes his version of historical materialism theoretically uninteresting. Why didn't Cohen simply assert the brute fact at once and then conclude his book? Presumably, he did not want merely to assert a fact but to explain it. But an explanation whose plausibility rests on an appeal to the very fact it is supposed to explain is a weak explanation indeed. The second difficulty is even more serious. Even if Cohen's factual appeal did work for the phenomenon of regression, it does not even begin to address the question of fossilization and miscarriage, occurrences that have by no means been rare in human history.

A first theoretical difficulty in Cohen's position, then, is the following. One has not explained production relations by saying that they change in order to facilitate productive growth, when one simultaneously admits the possibility of the production relations fossilizing, miscarrying, or regressing in a manner that prevents such growth. Rather than providing an explanation of history, this merely states the problem that an adequate theory of history must answer.

Interestingly enough, Cohen (1982a) himself admits as much in a later article. Since the publication of his book he and Jon Elster have carried on a running debate. The central issue in this debate is whether one needs to specify a mechanism suggesting how *B* functionally explains *A* in order to assert that *B* functionally explains *A*. Elster insists that such a mechanism must be supplied while Cohen thinks that "One can support the claim that *B* functionally explains *A* even when one cannot suggest what the mechanism is, if, instead, one can point to an appropriately varied range of instances in which, whenever *A* would be functional for *B*, *A* appears" (51).

I believe that Cohen is correct here. A comparative-historical method of establishing hypotheses is entirely appropriate in social theory.[4] This means, however, that Cohen's own hypothesis should be tested by examining whether in various cases in which a set of production relations would have promoted the advance of the productive forces, and not otherwise, that set of production relations in fact arose. Now consider the following passage:

> Suppose we found, *what I regret is false*, that wherever capitalism would promote the development of the productive forces, and not otherwise, capitalism arises; that it had arisen in the East at just that level of development at which it arose in the West, and that there were many other remarkable instances of such "fine tuning." Then Elster might not persist in his scepticism about consequence explanations which have not been elaborated, and he might agree that there must be a mechanism in virtue of which, because capitalism would develop the productive forces, it arose. (Cohen 1982a, 53. Emphasis mine.)

Cohen is here intent on defending a comparative-historical testing as sufficient in principle for asserting a functional explanation. He is so intent on this that he doesn't notice that with the emphasized words in the first sentence he himself has refuted his central hypothesis by his own standard for establishing hypotheses. For if it is false that "wherever capitalism would promote the development of the productive forces, and not otherwise, capitalism arises"—in other words, if it is possible for the productive relations to fossilize, miscarry, or regress—then there is no warrant for asserting that the rise of capitalism can be functionally explained in terms of the development of the productive forces.

A second theoretical problem in Cohen's account concerns his analysis of contemporary capitalist society. While the philosophies of history of Hegel and others attempt to reconcile us with the rationality of the present period, a central tenet of historical materialism is that present capitalist society must be criticized and replaced with socialist social relations. Cohen clearly intends to uphold this tenet. But from his perspective it does not seem possible to offer any convincing reason why capitalism must be overcome.

Before formulating this objection more fully we first must clarify one other aspect of Cohen's theory of history. Does he believe that the productive forces must have reached the maximum level of productivity possible under one set of production relations before a move to a new set of relations takes place? Cohen considers whether it is true that if an economic structure of kind S (just higher than kind R) appears, then an economic structure of kind R actualized its maximum productive potential. His answer (1978, 173) is unequivocal: "Yes. If S appears, R achieved its maximum productivity."[5]

We now must apply this general thesis to capitalism. A critique of capitalism grounded on his theory of history could only argue that at some point capitalism ceases to allow for advances in productive capacity and that the necessity for a move to new (socialist) production relations is functionally explained by this: "The productive achievement of capitalism is to create a surplus which permits the producers themselves to share in civilization, nor can power now develop any further unless they are culturally enfranchised. The past development of the productive forces makes socialism possible, and their future development makes socialism necessary" (Cohen 1978, 206).

This transformation of social relations is explained by "the exhaustion of the productive creativity of the old order . . . the expansion of produtive power has been blocked, and the revolution will enable it to proceed afresh. The function of the revolutionary social change is to unlock the productive forces" (Cohen 1978, 150). An elementary familiarity with the logic of capital accumulation and the relationship between capital accumulation and technological advance makes this argument extremely doubtful. As Ernest Mandel (1978) writes,

> The characteristic element in the capitalist mode of production . . . is the fact that each new cycle of extended production begins with different machines than the previous one. In capitalism, under the whip of competition and the constant quest for surplus profits, efforts are continually made to lower the costs of production and cheapen the value of commodities by means of technical improvements. (110–11)

In periods of economic growth the capitalist's need to maximize profits as a rule leads to a high rate of investment and a rapid rise of output per head. In periods of economic stagnation the overall rate of investment is significantly lower. Nonetheless as a rule the same need to maximize profits will continue to lead to the introduction of technologies that result in a continued rise of output per head. In fact, the demand for increased productive capacity is actually *heightened* during a downswing.[6] There thus appears to be no need for a "revolutionary social change . . . to unlock the productive forces"; their development is "blocked" in capitalism neither in periods of expansion nor in periods of stagnation.

This objection holds only if one takes the development of the productive forces in a purely technical and quantitative way. But would it not be possible to include a qualitative, emancipatory dimension in the concept of the productive forces? In that case, merely quantitative advancement of the productive forces would just enlarge the basis of potential emancipation. For the emancipatory potential of the productive forces to be realized, qualitative change–revolutionary social change–would be necessary. Thus the "unlocking" of the productive forces required under capitalism would refer to actualizing their emancipatory potential, and not to their quantitative expansion. This move would allow Cohen to avoid the difficulty presented above. But Cohen explicitly does *not* define the productive forces in this manner. He explicitly argues (1978, chap. 2, sec. 6) that the relevant standard for measuring growth in productive power is how much or how little labor must be spent with given forces to produce what is required to satisfy the inescapable physical needs of the immediate producers. This purely quantitative measure of social productivity is repeated in Cohen's subsequent articles in defense of his book (1980, 484; 1982a, 29). Also, Cohen (1978) explicitly rejects regarding the uses to which the productive forces are put (e.g., to further emancipation) as a way of measuring an increase in productive capacity: "Sub-optimal use does not entail a drop in the level of development of the productive forces" (56). Because technical advances fulfilling the criterion Cohen himself sets for determining development of the productive forces are built into capitalism, the above objection stands.

Theoretically there are two options open to Cohen at this point. The first is to claim that all that is necessary to ground a rejection of capitalism is that a productive level *sufficient* for socialism be present, and not that capitalism has exhausted its potential for developing productive capacity. Some passages suggest that this is what Cohen (1978) has in mind, for example: "What makes a *successful* revolution possible is *sufficiently* developed productive forces (203. Second emphasis mine). Cohen himself does not seem to realize how much this contradicts his own talk of an economic structure having to achieve "its maximum productivity" before a higher economic structure can appear. Even worse, he cannot make this move without betraying the central tenet of his theory of history. His major claim was that a change in the production relations is accounted for by a functional explanation that connects such change to the furthering of blocked productive growth. That connection would be lacking if the productive forces were not seen as "blocked."

Cohen's other option is to assert that eventually the cyclicial alternation from upswing to crisis and back in capitalism culminates in a final collapse. At that point the productive forces would indeed be "blocked." Cohen would then be able to derive an argument for abandoning capitalism from his general theory of history. But for good reasons Cohen (1978) explicitly rejects this breakdown theory: "There is no economically legislated final breakdown" (204). It follows that Cohen has presented no argument to establish that capitalism will ever achieve its maximum productivity. Therefore no compelling argument for a rejection of capitalism can be derived within the framework of Cohen's version of historical materialism.[7]

Practical implications. Besides theoretical cogency, an adequate version of historical materialism must also be relevant to emancipatory praxis. On this point, too, Cohen's position is lacking. For a theory to be relevant to emancipatory praxis, it is not required that it present a fully worked-out normative model. Nor is it necessary (or even possible) that specific tactics and strategies to be used in day-to-day struggles be derivable from it. These are the tasks of the three branches of social policy. However, for a model of historical development to have an immanent connection to praxis, it must sketch in a general fashion the direction that struggles for emancipation should take.

Cohen's view on the general direction of future development may be gleaned from his dictum that "history is the growth of human productive power" (1980, 129). Given Cohen's quantitative definition of "growth," the practical implication of this position is clear. The struggle for historical progress, for socialism, turns out to be not much more than a struggle for bigger and more efficient factories.

If this is indeed the practical implications of Cohen's theory, then it must be concluded that his version of historical materialism is not relevant to emancipatory praxis. Emancipation involves improving the economic position of working and oppressed men and women and strengthening their social position. It involves extending their political power and their political freedom, through extending democratic mechanisms. It involves reducing economic and social inequality and lessening the necessity and power of state coercion. There is no necessary connection, however, between struggle for a quantitative increase in the productive forces and struggle in any of these areas. Indeed, productivist arguments could even be (and have been) used to justify suppressing struggles for emancipation in these directions. The practical implications of Cohen's position are therefore ambivalent at best.

Habermas

Any comparison of Habermas's reconstruction of historical materialism and Cohen's theory of history should begin with the notions of "rationality" employed by the two theorists. The difference in their explication of this concept is the ultimate source of the divergences in their positions. After discussing this difference the general model of social evolution proposed by Habermas will be sketched. Finally this model will be evaluated. The theoretical and practical difficulties raised regarding Cohen's position are central issues that confront any version of historical materialism. The concluding evaluation, therefore, will focus on whether Habermas is in a better position to resolve these issues.

The Concept of Rationality

A statement asserting human rationality served as a premise for Cohen's argument for the development thesis. Cohen himself does not explicate this concept, but it is easy enough to extrapolate its meaning from his discussion of the productive forces. There Cohen points out that intentionality is a key factor in determining what counts as a productive force and what does not. The same entity may count as a productive force at one moment and not at another depending upon whether it is employed by laboring subjects with the intention of transforming material objects (1978, 48ff.). In Cohen's usage, "rationality" refers to the capacity for this type of intentionality. It may thus be termed *means-ends rationality* or *technical rationality*. A process of technical rationalization occurs whenever human actors oriented in this intentional structure, having discovered more efficient means for the fulfillment of this end of controlling nature, implement this discovery.

This same notion of technical rationality plays a central, if indirect, role in Cohen's other major argument, the argument for the primary thesis. We saw that this argument ultimately rests upon a claim concerning a supposed dispositional fact in the production relations that lead other classes in a society to form alliances with the class that can best further productive development. The structure of intentionality operating behind such alliances likewise is one within which means are sought to attain the end of increased technical control. To the degree that such alliances are successful and lead to the development of the productive forces, technical rationalization occurs; that is, the control of nature is accomplished in a more technically efficient manner.

The basic difference between Habermas and Cohen stems from the former's insistence that besides technical rationality there is another form of human rationality, practical rationality.[8] An adequate theory of social development, therefore, must take into account practical rationalization processes as well as processes of technical rationalization. One way in which the notion of practical rationality can be derived is the following. Let us call the realm constituted by the shared cultural traditions of a community the "life world."[9] In any communicative action within the life world three distinct worlds are opened to the speaker and hearer.[10] The subjective world of the wishes, feelings, and moods of the speaker is revealed in the making of a speech act. Likewise in the propositional content of the speech act both speaker and hearer refer to an objective world. Finally, the act of communication itself constitutes an interpersonal relationship between speaker and hearer. Here the social world comes into play. In communication different sorts of criticizable validity claims arise with respect to each of these worlds. Did the speaker truthfully reveal her attitudes? Is it true that the propositional content refers to an existing state of affairs? Is the interpersonal relationship constituted by the speech act one that is normatively correct? (see Habermas 1981b, 1:149).

In the present context we may concentrate upon the objective and social worlds and the claims to truth and normative correctness, respectively. Each realm has a distinct form of rationality. Habermas (1981b) writes, "The aspects of possible rationality of action depend in turn upon the world relations which we impute to the actor" (1:126). Technical rationality is oriented towards manipulations in the objective world. Its degree of rationality is measured by the extent to which certain truth-claims regarding the objective world are warranted, and the efficiency with which the actor can employ this knowledge. For instance, to do A in order to bring about B is technically rational (*wirksam*) only to the extent that there are good reasons for supposing the proposition "A causes B" to be true of the objective world (see Habermas 1981b, 1:130). In contrast, practical rationality is oriented towards interactions within the social world. Its degree of rationality is measured by the extent to which claims to normative correctness in the social world are warranted. For instance, a speaker's command that the hearer bring B about is practically rational only to the extent that there are good reasons for supposing the relationship of authority of the speaker over the hearer to be normatively correct. Technical and practical rationality are thus fundamentally distinct. It is impossible to derive the normative correctness of the speaker's command to bring *B* about from any knowledge of a causal connection between *A* and *B*, no matter how extensive.[11]

Having distinguished practical rationality from technical rationality, the notion of practical rationalization can be defined next. Practical rationalization takes place when the structures of moral-practical consciousness evolve in a way that leads to progressively more compelling justifications of claims to normative correctness. Habermas discusses this evolution in the structures of moral-practical consciousness within the context of a theory of social action. In the part of this theory of concern here, he distinguishes three structures within which practical activity takes place. These stages form a logical sequence of development in that (1) each succeeding stage presupposes the ones before it while adding some new content, (2) no stage can be skipped, and (3) the order of stages is invariant. Habermas feels that the developmental psychology of Piaget (1965) and Kohlberg (1971) provides empirical evidence for the ordering of stages he proposes. Here, however, I shall present a more philosophical argument. This argument is dialectical in structure, employing a paradigm first worked out in Hegel's *Phenomenology of the Spirit*. In that work Hegel begins with the most elementary forms of experience and shows how, on any given level of experience, reflection on the structure of that experience itself introduces a new element to the experience. In this manner a new structure is formed, a higher level of development is attained. Following a similar procedure, Habermas begins with the simplest structure of social action and traces a dialectic to more developed stages.[12]

In the first stage an acting subject *A* symbolically expresses a behavioral expectation, to which another subject *B* reacts with an action in the intention of fulfilling (or not fulfilling) *A*'s expectation. The consequences of the action of the one may or may not match the expectations of the other. In this manner the meaning of the action is reciprocally defined. This meaning is determined by the degree to which the consequences of the action of one participant fulfill the expectations of the other. Actions, the consequences of actions, behavioral expectations, and acting subjects are the basic units in this structure, and they are all perceived to lie on a single plane of reality.

A move of reflection occurs when the subjects involved not only adopt the perspective of the other but become able to exchange the perspective of a participant for that of an observer. With this move [13] the reciprocal behavioral expectation now can be thematicized explicitly as something apart from any specific action. It now can be formulated as a norm of action. With this the structure of social action becomes two-tiered. The reality plane of actions and their consequences form a surface level underlying which are norms and the intentions of actors to obey (disregard) established norms.

Just as reflection on reciprocal behavioral expectations leads to a thematicization of norms, so does reflection on norms introduce a new element into the structure of social action: the principles from which norms can be generated. Rather than simply being accepted as given, as in the second stage, on this more developed level of social action the norms that underlie action are treated hypothetically.[14] They may be either legitimate or illegitimate when confronted with the principles from which they stem. Now the structure of practical experience is three-tiered; principles occupy a deeper level than norms, which in turn underlie concrete actions and their consequences.

From this theory of stages in the development of the structure of social action a theory of practical rationalization can be derived. When social actors on the first stage attempt to justify their actions, they operate on a preconventional level of moral-practical consciousness.[15] In this limited framework only the consequences of actions are evaluated in cases of conflicts regarding the justification of actions. If these consequences fulfill reciprocally established expectations, the action is seen as justified. A conventional stage of consciousness is reached once intentions are assessed independently of the concrete consequences of actions. Here a system of norms is differentiated within the symbolic universe of the social actors, and their concrete actions are measured by the actors' intentions regarding these norms and not just by the consequences of their acts. Finally, when this system of norms is no longer accepted as given, moral-practical consciousness has reached a postconventional stage. This progression from a preconventional level of moral-practical consciousness, through a conventional level, to a postconventional stage captures the basic process of practical rationalization. On each successive level reasons for normative claims regarding the justifications of human actions can be given that are progressively more compelling. And, Habermas insists, rationalization in this practical sense is clearly distinct from the technical rationalization that allows us to acquire progressively greater control over external nature.

Habermas's Theory of Social Evolution

For Habermas, the object of the theory of historical materialism is to account for the move from one level of social evolution to the next. This does not imply a linear view of historical development in which "progress" is viewed as necessary. It is instead a reconstruction of history in which a line of progress is picked out amidst the whirl of progress and decline that together make up history.[16] The purpose of the theory is not to inform us of the inevitable next stage of history, but rather to persuade us that if history is to evolve we must orient our actions in a specific direction (without there being any metaphysical guarantees that we shall succeed.) Working out such a theory, Habermas insists, requires reference to both technical and practical rationalization.

We can take for our starting point a functioning social system at a given level of social evolution.[17] The move to the next level is initiated by system problems that arise in the basic domain of the social system. These system problems, of course, will be different at each level of social evolution. In evolutionary promising societies an endogenous learning mechanism in certain individuals creates a potential of available knowledge that in principle could resolve the system problems.[18] This knowledge fits under the heading "technical rationality"; it is knowledge of the means necessary to attain the end of resolving the system problems. For example, if the system problem in question stems from a low level of productive capacity, the knowledge would concern what is necessary to develop the productive forces.

Technical rationalization, however, does not occur automatically even when individuals possess the requisite technical knowledge. In cases where quantum leaps in social evolution are demanded the technical knowledge cannot be implemented within the given institutional framework. The creation of a new institutional system is thus required. This can be brought about only through successful social movements. Thus a necessary condition of the possibility of a new institutional system is that groups are able to organize themselves, struggle against, and defeat those groups allied in defense of the established institutional system. But something else is required as well. A new institutional system organizes social action in a new manner. It institutionalizes a new principle of social integration, which Habermas terms an "organization principle." Social integration is a matter of sharing a world view, a moral system, a group identity.[19] All of these in turn embody a rationality structure on a specific stage of moral-practical consciousness. Therefore, a further necessary condition of the possibility of a new institutional system is that the underlying rationality structure reflected in world-views, moral systems, and group identities has moved to a new level.[20] In short, practical rationalization must have taken place in which world-views, moral systems, and group identities move (not necessarily simultaneously, of course) from a preconventional level to a conventional stage, or from the conventional to the postconventional level. Only with this move to the next stage in the developmental logic of moral-practical consciousness is a new principle of social integration provided, which in turn allows a new institutional framework to be formed, a framework capable of exploiting the available technical knowledge, thereby resolving the initial system problems.[21]

The following passage nicely summarizes Habermas's version of historical materialism, as opposed to historical materialists, such as Cohen, who localize

> the learning processes important for evolution in the dimension of objectivating thought – of technical and organizational knowledge, of instrumental and strategic action, in short, of productive forces – there are good reasons meanwhile for assuming that learning processes also take place in the dimension of moral insight, practical knowledge, communicative action, and the consensual regulation of action conflicts – learning processes that are deposited in more mature forms of social integration, in new productive forces. The rationality structures that find expression in world views, moral representations, and identity formations, that become practically effective in social movements and are finally embodied in institutional systems, thereby gain a strategically important position from a theoretical point of view. The systematically reconstructible patterns of development of normative structures are now of particular interest.[22]

In contrast to the reductionism of Cohen's functionalist explanation of history we may term Habermas's theory of social evolution "structural pluralism." The fact that a change in the production relations would be functional for productive development is not a sufficient condition for that change. A plurality of different factors must be taken into account and not simply the development of the productive forces.

Evaluation of Habermas's Position

Theoretical issues. Can the explanatory model proposed in Habermas's theory of social evolution avoid the sorts of objections to which Cohen's position proved susceptible? With regard to the first objection made against Cohen's view above, fossilization and miscarriage can be accounted for within Habermas's framework. No matter how functional for productive development an advance in the production relations might be, unless a particular society undertakes a moral-practical learning process, no new principle of social organization will arise, and a move to a higher level of productive development will not occur.

Let us construct an ideal type of the transition from archaic societies to early civilizations as an example. Assume that two archaic societies face the same system problems (e.g., ecologically conditioned land scarcity and population density) and are identical in all other relevant respects as well. In both cases productive development could resolve these problems, and a shift in production relations allowing for that development therefore would be functional. But in society *A* the shift occurs while in *B* it does not. From Cohen's perspective there is no way to account for this sort of case. Habermas does offer help here. He would suggest that, other things being equal, society *A* completed the required practical rationalization process successfully, while *B* did not. More specifically, in both societies the system problems that were "irresolvable within the given framework, become more and more visible the more frequently they led to conflicts that overloaded the archaic legal institutions (courts of arbitration, feuding law.)" But society *A*, under the pressure of evolutionary challenges, made use of the cognitive potential in [its] world view and institutionalized—at first on a trial basis—an administration of justice at a conventional level. Thus, for example, the war chief was empowered to adjudicate cases of conflict, no longer only according to the concrete distribution of power, but according to socially recognized norms grounded in tradition. Law was no longer only that on which the parties could agree.[23]

As this move was stabilized the war chief became a political ruler; a new principle of social organization based on the state replaced a society organized along kinship relations. Since the ruler could best secure "the loyalty of his officials, of the priest and warrior families by assuring them privileged access to the means of production (palace and temple economy)," the rise of the state was accompanied by the rise of class distinctions in society. As the state thereby uncoupled the production process from the limiting conditions of the kinship system, the enlarged organizational capacity of class society was able to utilize cognitive potential already discovered in the neolithic evolution (e.g., regarding the intensification of cultivation and stock farming). The resulting development of the productive forces then allowed the initial system problems to be resolved in society A. Society B, on the other hand, either did not successfully undertake or failed to stabilize a learning process in the moral-practical sphere; it did not move from a preconventional to a conventional legal system. It thus was not able to move to new institutional systems that could exploit the available technical knowledge. This lack of practical rationalization explains why a miscarriage, fossilization, and even regression of the economic structure can occur even when a different type of change is functional for the development of the productive forces. Habermas has a way of accounting for miscarriage, fossilization, and regression, whereas Cohen does not. This provides us with a first reason for regarding his version of historical materialism as superior.

In all versions of historical materialism, socialism is seen as an advance over capitalism. Everything else equal, one version counts as superior to another if it can make this ordering more plausible. A second objection to Cohen's position was that it could not provide compelling theoretical arguments for rejecting capitalism once it is acknowledged that further technological development is always compatible with the logic of capital accumulation. Since the rejection of capitalism is a defining characteristic of historical materialism, Cohen's failure to provide this sort of argument undermined his claim to offer an adequate formulation of that position. Such arguments can be constructed within a Habermasian framework. We therefore have a second reason for regarding his perspective a more satisfactory version of historical materialism.

Before presenting these arguments one must show how modern capitalism fits into Habermas's theory of social evolution. In Habermas's view "modernity," that is, historically existing modern society, embodies structures characteristic of a postconventional stage of social evolution. Following Weber, Habermas points to the role played by the Protestant Ethic and modern law in ushering in modernity. Both the Protestant Ethic and modern law embody the post-conventional structure of moral-practical consciousness definitive of the modern stage of social evolution. The practical rationalization within the life world that occurred with the spread of the Protestant Ethic and modern law allowed for heightened complexity in the social system. This also occurred with earlier developments in moral-practical consciousness. What is unique to modernity is that now, for the first time, the social system, concerned with the material reproduction of the life world, breaks off from the life world. Specifically, these new forms of moral-practical consciousness break down traditional manners of organizing economic production and distribution and political administration. They allow economic and political organizations to arise in which members are no longer bound within traditional social roles but by individually chosen vocations.[24] Their action is now a function of the exchange of certain media (money and power, respectively). This breaking-off of economic and political systems from the life world allowed a tremendous increase in technical rationality. Unfortunately, these systems also set off recurrent crises and, later, social pathologies. Habermas derives arguments against capitalism from these tendencies to crises and pathologies, rather than from any failure of this system to develop the productive forces quantitatively.

Crises occur "[W]hen the achievements of the economy and state manifestly remain below an established level of claims and injure the symbolic reproduction of the life world by calling forth conflicts and reactions of opposition" (Habermas 1981b, 2:565). The phrase "established level of claims" refers to the perceived ability of the social system to satisfy human needs, given the stage of development attained. Habermas (1981b) accepts the traditional Marxist account of economic crisis in that he grants that the process of capital accumulation tends to cyclical breakdown for reasons internal to the system itself (585). He goes beyond economistic theories of crisis in pointing out that economic crises can be displaced to the political sphere.[25] In developed capitalist societies there is a constant swing from one crisis form to the other.[26]

In so far as both forms of crisis are indigenous to capitalism, the satisfaction of fundamental human needs is regularly threatened significantly for many groups, providing an argument for rejecting this social system even if it is not the case that the productive forces are ever "fettered" quantitatively. To the extent that this argument is widely accepted, the capitalist system loses its legitimation and its ability to motivate people to accept it.

Habermas, however, believes that the disruptions caused by crises in principle may be avoided to a considerable degree. Through various types of programs [27] the social state of advanced capitalism can compensate the victims of economic and political crisis enough to bring about what Habermas (1981b) terms a "pacification of class conflict" (2:505). To the extent that this pacification occurs,[28] the above argument against capitalism loses much of its force.

At this point Habermas introduces a second argument, an argument based upon the pathologies capitalism creates. The compensations offered by the social state are in the form of bureaucratic decisions and monetary rewards. It compensates by transforming individuals into clients and consumers. And it transforms individuals in this manner in more and more realms of their lives as capitalism develops.[29] Eventually the processes of cultural reproduction, social integration, and socialization are infringed upon. Habermas terms this the "colonization of the life world."[30] His main thesis here is that these sorts of processes cannot be undertaken by "consumers" and "clients." They require interpersonal communication, and not an exchange of money and administrative power, in order to operate.[31] When the social state, in order to resolve crises stemming from the economic and political subsystems, nonetheless infringes upon these processes, pathological consequences result: "In distinction from the material reproduction of the life world, its symbolic reproduction cannot be transformed by monetarization and bureaucratization without pathological consequences in the basis of systematic integration" (1981b, 2:576–77).[32] Habermas's second argument, then, is that a capitalist system must be overcome if the community is to retain its social identity as a community (1981b, 2:566). This argument holds even if the productive forces are not quantitatively fettered in capitalism and even if disruptions caused by economic and political crises can somehow be kept below the critical threshold.

A theory of the crises and pathologies that arise within capitalism is on a much more concrete level of analysis than a theory of social evolution. Since the latter is our topic here, we cannot discuss the former in further details. It is sufficient for our purpose here to have established that within the framework of Habermas's theory of social evolution arguments can be constructed that theoretically ground a rejection of capitalism while avoiding the sorts of difficulties that beset Cohen's view.[33]

Practical implications. What are the practical implications that follow from Habermas's version of historical materialism? The same question must be discussed here as was posed to Cohen's position. Can Habermas's version of historical materialism orient practical struggles for emancipation by sketching the sort of society to be brought about by these struggles? We can begin to answer this question by seeing what practical implications cannot be drawn from his perspective. First, history, for Habermas, cannot be reduced to simply productive advance. Thus a society that was devoted to increasing productivity almost exclusively would not provide a proper goal for action. Here too Habermas's position is in stark contrast to Cohen's. Second, any return to traditional societies is ruled out. This would count as a regression from the stage of social evolution already attained. Also ruled out by the theory is a practical orientation towards instituting bureaucratic socialism; it too is subject to crises[34] and to social pathologies.[35] What, then, does Habermas advocate? Regarding his own theory he (1981b) writes,

> Over against the reality of developed societies this theory is critical, insofar as these societies do not exhaust the learning potential which they have at their cultural disposal but instead give themselves over

to an uncontrolled growth in complexity. As we have seen, growing system complexity . . . does not only push back traditional life forms. It attacks the communicative infrastructure of extensively rationalized life worlds.(2:549)

The life world was initially rationalized by the move to postconventional structures of moral-practical consciousness. For contingent historical reasons the Protestant Ethic was the form in which postconventional structures were first historically embodied. This form led, of course, to capitalism and its eventual attack on the communicative infrastructure. However, The Protestant Ethic is not the only possible embodiment of a postconventional structure of consciousness. It is not even its only historical embodiment: "A moral consciousness directed by principles is not necessarily tied to a personal interest in redemption; it has actually stabilized itself in a secularized form, even if at first only in certain social strata" (1981b, 2:450). Habermas here refers to what he terms a "cognitive ethic." Within this perspective, defended by thinkers from Kant to Rawls, when conventional norms no longer retain their force, an appeal to the universalizable interests of the social actors in question provides the only compelling justification for practical decision.[36] Habermas himself has contributed to this viewpoint by establishing that the universalizable interests of the community can only be fixed within a discourse situation in which each participant has the opportunity to present and defend his perspective without coercion. The Protestant Ethic, with its egocentric doctrine of the particularism of grace thus is a most inadequate manifestation of a postconventional standpoint, as it excludes discourse of this sort (1981b, 2:450). Habermas therefore advocates struggling for a society in which a more adequate embodiment of a postconventional structure of moral-practical consciousness is attained. In this manner the "learning potential" implicit in this structure can be actualized.

From the perspective of Habermas's theory of social evoluation, the significance of progressive social movements is that they at least implicitly appeal to the postconventional principle of universalizable interests. These appeals are articulated by Habermas with reference to what he terms the "logic of practical discourse." Consider the struggle for worker control of the workplace. In "A Reply to My Critics," Habermas writes: "the justification of normative regulations that help this repressed interest obtain its rights follows the logic of practical discourse" (Thompson and Held 1982, 312). In other words, a lack of autonomy in the workplace can be criticized as illegitimate because those affected by this practice would not agree to it in an uncoerced speech situation. The practice therefore is not based upon a universalizable interest. From this we may conclude that Habermas's theory orients emancipatory struggles by proposing that their long-term goal be the creation of a society in which the institutionalization of uncoerced discourse ensures that the universalizable interests of the society are articulated and actualized: "Procedures of conflict resolution must arise which are appropriate to the structures of action oriented to understanding: discursive processes of will formation and deliberation and decision procedures oriented towards consensus" (1981b, 2:544).

This conclusion is still quite vague. I shall discuss the question of the institutionalization of discourse in much greater detail in Chapter IX. But the above is sufficient for us to affirm that Habermas does provide an orientation to those engaged in emancipatory struggles, one that seems clearly superior to the productivist orientation offered in Cohen's theory. There is an intrinsic connection between Habermas's contribution to the third branch of social theory and those branches devoted to social policy. The ethical principle of universalizability provides this connection.

PART THREE

SOME ETHICAL
EVALUATIONS
OF CAPITALISM

The second general area of social theory, social ethics, can be divided into three branches. These branches (value analysis, value selection, and evaluations) can be defined in terms of the fundamental questions to which they are devoted: What are the logical structures of different value systems? Which of these systems of values ought to be affirmed? How are social phenomena to be evaluated from the standpoint of the selected value system?

The two chapters that make up Part Three of this work are contributions to the sixth branch of social theory, evaluations.[1] Evaluations can be made of either general models of social systems or processes, or of specific structures or practices that have occurred. The concern here is with the former. In Part Two Habermas's contribution to branch five, his derivation of the ethical principle of universalizability, was defended. This principle now comes into play as the normative standard to be used in evaluations of social systems. According to this principle, all those social systems that for structural reasons do not allow the satisfaction of generalizable interests must be negatively evaluated, while those that do allow this can be affirmed. Given familiar empirical premises, normative critiques of social structures based on slavery, feudalism, or bureaucratic commands can be easily derived from this principle. No social system that grants one group of people unchecked power over other groups would be accepted by the latter groups in a speech situation without coercion.

Systems based on slavery, serfdom, or bureaucratic control all grant unchecked power to some groups. Therefore none of these social systems is compatible with the principle of universalizable interests.

What about capitalism? The chapters that follow consider two recent attempts to argue for affirmative evaluations of this social system. While neither employs Habermasian vocabulary, both invoke ethical principles that are either compatible with or identical to the principle of universalizability.

Chapter V examines Richard T. De George's *Business Ethics* (1982). While the subdiscipline of business ethics is mostly devoted to the evaluation of specific practices within capitalism, works in this field usually also include an evaluation of the basic institutional structure that defines capitalism. De George's book can be taken as a representative text. If De George's case that capitalism fully institutionalizes freedom and equality were compelling, then it would follow at once that this social system could be accepted in a speech situation without coercion. However, I believe that De George has failed to establish that capitalism is compatible with universalizable interests.

In an important recent article, N. Scott Arnold (1987) has presented a somewhat different case for a positive evaluation of capitalism, one based upon the essential goal of market transactions. In Chapter VI I consider Arnold's arguments. I hold that if the goal of economic transactions is defined satisfactorily, Arnold also fails to provide compelling grounds for a positive ethical evaluation of capitalism.

V

On Liberty and Equality

Richard T. De George's *Business Ethics* (1982) is one of the clearest and best-argued works in the field of business ethics. In this chapter I shall examine some of its central arguments (all page references in text are to this work). Prior to this, however, I would like to situate the rise of business ethics within a social context. This situation will allow us to appreciate better what is at stake in the arguments to be discussed.

It is surely no accident that business ethics as a branch of philosophical inquiry including countless articles and books, entire journals, well-funded conferences, and so on, arose when it did in the early and mid-1970s. Vietnam and Watergate had resulted in widespread cynicism towards political institutions the like of which had not been seen before in the United States. This cynicism extended into the business world as well. Almost daily headlines announced that another corporation was caught making illegal campaign contributions, or was engaged in bribery overseas, or had conspired to create artificial shortages, and so on and so on. There was, in short, the beginnings of a general *crisis of legitimacy*.[1] In the long run a legitimation crisis can undermine the stability of a social system as throughly as an economic crisis (see Habermas 1975). And when a crisis in legitimacy is combined with economic crisis (as was the case during the recessions of 1974–75, 1980, and 1981–82) the situation is potentially explosive. This remains the case even if extensive apathy and despair has been the typical response rather than direct mass action.

One response to this situation was the rise of the new right. This position turns a deaf ear on criticisms of "the American way of life." It instead calls for a return to traditional American values (God, family, patriotism). If this social fundamentalism were widespread enough, the legitimation crisis would be overcome.

Whatever the private psychological intentions of philosophers engaged in business ethics might be, from a sociological perspective business ethics as a discipline has an objective function similiar to that of the New Right. It too functions as a mechanism for reestablishing the moral legitimacy of the fundamental economic and political institutions of the United States. Its strategy of accomplishing this, however, is in stark contrast to that of the New Right. Rather than denying the moral force of criticisms of the "American way of life," it explicitly acknowledges the validity of many criticisms of specific practices. It then goes on to consider how our capitalist system could be tinkered with in order to eliminate the morally objectionable practices *without radically transforming the underlying structure within which the practice occurs.*[2] In this more sophisticated fashion the same conclusion is reached as that attained by the New Right: the underlying structure is morally justifiable. If this conclusion were accepted by enough students and communicated effectively to their relatives and friends, business ethics would contribute significantly to avoiding any crisis of legitimacy.

A single example should be sufficient to illustrate this point. "Whistle-blowing" on the part of employees is often morally justifiable (or even morally obligatory) when the corporations for which they work are engaged in certain activities. But those employees who have "blown the whistle" often enough have suffered punitive measures at the hands of their company. De George grants that this is clearly immoral. His solution is to institute an ombudsman or standing committee within the corporation "whose job it is to uncover immoral and illegal practices, and whose job it is to listen to the moral concerns of employees at every level about the firm's practices. He should be independent of management, and report to the audit committee of the board, which ideally should be a committee made up of independent board memebers" (163). Through measures such as this the basic structure of the corporation can be retained while simultaneously overcoming the morally objectionable practices. In this manner the moral legitimacy of the institution is established precisely by taking the criticisms directed against the institution seriously.

For any ethical problem connected with specific business practices this sort of tinkering can be attempted. In different cases the claim that such tinkering is an adequate response to the morally objectionable practice in question will have varying degrees of plausibility. For the most part I shall not examine specific cases here. Even plausible suggestions for reforming specific practices are not independent moral justifications for the basic structure underlying those practices. As De George states, even a slaveholder who personally treats his slaves fairly is still participating in an unjust system (89ff.). Arguments providing direct justification for the basic structure are therefore necessary. De George devotes two central chapters to this more foundational level of business ethics. It is the arguments on this level that I wish to consider.

De George lists three features which together define a capitalist structure: available accumulation of industrial capital,[3] private ownership of the means of production, and a free-market system (97ff.). In defense of the moral legitimacy of this structure De George throws out a great number of arguments, all of which cannot be considered here. I shall limit myself to an examination of the three arguments De George himself develops the most fully.

The first argument might be termed the *argument from consensus*. Here De George contrasts the model of a capitalist system with three models with different defining features: bureaucratic socialism (which he terms "socialism" without adding the qualification necessary to distinguish it from the third model, which is also a form of socialism), libertarianism, and workers' democracy. He notes that there is no widespread consensus that any of these alternative models is morally superior to that of capitalism. "The consensus in America is that we do not need another system. No other system is morally preferable or waiting to be adopted" (127).

This is, of course, an extremely weak argument. It is guilty of the naturalistic fallacy of attempting to derive an "ought" (regarding the moral justification of institutional structures) from an "is" (an existing political consensus). That there is a fallacy here can be shown by a simple example. It is quite possible (and, unfortunately, not uncommon) for a nation to attain a consensus that waging an unjust war of aggression is morally justifiable.[4]

The second and third arguments to be considered are much stronger. They can be termed the *arguments from equality* and *liberty*, respectively. The equality referred to in the second argument is not an equality of results. A capitalist society inevitably will generate inequalities in the distribution of social goods. De George even concedes that the inequalities which exist today exceed what is morally permissible. He therefore proposes progressive taxation as a way of reducing the inequality to morally acceptable limits: "The overall system can reduce the differential between the highest and lowest paid, or it can equalize the two considerably more than it presently does through a different tax structure. Such injustices can be handled within the system" (122). Even if such taxation schemes are enacted,[5] however, inequalities will still remain inherent in the system. Therefore "Obviously a view of justice which demands equality of results will not be compatible with capitalism" (106). But this is not De George's view of justice. For him it is equality of opportunity, and not of results, that determines whether a situation is just or not. He expresses this idea with an analogy between a capitalist system and a race:

> In the capitalist system, justice demands equality of opportunity. It does not demand equality of results. The best way to tell who is the fastest runner is to have all runners compete under the same conditions. Someone will finish first, someone will finish last and others will finish somewhere in between. . . . [A]s long as there is equality of opportunity . . . justice has been served. (106)

Of course specific practices such as racial and sexual discrimination prevent such equality of opportunity. But these practices are accidental to a capitalist system. They can be removed by reforms without drastic alteration in the structure of the system being necessary (De George 1982, chap. 10). Because the structure essentially allows for equality of opportunity, it is morally legitimate.

We have discussed (1) an initial starting point in which the overcoming of racial and sexual discrimination ensures equality of opportunity, and (2) an end point in which any inequality of results great enough to be morally objectionable can be avoided through progressive taxation. De George's third argument fills the gap between the starting and end points by stating that the capitalist system is morally legitimate because the process of moving from the initial equality of opportunity to the eventual inequality of results is intrinsically one in which liberty is exercised: "The free market system . . . values freedom. Each individual within the system makes free choices in each transaction into which he enters" (101). "This freedom is significant from a moral point of view. An argument in defense of free enterprise trades heavily on the maturity, intelligence, and responsibility of those operating within the economic system" (109).

Two forms in which liberty is exercised should be singled out as especially significant. First, some participants freely choose to undertake initiatives and to take on risks. Those successful in initiatives and risk taking will "win the race" ("Differences in income are to be expected in a competitive system and in a system in which monetary reward is a prime incentive for creativity in production.") Yet as long as this results from fair transactions freely entered into, no one has cause for complaint. A second area in which liberty is exercised comes in the agreements made by some to work for others. Whereas Marxists see exploitation in all such transactions, De George sees a free exchange between buyer and seller such that "The workers are not oppressed. There may be some exploitation, but exploitation consists of paying the worker less than the productivity of a worker at the margin. It is not built into the system" (116).

De George is, of course well aware that in capitalism many transactions are not based upon the exercise of liberty. But here too it is a question only of specific practices (concealing information, misrepresentation, intimidation, etc.). Reforms can be made that significantly reduce the occurrence of such practices. They are not intrinsic to the system and hence do not undermine its moral legitimacy.

In the argument from equality De George could be accused of not taking seriously enough just how vital racial and sexual discrimination are to a capitalist system. These practices provide capital with a ready source of cheap labor and fragment the working class so that it becomes harder for it to articulate its class interests (see especially Reich 1981 and Mitchell 1977). But let us grant for the sake of argument that inequality of opportunity stemming from sexual and racial discrimination is not intrinsic to the structure of a capitalist system. There remains another type of inequality that De George himself notes *is* intrinsic to this system, indeed is one of the three factors that define this system for De George: "[N]ot everyone owns the means of production. The majority of people in our model of capitalism do not individually own the means of production which they use. They are employed by others and work for wages" (99).[6] *This* form of inequality is not a practice that can be tinkered with; it is constitutive of the system within which all practices occur. And this inequality is an inequality of *opportunity*, not of results. The economic power that comes from ownership of the means of production brings with it the opportunity for further economic gain, political influence, and social status—in short, more favorable life opportunities than those of nonowners of the means of production (at least these things tend to be connected with ownership of the means of production). Thus the analogy with a race in which all begin at the same point hardly seems appropriate. Intrinsic to the structure of capitalism is the fact that when the "race" starts those who privately own the means of production are already close to the finish line. A few may still "stumble" and lose the race, but that is not the same thing as all starting out together.

De George would reply that while the above may have been accurate for nineteenth-century capitalism, the emergence of pension fund ownership of stocks shows that it is not intrinsic to the structure of capitalism. "Through pension plans and insurance policies American workers are in fact the owners of the means of production to a considerable extent" (116). This response is inadequate for a number of reasons. First, pension plans, while growing, are still a relatively insignificant source of stock ownership (less than 10 percent of outstanding shares [Ackerman and Zimbalist 1978, 301]). Second, almost without exception pension funds are controlled by bank trust departments or other financial institutions rather than by the workers themselves, so "their wealth is not a source of power or current income for workers in the same sense that personal wealth is a source of power to capitalists" (Ackerman and Zimbalist 1978, 301).[7] Third, of personally owned corporate stock the wealthiest 5 percent of the population own 83 percent (the wealthiest 1 percent own 55–65 percent) of the corporate stock in other businesses and hands. It is simply not plausible to assert that a worker who participates in a pension plan and a member of that top 5 percent have equal opportunity. Finally, it also would not be plausible to suggest that all the above is not necessary to the structure of capitalism, that pension fund ownership could grow in significance and be under worker control without going beyond that structure. Based on De George's own contrast of capitalism with alternative structures, one must conclude that the more extensive worker-controlled pension fund ownership was, the more the society in question would have moved away from capitalism and towards worker democracy (125).

The inequality of opportunity constitutive of (intrinsic to) the structure of capitalism has ramifications for an evaluation of the extent to which that structure intrinsically involves liberty. We have mentioned two alleged examples of how the exercise of liberty is intrinsic to the system. The first had to do with risks freely taken on by entrepreneurs. But given that the means of production are privately owned/controlled by a few, it is not sufficient simply to say that these risks justify a resulting inequality of results. It is true that capitalists can decide which risks they wish to face. But day in and day out, workers suffer risks such as that of industrial accidents from speed-ups, long-term physical and psychological health erosion from the work environment, declining standards of living if not unemployment in periods of economic downswing, and so forth. To the extent that it is possible to measure such things quantitatively, these risks are surely more than the risks to which the owners of the means of production subject themselves. After all, the greatest danger risked by the members of the latter class is usually that they find themselves reduced to being a member of the former class! Capitalists are exposed to the risks that come from owning the means of production; workers are exposed to the risks that come from *not* owning the means of production. Thus the taking-on of risk has much less to do with an individual's autonomous free choice and much more to do with his or her class position.

The second alleged example of liberty was the wage contract. When labor and management are allowed to bargain freely, the mechanism of the market intrinsically tends towards a voluntary agreement in which workers are rewarded in proportion to their contribution. Deviations are accidental and may be corrected through various reforms. Accepting De George's perspective for the moment, he forgets that it is only the least efficient worker who is paid based on his or her productivity at the margin. Given that competition in the labor market supposedly tends to equalize wages for those doing the same work, this means that all other workers are paid according to the contribution of the least productive worker and not according to their own contribution. All but the last worker are, therefore, intrinsically "exploited," even in the terms of De George's own framework.

De George's framework, however, should not be accepted. Here, too, the lack of equality discussed above is intrinsically connected with a lack of liberty. The controllers of capital possess the buildings, the tools, the machines and the raw materials necessary for production of office work, as well as an ample reserve of funds. They do not engage in economic activity in order to ensure their subsistence but in order to accumulate yet further wealth. Their subsistence is guaranteed, at least for a number of years. In stark contrast workers do not possess any reserves beyond their hands and minds, which they *must* hire out if they and their families are to survive. The confrontation of labor and capital would be fair only if workers too possessed reserves of foodstuffs, or money, that would enable them to supply their needs and those of their families for several years. Then and only then could an agreement between the two be a "free" one. Short of this the two groups do not negotiate on an equal footing; the workers are eventually *compelled* to seek employment or else starve. "Free" enterprise is built upon this compulsion, not upon liberty. Just as social systems based on slavery, feudalism, and bureaucratic command grant one group unchecked power over other groups, so too does capitalism. Just as they cannot be said to be compatible with generalizable interests, so too is this the case for capitalism.

Conclusion

This chapter has been entirely critical up until this point. I would like to conclude on a more constructive note by proposing a view of liberty and equality that can avoid the difficulties De George has fallen into. Liberty is, I believe, the more fundamental category, and so we can begin with it. What follows is quite sketchy. I shall return to this general topic in Part Four.

First, "private" decisions must be distinguished from decisions that are "public" in scope. Liberty involves something quite different in the two cases. With respect to private decisions the call for liberty is a demand that the individual's right to decide not be infringed upon (subject to the usual qualifications, e.g., that in exercising this right the individual is not infringing on the rights of others). But with respect to public decisions the call for liberty is a claim that an individual's right to decide *is* infringed upon through being subject to public control. For example, the decision-making of a president of a republic is restricted (through elections, impeachment, recall, etc.) relative to the decision-making of an absolute monarch. Yet we would all predicate "liberty" of the former arrangement and not of the latter. A positive conception of liberty on the sociopolitical (rather than private) plane would be: "Liberty is an institutional arrangement in which exercises of public power are subject to public control." This allows us to talk of degrees of liberty; an institutional arrangement can allow for greater or less liberty depending upon the extent to which exercises of public power are subject to public control.

With this positive conception of liberty it is easy to spot the root cause of De George's theoretical difficulties. His work, the work of all texts in business ethics, and indeed the entire capitalist system, is based on a fundamental category mistake: he conceptualizes decisions that are intrinsically public in nature (those that follow from ownership/control of the means of production) as decisions that are private in scope. He then attempts to apply the notion of liberty appropriate to the private sphere, when an entirely different notion of liberty is called for. This cannot be done in a convincing or even consistent fashion.

There was a time, not very long ago at all, when state offices were seen as private possessions that could be passed from individual to individual through inheritance, gift, or purchase. Today the question "Who owns a state office?" strikes us as odd. A state office is not a "thing" that someone can own as a private possession. It is rather a social relation in which political authority is exercised, with this exercise ultimately resting upon the consent of the governed.

This is political liberty, and the world-historical task of the eighteenth century was to introduce and spread this principle. We today still think of the means of production as private possessions that can be inherited, given, or purchased by individuals. But control of the means of production is instead a social relation in which economic authority is exercised. This exercise, too, should rest upon the consent of the governed. This would be economic liberty, and the world-historical task of our century is to introduce and spread this principle. Only when the inequality that stems from private ownership of the means of production is overcome will liberty be taken to the next higher stage.

VI

Are Entrepreneurial Profits Prima Facie Deserved?

N. Scott Arnold's "Why Profits are Deserved" (1987, all page references in text are to this work) is an extremely important essay that falls on the sixth branch of social theory. Like De George, Arnold too is concerned with the normative evaluation of capitalist market societies, an essential element of which is entrepreneurial profits.

Arnold's basic argument seems extremely well constructed: institutional desert claims are based on appeals to the essential goal of the institution. The essential goal of markets is "to meet the wants and needs of the consumers that can be satisfied by scarce and exchangeable goods and services" (396). Entrepreneurs are those who rearrange the structure of production in order to overcome a perceived malallocation of resources. They do this in the hope of a reward, termed "pure profits" (as opposed to the "interest" received by providers of capital goods). Allowing them to receive and retain these profits if they successfully identify a malallocation – or to suffer losses if they are mistaken – furthers the essential goal of markets. Overcoming such malallocations better allows the wants and needs of consumers to be met. Therefore these profits (losses) are prima facie deserved. Therefore, too, capital gains taxes are prima facie undeserved.

The Goal of Market Exchange

Arnold does not invoke the principle of universalizability in his article. However it might well appear that meeting "the wants and needs of . . . consumers" is a goal to which participants in a discourse anticipating an ideal speech situation would agree. If this were granted, then it might seem plausible that capitalist market societies based upon entrepreneurial profits should be evaluated positively (at least prima facie) based upon that principle.

However, would participants in such a discourse agree to Arnold's formulation of this goal? I believe that they would find it both narrow and arbitrary. Arnold insists his formulation of the goal is true "even if the allocation is not optimal and even if not all exchangeable goods and services are (or should be) allocated by market mechanisms" (396). Arnold thus seems to define the goal of market exchange to be "meeting the wants and needs of the consumers" *whether or not* this involves an optimal allocation of goods and services that should be allocated by market mechanisms.

Would social agents discussing the proper goal of economic institutions in a speech situation without coercion agree to this? It seems unlikely. Even Arnold cannot avoid the notion of optimality altogether. He has argued that entrepreneurial profits are prima facie deserved precisely because they address a malallocation of resources. The act of correcting a malallocation *presupposes* the ideal of an optimal allocation, even if Arnold has failed to make this explicit.

This presupposition leads us to the next problem. The notion of an optimal allocation implicit in Arnold's discussion of the goal is limited to the provision of consumer items. With this, Arnold's argument becomes tautologous. An attempt to justify something should appeal to some principle that is conceptually distinct from what is to be justified. Such is the case with Arnold's example of the World Series. The goal of that institution is the determination of the best baseball team in the United States. The team that is best deserves to win precisely because that would best fulfill the goal of the institution. Here the goal is conceptually distinct from the success of the deserving team. Luck and other factors might interfere so that the most deserving team turned out not to win on this or that occasion. Talent in baseball can be assessed separately from success in World Series competition. Contrary to Arnold's supposition, the case of entrepreneurial profits is not analogous. Entrepreneurial profits are *defined* in terms of satisfying effective demand: no sales to consumers, no profits. In other words, if entrepreneurial profits are supposed to be prima facie deserved due to meeting effective demand, and if profits by definition follow from sales to consumers, then the argument comes down to saying that entrepreneurial profits are justified because they are entrepreneurial profits. This clearly will not do.

Arnold would insist that the connection between deserved profits and the goal of market transactions is not trivially true on his account. For one thing, "the usual vagaries of luck" (400) can prevent those who deserve profits from receiving them. But what would "bad luck" mean in this context? Imagine an entrepreneur who has invested in a low-cost way of producing a superior product. Despite this the entrepreneur failed because the start-up ad campaign didn't work, or because the trucks taking the product to market broke down. Is this bad luck? Surely meeting the wants and needs of consumers includes successfully informing consumers of the availability of products and distributing them to sales outlets. If these things are left to chance, if no back-up plan was formulated and implemented, then this is a failure on the part of the entrepreneur *qua* entrepreneur, and not simply bad luck. On Arnold's own principles, profits would *not* be deserved.

In trying to avoid the appearance of tautology Arnold makes a second move. He points out that market systems may not automatically apportion the objects of desert to those who deserve them. A worker whose suggestion resulted in pure profits for a firm may not receive the profits she deserves. This response does not address the issue at hand. We must distinguish two questions. In the World Series example, we can distinguish the question whether a team deserved to win from the question whether the fruits of victory were divided up properly among the team's owners, coaches, and players. Similarly, the question whether the profits appropriated by a particular firm are deserved can be distinguished from whether the profits are divided up properly among the firm's investors, managers, and workers. The latter question is indeed important, and I shall return to it in this chapter. But however it is answered the fact remains that

Arnold provides only a tautological answer to the former question in the profits case. Given Arnold's restricted definition of the end of market exchange, the connection between that end and the entrepreneurial profits appropriated by the firm is a trivial one. This remains true no matter what the reward system within the internal organization of the given firm. In order to avoid this tautology the goal of market exchange should be formulated as "to approach the optimal allocation of economic benefits and burdens," rather than "to meet the wants and needs of . . . consumers." Arnold's reason for avoiding this wider interpretation of the goal of market exchange is clear enough. On the wider interpretation we cannot say a priori whether entrepreneurial profits are prima facie deserved or not. We would first have to know whether those profits generally aimed at an optimal allocation of economic benefits and burdens. By eliminating the wider interpretation without providing grounds for doing so, Arnold has quite clearly committed a petitio: he has defined the goal of the market in terms that allow him to arrive at the results he wished to attain.

Entrepreneurial Profits: Genus and Species

There is a second aspect of Arnold's position that is equally questionable. Even if a given reward can be shown to be deserved in terms of the goal of a specific institution, this obviously counts for little if that institution itself is morally objectionable. Arnold is well aware that if this were the case here "the desert claim of entrepreneurs would be of little ultimate significance." However he writes that "this turns out not to be a very serious problem" (401). After all, even many socialists today advocate the use of markets. Therefore the moral legitimacy of the market is not a contentious issue.

There are reasons to be wary of Arnold's claim that "socialists who think seriously about economics" all accept the necessity of the market for the foreseeable future.[1] But even if this claim is overlooked, his move here is truly astounding. Arnold seeks to justify the claim that as a *genus* entrepreneurial profits are prima facie deserved: "the account of who deserves profits defended in this essay is completely general" (401). The contentiousness of this claim is not lessened in the slightest by the fact that socialists accept one particular *species* of that genus. It is very often the case that a general type of action is morally objectionable except when quite specific conditions are met. Arnold's point is analogous to saying that there is nothing morally problematic about the genus "shooting a gun at another" on the grounds that even most members of gun control lobbies find a certain species of it acceptable (e.g., shooting when engaged in a just war). Any attempt to justify a general type of action by referring to those who accept it only under quite restricted conditions is inherently sophistical.

Why do socialists hold that entrepreneurial profits in general are not deserved, but are at most deserved in specific circumstances? Because the goal of the market includes approaching an optimal allocation of economic benefits and burdens; market success in general does *not* prima facie further that end. It furthers that end only when certain conditions are met. There are at least three respects in which entrepreneurial profits generally fail to attain that end. These points have been made often enough before. But as Arnold is surely not alone in overlooking them, they bear repeating. Surely they would be crucial in any attempt to evaluate whether capitalist markets were consistent with generalizable interests.

Social Costs

An optimal allocation of economic benefits and burdens requires that all social costs be taken into account when goods and services are provided. Now the market is an extremely efficient mechanism of ensuring that *some* categories of social costs are minimized. For instance, part of the social cost of a production process is the depletion of natural resources. Let us suppose a given natural resource is expensive. Entrepreneurs will invest in firms that have discovered either technological processes that use expensive raw material more efficiently or cheaper synthetic substitutes. These approaches generally will generate pure profits for those entrepreneurs. Other enterprises, funded by other entrepreneurs seeking similar profits for themselves, will emulate these practices. As a result of this mechanism the social cost of employing this input will be minimized over time.

This is not the whole story, however. The minimization of a firm's input costs can in no way be equated with the minimization of the social costs in general. While the market efficiently deals with the former, it typically and systematically ignores the costs of a production process imposed on the society as a whole rather than the producing enterprise. This is why these costs are termed "externalities" by economists.[2] They are social costs external to the entrepreneur's decision-making, concerned as it is with profit maximizing. But it is not only the case that entrepreneurs, concerned only with the difference between factor prices and output prices, according to Arnold, typically have no incentive to minimize these sorts of social costs. In most market contexts they have a strong *disincentive* to do so. If a firm installs, say, expensive pollution control equipment while its competitors do not, then those competitors will be able to undercut its prices. Everything else being equal, they will have lower production costs.

There is no reason to assume a priori that the social costs the market systematically tends to ignore will be less significant morally than those it systematically tends to minimize. Therefore there is no reason to assume a priori that an acceptable trade-off between the provision of goods and services and the social costs of providing them always accompanies a successful sale. There is no reason to assume a priori that an essential goal of market transactions, the approximation of an optimal allocation of economic benefits and burdens, has been met even when entrepreneurial investments result in the provision of goods and services to consumers. And, finally, there is no reason to assume a priori that the ensuing entrepreneurial profits are prima facie deserved. We would first need much more information regarding the externalities imposed on the society before we could begin to judge.

Consumer Wants and Needs

When Arnold defines the goal of the market in terms of the wants and needs of consumers, he fails to note a crucial ambiguity in the term "consumer." On the one hand it could mean all those in market societies who must turn to the market in order to meet their wants and needs. On the other hand it could mean all those with sufficient purchasing power to engage in market exchange successfully. Arnold clearly employs the term in the latter sense. But, once again, this makes the connection between entrepreneurial profits and the satisfaction of the wants and needs of consumers trivially true by stipulation. If this is to be avoided, then just as the end of market activity must be taken in a broader sense than Arnold's formulation, so must "consumer" be taken in the former, broader, signification.

The principle of consumer sovereignty to which Arnold appeals gets much of its rhetorical force from echoing the democratic ideal of popular sovereignty. But the principle of a consumer "voting" with his or her dollars means that a person with a million dollars gets a million votes, while a person with one dollar gets one vote. In other words, entrepreneurial activity generally does not match supply with consumer demand per se, but with *effective* demand only, demand backed by purchasing power. While it generally meets the wants and needs of those with effective demand quite efficiently, it systematically neglects the wants and needs of consumers who lack purchasing power. As a result market economies often actually result in an absolute lowering of the standard of living of a majority of consumers. This was the case in the countries of the West for much of the eighteenth and nineteenth centuries. It is still the case today for the inhabitants of the Southern Hemisphere. In this context Sen (1981) has established that the worst famines in Africa were caused by the lack of purchasing power of the poor rather than any shortage of food. Consider the entrepreneurial profits that resulted in Africa from shifting food production from the production of foodstuffs for local nutritional needs to luxury items of low nutrition for the export market (see Dinham and Hines 1984). Surely these pure profits cannot be justified prima facie in terms of satisfying consumer needs, at least not on the broader, more adequate, interpretation of "consumer."

Of course the average standard of living of the majority of consumers in the West did rise in the thirty years preceding World War I and the quarter of a century following World War II. But even then significant consumption needs (let alone wants) of entire sections of the population (e.g., racially oppressed groups, the elderly, the unemployed, single mothers) have been left unmet by entrepreneurial activity concerned solely with effective demand.

Further, it is even possible in principle to imagine market societies that ignore altogether the consumer needs of all but a tiny minority. Suppose that progressive automation makes the working class economically redundant, surviving on charity or else starving to death. The private owners of means of production could still circulate money and generate incomes through buying and selling machines, spare parts, raw materials, and consumption goods amongst themselves. This society would allow plenty of scope for entrepreneurial profits, even though the consumer wants and needs of all but a few were *entirely* left out of the circuit of market activity (Hodgson 1982, 83–84). Surely it would be most implausible to argue that this species of entrepreneurial profits could be prima facie deserved in terms of the satisfaction of consumer wants and needs.

If the essential goal of market activity includes the provision of consumer demand, and if "consumer demand" is defined in the broad sense required to avoid trivialities and to be consistent with the idea of aiming at an optimal allocation of economic benefits and burdens, then we cannot assume a priori that entrepreneurial profits are prima facie deserved on the grounds that they further the goal of the market. Once again we do not have enough information to judge. We would first need to know more about the wants and needs that were systematically *not* met due to entrepreneurs' exclusive concern with those fortunate enough to have purchasing power.

Social Labor

Defining the goal of market activity solely in terms of the provision of goods and services to consumers abstracts from the fact that labor is inherently related to consumption both quantitatively and qualitatively. First, as already noted, the extent of one's ability to consume in market societies generally depends on one's purchasing power. And purchasing power is generally a function of one's place in the social division of labor. Those who own and control the means of producing and distributing goods and services typically have the greatest purchasing power, those who are unemployed typically have the least. Those in between typically have an ability to consume corresponding to their closeness to or distance from these two poles, with upper-level management having considerable more purchasing power than those marginally employed. Second, the types of activity one engages in within the realm of consumption is generally a function of one's place in the social division of labor. A person returning from de-skilled work in a state of physical and psychological exhaustion will hardly be in a position to engage in forms of consumption that require strenuous mental or physical exertion. Only the more passive forms of consumption will generally be realistic options. Conversely, a worker in a skilled position with considerable control over his or her activity during the workday will typically be in a much better position to engage in active forms of consumption. These two points suggest that in reflecting upon the optimal allocation of economic benefits and burdens the realm of work is as central as the realm of consumption. If an allocation truly approached the optimal it would include a provision of work for the members of society that was as materially rewarding and as creative and meaningful as possible.[3]

Is there any inherent connection between entrepreneurial profits and the attainment of this end? Turning to the qualitative dimension first, Arnold does acknowledge that in some market situations there may be considerable worker self-management. There is every reason to believe that in such situations the workers would ensure that labor was as creative and meaningful as possible. But of course this is not generally a feature of market societies. For the most part in Arnold's own discussion the entrepreneur is the only true subject of production. Wage laborers are lumped together with that which lacks subjectivity—machines and land—as "factor inputs" to be purchased by entrepreneurs or their delegates. All these factor inputs then stand at the disposal of the entrepreneurs. Is there any reason to assume a priori that entrepreneurs will dipose of "labor inputs" in a way that enhances the creativity and meaningfulness of work? Clearly there is not. In some circumstances this may be compatible with the entrepreneur's interest in maximizing his or her profits. In many others it may very well not be.

From a quantitative standpoint Arnold is in something of a dilemma. He cannot assert that labor (or other factor inputs for that matter) receives an income proportional to its contribution to production. This would leave him open to the Sraffian critique proposed by Nell (1987). It would also undermine his own account of entrepreneurial profits, in which pure profits result from entrepreneurs hiring factor inputs at *less* than their marginal productivity. But he also ought not to consider that which factors receive to be totally indeterminate when he considers whether entrepreneurial profits are prima facie deserved. The activity of entrepreneurs is inherently within a network of social relationships. The question whether they prima facie deserve their rewards cannot be adequately considered in abstraction from whether other participants in that network prima facie receive what *they* deserve. If the entrepreneur's profits generally turned out to be essentially connected to a specific factor input systematically receiving less than its desert, then the claim that profits were prima facie deserved would be seriously undermined.

There are good reasons to think that in most species of market societies wage laborers typically do not receive what they deserve. Fortunately, this point can be made without having to construct a complete theory of economic desert here. However one defines desert, in an asymmetrical situation where structural power is operating, the party subjected to that power will generally tend to receive less than what is deserved.[4] In particular cases this may not occur. But the tendencies are in that direction, and as Arnold says in a different context, "in justifying institutional rules, that is the relevant consideration" (413). If this point is granted, then what must be done here is to show how the wage contract is an asymmetrical situation in which structural power is operating. This can be established simply by considering the lack of symmetry typically inherent in the wage contract. On the one side stand those who are extremely lucky if they are not suffocating with debt, let alone able to accumulate more than relatively insignificant savings. On the other side stand those who own and control both the productive resources of the society and considerable reserve funds for personal consumption. Given this structural inequality built into the starting point, any resulting agreement will tend to favor systematically the interests of entrepreneurs over the interests of wage laborers so that we may say that, in general, a form of structural coercion is operating. Entrepreneurs, in general, can simply afford to wait until the terms it receives are most favorable while wage laborers, in general, cannot. This does not imply that wages always remain at a mere subsistence level or worse. Depending upon the profitability of specific firms, conditions in the labor market, the degree of unity and combativeness among workers, the level of competition among entrepreneurs, and so on, wage contracts can incorporate labor's interests to a greater or lesser degree. But structural power remains operative. Entrepreneurs hold the trump card. If wage contracts begin to favor labor to the point where the profit interests of entrepreneurs as a group are threatened, they will take advantage of their private control of investment decisions and call a capital strike. Investment funds would be hoarded, or devoted to speculation, or diverted to overseas investment. Unemployment would rise drastically, thereby weakening labor's position in the wage contract, thereby restoring the asymmetrical situation entrepreneurs euphemistically refer to as a "favorable business climate."

The very least one can conclude from all this is that there is no reason to assume a priori that entrepreneurial profits are prima facie deserved on the grounds that they further the goal of an optimal alocation of economic benefits and burdens. Here too we do not have enough information to be able to judge. It could very well be the case that these profits are a direct function of a malallocation of economic benefits and burdens to wage laborers, a malallocation with both qualitative and quantitative dimensions.

Conclusion

The idea that institutional desert is to be assessed in terms of the essential goal of the given institution is appropriate to evaluating whether an institutional arrangement is consistent with generalizable interests. In trying to evaluate whether entrepreneurial profits are prima facie deserved, however, Arnold makes things too easy for himself. If the goal of market exchange is defined in terms of meeting the effective demand of consumers with purchasing power, then it follows trivially that entrepreneurial profits are prima facie deserved in terms of that end. But this is a one-sided and inadequate way of defining the end of market transactions. Arnold's own homage to entrepreneurs for correcting malallocations of resources suggests a more adequate and comprehensive ideal for market activity: the optimal allocation of economic benefits and burdens. I have argued that there is no reason whatsoever to assume a priori that entrepreneurial profits contribute to attaining this end. This could be asserted only if certain specific conditions were met. Entrepreneurial activity would have to be subject to strict social controls to ensure that all social costs are taken into account, that investments do not systematically neglect the areas of the greatest social needs, that there is no asymmetrical structural power underlying the relationship between wage laborers and entrepreneurs, and so on. Such conditions are clearly *not* met in the entrepreneurial activity of those whose profits Arnold is most concerned to justify, "the independent businessman, the promoters, the managers of large corporations with significant stock holdings, the arbitrage experts in the stock market, the instigators of hostile takeovers, and so on" (397). The moral rot at the heart of the all-too-pervasive phenomenon of Boeskyism gives the lie to Arnold all too obviously. Arguing that entrepreneurial profits are prima facie deserved in terms of the goal of exchange applies only to certain species of entrepreneurial profits. It by no means works for the genus as a whole, as Arnold supposes.

PART FOUR

THREE NORMATIVE MODELS

After descriptions and evaluations of social reality have been made, there is still the "What is to be done?" question; within social theory, social policy has a place alongside social science and social ethics. Social policy obviously includes the formulation of strategies and tactics. However, specific strategies and tactics always presuppose an ultimate end, a goal that the strategies and tactics will hopefully allow us to approach. The task of the seventh branch of social theory is to construct a normative model of institutions that makes the ultimate goal of our social policy explicit.

Given the ethical principle of universalizability derived by Habermas, the question to be answered in branch seven can be made more concrete: What sort of social system would be most compatible with universalizable interests?[1] Universalizable interests are those about which a consensus could be attained in an uncoerced discourse. This implies that the model we are seeking must be one in which exercises of public power are based upon a discourse that anticipates an ideal speech situation. I believe that *council democracy*, a model of institutions defended by Marx, Rosa Luxemburg, Trotsky, Gramsci, and Ernest Mandel, provides the answer.

In Chapters VII–IX I present the argument for council democracy somewhat indirectly. I discuss three philosophers who have accepted the ethical principle of universalizabity: Kant, John Rawls (*A Theory of Justice*), and Habermas himself. All three have constructed normative models within which that principle is supposedly institutionalized. None of these models is based on council democracy. I examine each model in detail, and show that all are fundamentally

111

flawed. In Chapter VII, I discuss some developmental tendencies in the model of simple commodity production Kant advocated, and the relevance of these tendencies to the normative adequacy of his model. In *A Theory of Justice* Rawls argued that liberal capitalism is just as long as the state fulfills certain tasks. In Chapter VIII, I claim that the functioning of a capitalistic economy tends to prevent the state from fulfilling these tasks. Finally, in Chapter IX, I maintain that the normative model of institutions Habermas defends can be criticized from the standpoint of Habermas's own value commitments. In each case I argue that council democracy provides a more adequate institutionalization of the universalizabilty principle.

One last point must be made. Many of the arguments considered here in Part Four involve ethical evaluations of capitalism similar to those undertaken in Part Three. However, in Part Three the evaluations were directed at capitalism taken as an existing set of structures and processes. In Part Four, capitalism is considered as a normative ideal. Of course there is some overlap between the two. But the difference, which is the difference between the sixth and the seventh branch of social theory, is sufficient to justify a separate treatment of the two themes.

VII

Kant's Political Philosophy: *Rechtsstaat* or Council Democracy?

Most studies of Kant's political philosophy explore the relationship between Kant's political philosophy and the remaining parts of his philosophical system.[1] Like the remainder of his system, Kant's political philosophy seems at first glance to be constructed entirely a priori. A political philosophy that is not solely on a transcendental level, he seemed to insist, cannot deal adequately with the central issue of political philosophy: What is right? The theorist who remains on a merely empirical level,

> can, of course, tell us what the actual Law of the land is (*quid sit juris*), that is, what the laws say or have said at a certain time and at a certain place. But whether what these laws prescribe is also just and the universal criterion that will in general enable us to recognize what is just or unjust (*justum et injustum*)–the answer to such questions will remain hidden from him unless, for a while, he abandons empirical principles and searches for the sources of these judgments in pure reason. [To do so is necessary] in order to lay the foundations of any possible positive legislation (Kant, 1965), 34).[2]

A transcendental political philosophy along these lines would appear to unfold in two stages. First, certain fundamental normative principles operative throughout the practical sphere would be formulated. To these other normative principles specific to the political sphere must be added. Second, a model of basic institutions embodying these normative principles would be derived. In this manner the claim that the model of institutions so derived was "just" or "right" could then be grounded a priori in terms of the fundamental normative principles it embodies.

A first thesis of this chapter is that Kant's political philosophy is more complex than the above account suggests. I shall briefly present Kant's fundamental normative principles. For our purposes here we may regard these principles as equivalent to the ethical principle of universalizability that Habermas claims is immanent in all speech. Given this principle, taken from what I have termed the fifth branch of social theory, the question that defines the seventh branch can be formulated at once: What normative model of institutions best embodies this ethical principle, thus providing an ultimate goal for social policy? After presenting the model Kant advocated, I shall argue that normative claims regarding the rightness of this model cannot be derived solely from Kant's normative principle. Further premises are required for the argument to work, premises that are empirical in nature. Despite the passage quoted above, Kant himself was quite conscious of the need to make certain empirical assumptions in order to justify his claims, and he stated many of these assumptions explicitly. My second thesis is that there are good reasons for regarding a number of these empirical assumptions as doubtful. My third and final thesis is that if one inserts more plausible empirical assumptions into the argument a quite different model of fundamental institutions follows. More specifically, I shall argue that with these different empirical assumptions a model of a democratic form of socialism follows from the principle of universalizability that Kant accepted.[3]

Kant's A Priori Argument for a Pure Republic (*Rechtsstaat*) and Federation of Republics

The concept of transcendental *freedom* (rational *autonomy*) is the starting point of Kant's entire practical philosophy.[4] Freedom has a first, merely negative, sense in which agents are viewed as freed from the strict necessity of causal determination. Agents are free in a second, positive, sense insofar as they follow the moral law. Following the moral law (the "categorical imperative") is a matter of subjecting the maxims or fundamental intentions behind one's activity to the test of seeing whether they could be *universalized*. Implicit in this is the notion of *respect* for other persons; it is my respect for others as ends in themselves that leads me to test whether my particular maxims can be made universal, that is, compatible with the autonomy of others. Insofar as I too am in turn worthy of the respect of others, also implicit in universalization is the notion of furthering a *kingdom of ends*. This principle conveys the idea of an entire system of moral agents, each of whom respects the autonomy of others and is in turn respected by these others (see Hoffe 1977; Shalgi 1976; Rollin 1976). "Autonomy," "respect," and "the kingdom of ends" are fundamental normative principles ultimately equivalent to the principle of universalizability that has been referred to throughout this book. This principle is operative throughout Kant's practical philosophy.

One can strive to bring about the kingdom of ends as a result of an inner disposition (a good will) to follow the moral law. One part of Kant's practical philosophy, the *doctrine of virtue*, discusses the system of specific normative principles that grounds activity internally motivated by the desire to fulfill our duty to ourselves and to others. This realm of practical philosophy does not concern us here. The area of practical philosophy dealing with the sociopolitical sphere has a different problematic: to establish an institutional setting within which the activities of persons cohere in a manner that approximates the kingdom of ends, even if the agents themselves are *not* motivated by the duty to bring this about. This problematic must be considered because our self-love regularly prevents us from acting in accord with duty. The absence of the good will necessitates the presence of politics. The institutional setting approximating a kingdom of ends is derived within what Kant termed the *doctrine of right*.[5] While Kant placed action done from duty on a higher ethical plane than action which is merely right, in the existential order right has a certain priority over duty. A moral commitment to duty needs an institutional setting in order to flourish: "We cannot expect . . . moral attitudes to produce a good constitution; on the contrary, it is only through the latter that the people can be expected to attain a good level of moral culture" ("Perpetual Peace," in Kant 1970, 113).

The first necessary condition for the possibility of right action, that is, action at least externally in accord with a kingdom of ends,

115

is the establishment of a civil constitution. In any "state of nature", that is, any society imagined to be without a civil constitution, the danger is ever-present that others may interfere with my free action with no judge set above us. This would leave me with no recourse besides force. Instead of a situation in which the autonomy of each is mutually respected, a state of war holds, even if actual outbreaks of physical violence are limited. From this it follows as an a priori demand of reason that the state of nature must be abandoned. Rational agents must agree to enter a social contract establishing a civil constitution. Only under a civil constitution can freedom be exercised under external laws.[6] Here the existence of coercive laws enforced by a public authority ensures an approximation of a situation in which the exercise of one's freedom is limited only by the freedom of others. This is, for Kant, the very definition of justice or right: "Justice is . . . the aggregate of those conditions under which the will of one person can be conjoined with the will of another in accordance with a universal law of freedom" (1965, 34).

The notion that the civil constitution ultimately rests on a united will of all rational agents (a "social contract") provides a first normative principle specific to the sociopolitical sphere. This is the principle of the *general will*. A just system of institutions is one compatible with the general will as the ultimate ground of the civil constitution. The social contract, Kant (1970) wrote,

> is in fact merely an idea of reason, which nonetheless has undoubted practical reality; for it can oblige every legislator to frame his laws in such a way that they could have been produced by the united will of the whole nation, and to regard each subject, insofar as he can claim citizenship, as if he had consented within the general will. This is the test of the rightfulness of every public law. ("On the Common Saying," 79).

To this Kant (1970) added three further normative principles specific to the sociopolitical sphere:

> The civil state, regarded purely as a lawful state, is based on the following *a priori* principles:
>
> 1. The *freedom* of every member of society as a *human being*.

2. The equality of each with all the others as a *subject*.

3. The *independence* of each member of a commonwealth as a citizen.

These principles are not so much laws given by an already established state, as laws by which a state can alone be established in accordance with pure rational principles of external human right. ("On the Common Saying," 74)

"Freedom" here does not refer to the transcendental freedom discussed above, but rather to a principle of political liberty. It asserts that a model of just institutions must not contain any paternalism.[7] "Equality" here means equality before the law, and not any equality of possessions.[8] "Independence" means that in a just society only those who are economically self-sufficient and not dependent upon another person for their livelihood can participate fully in the commonwealth as active citizens.

Armed with both the general a priori ethical principle of universalizability and a priori principles specific to the sociopolitical sphere, Kant proceeded to construct a normative model of basic institutions embodying these principles to the greatest degree possible. On the national scale he terms this model a pure *republic*, while on the international plane he calls for a *federation of republics*. This model fixes what for Kant is the proper long-term goal of all practical activity in the sociopolitical sphere. It constitutes Kant's contribution to the seventh branch of social theory.

The republic or *Rechtsstaat* can be viewed as a social system uniting two distinct subsystems. The first subsystem is that of *socioeconomic activity*. Here individual citizens all have an equal right to exercise their liberty under law. In order to ensure this liberty and equality Kant derived a priori a number of fundamental rights, including the rights to choose a religion, to choose a marriage partner, to choose an occupation, to accumulate property through one's labor, to trade one's property with others, and so on.[9] The socioeconomic relationships of master and slave, or feudal lord and serf, are not compatible with these rights. Instead the networks binding the members of society together in Kant's republic are based upon free transactions among individuals, central among which are contractual transactions in the marketplace. The second subsystem is the *state*.[10] Here laws ensuring that those exercising their freedom in society do not

117

infringe upon the freedom of others are passed, enforced, and judged in their application. The state therefore is divided into the legislative, executive, and judicial branches of government, respectively ("Public Law," in Kant 1965, 78, #45).

In Kant's model a number of institutional mechanisms are proposed whereby the state and the socioeconomic realm are united. Of course all laws made, administered, and judged by the state affect society. But the state affects socioeconomic activity directly through such measures as taxing individuals to provide itself with revenues ("Public Law," in Kant 1965, 92–93). These revenues support what Kant termed "charitable or pious institutions" (93–94; today we would speak of welfare measures). The revenues also support the provisions of an infrastructure, that is, "help for the national economy . . . (e.g. for improvements to roads, new settlements, storage of foodstuffs for years of famine, etc.) ("Perpetual Peace," in Kant 1970, 95), and the enforcement of punishment. It is important to note that state intervention is limited to these sorts of activities. Specifically, the state may *not* infringe on the free transactions of individuals in the marketplace. Indeed, the preservation of property is a central motivation for the social contact which constitutes the state (see Brandt 1974; Kant 1965, 71–72, #42).

The individuals in society have input into the state in a number of ways. First, all those who as a result of their own efforts have attained the self-sufficiency required for being active citizens have an equal right to vote for members of the legislature, for "every true republic is and can be nothing else than a representative system of the people if it is to protect the rights of its citizens in the name of the people (Kant 1965, 113). Second, individual citizens also participate in the state's judicial activity, for "only the people can judge one of themselves, although they do this indirectly by means of their delegated representatives (the jury)" (Kant 1965, 83). These are mechanisms whereby Kant seeks to ensure that the formulation and enforcement of the laws of the state approximate to the general will. This end is also to be attained through institutionalizing public discourse.[11] In Kant's model of just institutions individual citizens possess a right to unrestricted free speech. Each has an equal right to propose and to evaluate policies. At first these policies will reflect the narrow horizons of the individual's self-interest. But the sharing of proposals in discussion sets off a process of enlightenment. Individual citizens gradually learn how to transcend the limits of their initially private horizons, and to attain a horizon which includes the interests of others. "For enlightenment of this kind," Kant writes, "all that is needed is *freedom*. And the freedom in question is the most innocuous form of all – freedom to make *public use* of one's reason in all matters."[12] When this occurs the empirical "will of all" approximates the a priori and normative "general will." State officials inevitably then use this general will as a guide in their policy making.

On the international plane, the relationship among states is exactly analogous to that among individuals prior to their entering under a civil constitution. Here too even if a condition of injustice is avoided a situation without justice obtains. Kant's solution here is, however, somewhat different. He did not call for a social contract on an international scale to enter into a world state. His (1970) view is that this would be conceptually incoherent ("Perpetual Peace," 102), impossible from an administrative standpoint, and would lead to despotism even if it were possible ("Perpetual Peace," 113; 1965, 123). His proposal instead was for a federation of commonwealths. This federation would establish an approximation to a condition of universal peace.

The Empirical Premises in Kant's Argument

It would certainly be worthwhile to examine in detail the a priori arguments Kant employed in the derivation of his model of a pure republic and a federation of republics. Here, however, I would like to examine a more neglected area of Kant's position. For Kant to conclude that his model of basic institutions is a suitable long-term goal of social policy he must do more than simply refer to certain normative principles. He also must suppose that were the model to be institutionalized it would function over time in a manner consistent with those principles. This means that his argument requires a set of empirical assumptions as to how his model would function. Without these further premises it is impossible to get from the premises stating Kant's normative principles to the conclusion that the model of institutions he advocated is acceptable. In previous chapters I have argued that normative considerations permeate the branches of social

119

theory devoted to empirical research, empirical theory construction, and the formulation of empirical models of social processes and structures. A corresponding point must be insisted upon here: the results of empirical studies are of great relevance to the normative branches of social theory. Despite his fondness for a priori arguments Kant himself was well aware of the need for such empirical premises in political philosophy. The task now is to present a list of Kant's eight empirical assumptions, stating briefly why they are necessary to Kant's position even though his intention is ultimately to establish normative claims. These empirical assertions fall into two groups: 1–4 offer four empirical presuppositions regarding the key elements of the model; 5–8 assert the four states of affairs that would follow as consequences of the model.

1. *Small independent producers are (or at least could be) the basic economic units in a market society.* Kant needed this empirical claim for two reasons. "Autonomy" is a central principle for Kant's practical philosophy. Any institutional framework defensible on Kantian grounds must embody this principle to the highest degree possible in the external world. Small independent producers control their own process of laboring. They are thus (externally) autonomous in their concrete day-to-day activity. Secondly, this has political implications. Kant (1970) supposed that only those who are economically independent are capable of truly independent participation in the political process. Small independent producers are therefore the bulk of the active citizens of the republic:

The only qualification required by a citizen (apart, of course, from being an adult male) is that he *must* be his *own master* (sui iuris), and must have some *property* (which can include any skill, trade, fine art or science) to support himself. In cases where he must earn his living from others, he must earn it only by *selling* that which is his, and not by allowing others to make use of him; for he must in the true sense of the word *serve* no-one but the commonwealth. In this respect artisans and large or small landowners are all equal, and each is entitled to one vote only ("On the Common Saying," 102; see also Saage 1973).

2. *Effort, merit, and brute luck are (or at least could be) the chief principles of distribution in a market society.* In other words, in such

a society there is an equality of opportunity. Kant (1970) did not at all claim that his model ensures equality of results: "The uniform equality of human beings as subjects of a state is, however, perfectly consistent with the utmost inequality of the mass in the degree of its possessions" ("On the Common Saying," 75). In fact, Kant's model allows inequalities such that some members of the society ("passive citizens") do not exercise significant autonomy in the external realm (servants, apprentices, wage laborers, etc.). The model, he continues, is nonetheless not unjust so long as "[E]very member of the commonwealth (is) entitled to reach any degree of rank which a subject can earn through his talent, his industry and his good fortune" (75).

3. *All exercises of public power are exercised by the state.* The idea of the social contract established for Kant the principle that all exercises of public power should be subject to public control, that is, to the general will. In his model the unrestricted freedom of speech in the public sphere, the direct election of members of the legislature, and so on, provide a public control over the exercise of public power by the state, ensuring that it approximates the general will. This is sufficient so long as it is assumed that only the state exercises public power.

4. *The equal right to free speech will lead to a process of enlightenment.* Kant (1970) wrote, "Men will of their own accord gradually work their way out of barbarism so long as artificial measures are not *deliberately* adopted to keep them in it" ("What is Enlightenment," 59). The thesis here is that the only checks on the formation of a rational public opinion are the restrictions imposed by the state in censorship. When these artifical restrictions are removed, public discourse will inevitably tend toward articulating a consensus approximating the general will.

We now come to the second set of empirical assumptions, those concerned with the consequences that allegedly would follow from Kant's model of institutions. All these points have the same form, captured in Max Weber's phrase, "The paradox of unintended consequences." Remember that Kant's project was to construct a system of institutions that would embody

121

principles of justice *even if those acting within these institutions are oriented by self-interest rather than by an inner intention to follow their duty.* (This is what distinguishes the doctrine of right from the doctrine of virtue.) Empirical assumptions 5 through 8 specify mechanisms that Kant believes would be operative within his model and that would lead to a just state of affairs even when this state was not intended by the agents themselves.

5. *Actions taken by the ruler out of self-interest will have the unintended consequence of increasing liberty.* Kant supposed, first, that the self-interest of the ruler demands that her state be economically powerful and, second, that economic vitality depends upon furthering civil freedom. Therefore, he concludes, the ruler's self-interest leads to a furthering of civil freedom:

Civil freedom can no longer be so easily infringed without disadvantage to all trades and industries, and especially to commerce, in the event of which the state's power in its external relations will also decline. But this freedom is gradually increasing. If the citizen is deterred from seeking his personal welfare in any way he chooses which is consistent with the freedom of others, the vitality of business in general and hence also the strength of the whole are held in check. For this reason, restrictions placed upon personal activites are increasingly relaxed. . . . It is a great benefit which the human race must reap even from its rulers' self-seeking schemes of expansion, if only they realise what is to their own advantage.[13]

6. *The pursuit of private self-interest by those engaged in international trade will have the unintended consequence of bringing the world closer to perpetual peace.* Suppose that a good deal of trade is conducted between state *A* and state *B*. The self-interest of *A* is now tied up with the fate of *B*. If some third country *C* were to threaten *B*, *A* has good reasons to intervene in order to preserve the peace, for example by offering itself as a mediator. It does so even if it lacks any commitment to peace as a duty and is motivated purely by self-interest:

The *spirit of commerce* sooner or later takes hold of every people, and it cannot exist side by side with war. . . . Thus states find themselves compelled to promote the noble cause of peace, though not exactly from motives of morality. And wherever in the world there is a threat of war breaking out, they will try to prevent it by mediation, just as if they had entered into a permanent league for this purpose. ("Perpetual Peace," in Kant 1970, 114).

7. *The pursuit of self-interest by the capitalist state through war and preparations for war will have the unintended consequence of leading to peace.* Kant's argument here is that the national debt resulting from even successful wars imposes such a burden that peace is soon seen to be in the self-interest of nations. This is so even when there is no commitment to peace as a duty.

War itself gradually becomes not only a highly artifical undertaking, extremely uncertain in its outcome for both parties, but also a very dubious risk to take since its aftermath is felt by the state in the shape of a constantly increasing national debt (a modern invention) whose repayment becomes interminable. ("Idea for a Universal History," in Kant 1970, 51).

8. *An approximation of perpetual peace will be the unintended consequence of imperialistic policies.* Kant was one of the first philosophers to sketch a theory of imperialism.[14] He had a clear sense that market societies have an innate tendency to expand beyond their own shores. He himself defended a right to initiate trade with foreign countries: "[All nations] have a right to attempt to trade with a foreigner without his being justified in regarding anyone who attempts it as an enemy" (Kant 1965, 125). Kant even defended the right to settle in foreign territories without the permission of the indigenous population so long as the lord of the territories agrees and no land is taken from the inhabitants: "The lord of a country has the right to encourage foreigners (colonists) to immigrate and settle in his country, even though his native subjects do not regard this action favorably. He may do so, however, only providing that the private ownership of the land of the natives is not diminished" (Kant 1965, 109). But Kant (1970) also felt that in market societies there is an innate tendency to go beyond these limits and to subject foreign territories to plunder:

If we (consider) the inhospitable conduct of the civilised states of our continent, *especially the commercial states, the injustice which they display in visiting foreign countries and peoples (which in their case is the same as conquering them) seems appallingly great.* America, the negro countries, the Spice Island, the Cape, etc. were looked upon at the time of their discovery as ownerless territories; for the native inhabitants were counted as nothing. In East India (Hindustan), foreign troops were brought in under the pretext of merely setting up trading posts. This led to oppression of the natives, incitement of the various Indian states to widespread wars, famine, insurrection, treachery and the whole litany of evils which can afflict the human race. ("Perpetual Peace," 106; see also 117)

Kant (1970) however, did not see this as a long-term problem. His view was that this activity will be self-correcting. Imperialist policies, he asserted, are not profitable. And so those who would otherwise engage in them will be led by private self-interest to refrain:

The worst (or from the point of view of moral judgments, the best) thing about all this is that the commercial states do not even benefit by their violence, for all their trading companies are on the point of collapse. The Sugar Islands, that stronghold of the cruellest and most calculated slavery, do not yield any real profit. ("Perpetual Peace," 107)

These eight assertions are all empirical. And yet they must be combined with Kant's normative premises in order to derive the normative conclusion that Kant's *Rechtsstaat* is the proper ultimate end to be sought by social policy. In other words, these eight statements must be granted if we are to conclude that the institutional framework Kant advocated is the closest approximate to a kingdom of ends possible in a situation where one cannot assume that all are motivated by the duty to follow the moral law. These eight assertions, however, are either simply false or at least extremely doubtful from the present perspective of 200 years of capitalist market development subsequent to Kant. Unfortunately, it is not possible here to do more than run through the eight assumptions briefly, suggesting why they are at the least implausible and why this fact undercuts the model of institutions Kant advocated in his *Rechtslehre*.

1. This assumption is simply false. Kant wrote at an early stage of European capitalist development termed merchant capitalism.

While many residues of feudalism remained, small commodity production was growing. Here goods were produced by small-scale independent producers who owned their own tools and controlled their own labor. They then sold these goods to merchants who resold them for a profit. Kant extrapolated from this to a future in which all production would be organized in this manner. But as merchants gradually accumulated a great deal of wealth, it was all but inevitable that they would come up with the idea of increasing their profits by directly controlling the labor process themselves. Their far-greater financial resources allowed them to purchase machines that independent producers could not afford, which in turn allowed them to take advantage of economies of scale that independent producers could not attain. In this manner, the social basis of Kant's *Rechtslehre* – the independent artisan and peasant landholder, in short the petite bourgeoisie – was totally surpassed as a significant economic class throughout the developed capitalist world.[15] The vast majority of people were now forced to sell their labor power in order to survive. This development undercuts Kant's model because now the vast majority of people are *not* able to exercise significant autonomy in the control of their concrete daily lives at the workplace. Regarding when labor is performed, how the work process is organized, the pace of the labor process, and so forth, the laboring classes today have less say than under the artisan production of Kant's model.[16] They therefore also lack the economic self-sufficiency that Kant insisted was a necessary condition for being an active citizen. He wrote (1965) that, "generally anyone who must depend for his support (subsistence and protection), not on his own industry, but on arrangements by others (with the exception of the state) – all such people lack civil personality" (79).

2. This assumption too seems to be quite clearly false. With the eradication of a society based upon the small independent producer owning his own means of production, equality of opportunity is eradicated as well. Those who own or control capital have far, far greater opportunities than those who do not, whatever the effort, merit, and luck of the latter might happen to

be. It is now not these three factors stressed by Kant that determines the distribution of wealth and one's ability to be autonomous in the external realm so much as it is one's class position.[17]

3. In a society of small independent producers the only form of public power is indeed located in the state. It is most doubtful that this remains the case with the rise of industrial capitalism. There is now a class of people that has the power to decide which areas shall flourish and which communities will decay, which types of technologies will be developed and which not, and so on. This is the power of allocating capital. These sorts of decisions affect the public as much, if not more, than the decisions made by state officials. Yet in Kant's model there is no direct public control over *these* exercises of public power.

One might reply that while there is no direct control over the power of capital, there is indirect control in that the public may operate through the state legislature. But the state is *itself* subject to the exercise of public power by the large holders of capital. The most obvious manner in which this occurs is the tendency for officeholders to be either wealthy themselves or dependent upon the backing of the wealthy (see Nichols 1974). But even if we imagine a state legislature that did significantly attempt to control capital, this attempt would be met by a combination of an investment strike at home and a flight of capital outside the nation. The domestic economy would be brought to the point of collapse. The state would then be forced to rescind its reforms in order to restore "investor confidence." As long as the state acknowledges private rights to the ownership and control of capital, the private holders of capital thus in effect possess a veto power over state legislation.

We shall discuss only one example of a public power not checked by public control that follows from the eradication of the small independent producer: the systematic coercion underlying the wage contract. The owners/controllers of capital possess both the productive resources of the society and a considerable reserve of funds. Their subsistence is not immediately threatened. Generally they can afford to wait before coming to an agreement over wages. In contrast, wage laborers do not possess any reserves to speak of beyond their hands and minds, which they *must* hire out within a relatively short period of time if they and their families are to be at least minimally secure. In negotiations, therefore, the two groups do not meet on an equal footing. Because of this there is an irreducible element of coercion in the ensuing wage contract.[18] This institutionalized coercion is incompatible with the claim that a kingdom of ends has been approxiimated. Instead, a large holder of capital would seem to fit a description Kant (1970) proposed for a member of the feudal nobility: "He would be allowed to practice coercion without himself being subject to coercive countermeasures from others, and would thus be more than their fellow-subject" ("On the Common Saying," 76).

4. Even when all legal constraints on free speech are abolished, this does not guarantee by itself that public discourse will tend towards an enlightened consensus approximating in the external realm the a priori general will. While all may formally have an equal chance to express their perspective, public debate will tend to be dominated by those whose financial resources grant them disproportionate access to the media, schools, and other institutions whereby views are transmitted. Given that these institutions are disproportionately influenced by controllers of capital through the private ownership of the mass media, the funding of research projects in the university, and so on, it is certainly implausible to assume that their interests will not be disproportionately represented in public discussion.[19] If this is the case, then public discourse may be channeled. Certain issues can be filtered out of general discussion altogether while others are formulated in categories that make sense of the social world from a capitalist perspective. For example, discussion of new technologies in the media and the classroom will employ exclusively the category "increased efficiency" in cases where the concept "increased capitalist control of the labor process" is no less descriptive. If this is the case, then the articulation of a truly enlightened public opinion on something like technical change, one incorporating the interests of all, will be extremely difficult despite the lack of legal restrictions on speech.

127

5. The formation of more or less fixed class divisions makes this assumption doubtful also. In a system of small independent producers, "economic vitality" can indeed be spurred by an increase in civil liberties. But at least in certain circumstances a *constriction* of liberty is a more plausible result of the attempt to stimulate "economic vitality" in a more-developed capitalist market society. Assume that at some T_1 citizens enjoy a considerable degree of freedom. Assume further that workers and consumers use this freedom to organize strong trade unions, active consumer organizations, and so on. As a result, significant wage gains are won, worker safety and consumer protection legislation is passed, and so forth. Now such things impose a cost on business. If this cost is judged to be too high by those who own/control capital, they will cease productive investment in the country and invest their funds in speculation on, say, gold, real estate, art works, or in overseas markets where the liberty to organize is not granted. As a result, by some T_2 there is widespread economic stagnation. In this circumstance a government, seeking the "economic vitality" of which Kant speaks, will be led to institute policies that directly or indirectly make it *more* difficult for workers and consumers to exercise their liberty in organizing. Or imagine some other capitalist country which at T_1 does *not* grant its citizens such liberty. What motivation does it have to institute policies it knows will make it harder to attract business investment, the source of economic vitality in a capitalist society?[20] At the least these thought experiments suggest that it is quite contingent whether or not the pursuit of "economic vitality" will lead to the unintended consequence of increased civil liberty.

6. Unfortunately for humanity this empirical thesis has been thoroughly refuted by history. Access to foreign raw materials, markets, and labor is often highly desired and even seen as a necessity to capitalist states. This has led not to international peace, but to military intervention on the part of the strongest capitalist states in order to attain and preserve this access. This military involvement can take two forms, either against other developed capitalist states which are trying to ensure *their* access

to overseas materials, market, and labor, or against those nations whose materials, markets, and labor are the objects of desire. Both forms of international conflict have occurred again and again since Kant's day. This is not to imply an economic reductionism that reduces *all* political-military policy to economic self-interest. The point is simply that Kant's thesis that economic self-interest leads capitalist nations closer to perpetual peace is implausible.[21]

7. Nor is it clear that the preparation and making of war by capitalist states itself leads to peace as an unintended consequence as a result of ever-increasing debts. In certain circumstances, at least, the costs of preparations for war can be a positive spur to a capitalist economy. It can provide an outlet for the investment of capital that otherwise could not be profitably employed, thereby helping the economy avoid stagnation. Kant (1970) himself envisioned a positive function of what is today termed "military Keynesianism":

A credit system, if used by the powers as an instrument of aggression against one another, shows the power of money in its most dangerous form. For while the debts thereby incurred are always secure against present demands (because not all the creditors will demand payment at the same time), these debts go on growing indefinitely. This ingenious system, invented by a commercial people in the present century, provides a military fund which may exceed the resources of all the other states put together. It can only be exhausted by an eventual tax-deficit, which may be postponed for a considerable time by the commercial stimulus which industry and trade receive through the credit system. ("Perpetual Peace," 95)

Kant may yet prove correct that the increase of public debt eventually will lead to the bankruptcy of military Keynesianism. But the ways in which military spending can be functional for a capitalist system makes Kant's assumption that it will lead to perpetual peace most questionable.

8. This final thesis falls in the group of those assumptions by Kant that are simply false. In most underdeveloped countries of the capitalist global system, conditions today are barely bet-

ter off than in the Sugar Islands of Kant's day. Capitalist investment goes hand in hand with the ruthless exploitation of indigenous human and natural resources. Declining standards of living for the vast majority, rates of unemployment often reaching 30 to 40 percent of the labor force, misery, malnutrition, and even starvation, is the norm. The all-but-inevitable complement of this is brutal police–military power. And this investment is incredibly profitable: "In the 1966–1978 period the outflow of capital (from U.S. corporations) to these (i.e., underdeveloped) countries was only $11 billion, while the return flow of income was a fabulous $56 billion" (Magdoff and Sweezy 1981, 164). Kant's assumption that control of foreign economies is unprofitable must therefore be regarded as wishful thinking.

Sketch of an Alternative Model of Institutions Embodying Kantian Principles

In the part of Kant's work that falls within the seventh branch of social theory Kant attempted to derive a priori an institutional system that would embody his fundamental normative principles. However he could claim that the model he derived embodied those principles only by making certain empirical assumptions that I have suggested are not plausible. There is thus a conflict between the normative principles Kant defended and the model of institutions he advocated.

At this point three options are open. First, one could keep the Kantian model of institutions but shift the underlying normative principles so as to make them consistent with the model. This would take us in the direction of Robert Nozick (1974). Nozick claims to be a Kantian, and his "minimal state" is indeed quite close to Kant's *Rechtsstaat* in its defense of private property rights and its denial that the state has any right to intervene in market transactions. But Nozick has abandoned the central Kantian principle of "autonomy." Kant's (1970) principle of autonomy implies that a citizen in the full sense cannot "allow others to make use of him" ("On the Common Saying," 78). The principle of an individual's right to liberty in Nozick's formulation, however, allows this. It is thus quite impoverished from a truly Kantian perspective; it is not consistent with generalizable interests (see the discussion of "liberty" in Chapter V, this book).

A second option is to tinker with the model of institutions Kant advocated so as to bring it into harmony with the principle of universalizability Kant accepted. This would take us in the direction of John Rawls (whose major work, of course, is *A Theory of Justice*) and Jürgen Habermas. Both thinkers grant the state a right to intervene in the market that goes far beyond anything Kant envisioned. But both do so in order to assert that a market society *can* be made congruent with the above principle. For reasons that will be explored in depth in the next two chapters, I believe that these attempts to modify Kant's *Rechtsstaat* cannot be judged successful.

This leaves a final option. The model of institutions proposed by Kant in his *Rechtslehre* could be radically transformed, so as to bring it in line with Kantian principles. It is this path I find most promising. It leads, I believe, from Kant to Marx. The system of institutions Marx advocated can be termed "council democracy." A sketch of this model will be presented. I shall then argue that this model fulfills the tasks assigned by Kant to a just republic.[22]

In this model the basic units are worker councils and consumer councils, at both local and regional levels. Local-level worker councils are self-managing units of production organized at the workplace. Within them workers themselves formulate proposals regarding what is to be produced, how the production process is to be organized, who among them is to oversee the production process, and so on. These decisions are made democratically, as are all council decisions. They are based on a principle of consensus, with majority vote being resorted to only if time constraints demand. Higher-level worker councils will be made up of democratically elected representatives from local worker councils. Their tasks will include deciding on questions regarding production that cannot be made at a local level. (For example, the question of whether one large steel mill should be built to take advantage of economies of scale as opposed to building a number of small mills close to places of production could not be answered appropriately on the local level.) They also will have to ensure that the plans of local worker councils ultimately fit together coherently. Local-level consumer councils are to be organized at the neighborhood level. Their tasks would include articulating the needs of their members, formulating requests that items of consumption be produced to satisfy these needs, and formulating principles for the distribution of consumption items. Higher-level consumer councils have the task of ensuring that the requests of the various local-level councils ultimately cohere, and also of dealing with consumption goods that transcend the local level. (An example of the issues that would arise here would be those involving public goods such as regional parks and cultural centers.)

This model would function as follows. Everyone would be both a member of a worker council and of a consumer council. As such, everyone would have an opportunity to present her ideas regarding what should be produced and how, and what should be requested for consumption. After a period of discussion the local-level worker councils would democratically agree on a proposal to produce so many units of various sorts of goods or services, while the local-level consumer councils would agree on a proposal to request to consume so many units of various sorts of goods and services. These plans would then be punched into a local terminal connected by a main computer to the terminals of every other local council. Armed instantly with information regarding the decisions of every other council, each local council would then voluntarily adjust its proposals to better match future production with articulated social needs. This process could be repeated a number of times within a given time-period, with the higher-level councils having the final responsibility of matching production plans with consumption needs to the greatest extent possible at the given level of productive capacity.

Of course, the functioning of this model too will have consequences unforeseeable at present. But there does exist today a body of knowledge that is relevant when considering those consequences that are rationally foreseeable at present. Many corporations, searching for greater worker productivity, have toyed with systems providing greater variety in workers' tasks and greater worker participation in management decisions. No matter how the experiments were organized, changes that provided workers with more power in production all increased worker productivity. This suggests that the model of council democracy could function over time in an efficient manner. The question now is whether it could function over time in a manner consistent with Kantian principles.[23]

Brief as this sketch of a system of council democracy has been, I believe that it is sufficient to establish that some such institutional system fulfills the intentions behind Kant's political philosophy to a far-greater degree than does a social system including a capitalist market society. I shall close this paper by arguing (1) that this model embodies central normative principles advocated by Kant, and (2) that there are no fundamental Kantian normative principles with which it is incompatible.

First, let us recall Kant's key normative principles: (a) any system of basic institutions must provide for the greatest degree of autonomy possible; (b) one specific area of autonomy must be the independence Kant associates with active citizenship; (c) the system of basic institutions must be structured so as to lead to social choices which approximate the general will, that is, which lead to a state of affairs approximating a kingdom of ends; and (d) there must be reason to think that empirical decisions approximating the normative general will result from the institutional framework without supposing that those acting within the framework are motivated by the duty to bring this about. Does the model of council democracy fulfill these principles?

(a) Workers managing the production process themselves and consumers controlling the affairs of their neighborhoods are acting autonomously to a degree impossible when investment decisions affecting the workplace and community are in the hands of those who privately own/control capital. Because large corporations, whatever the good intentions of those who run them, are forced by the logic of competition to treat workers and consumers primarily as means to further their profits, council democracy furthers the treatment of people as ends in themselves.

(b) In council democracy it is in principle possible for everyone to be an independent active citizen in Kant's full sense. That is, no one here is forced to sell his labor power to another in order to survive. Instead each person, to quote Kant's (1970) demand, "in the true sense of the word serves no-one but the commonwealth" ("On the Common Saying," 78).

(c) In the process whereby individuals and local councils formulate proposals and then revise those proposals when the views of other individuals and local councils are made public, an institutionalized mechanism is established which allows for an empirical consensus to be attained that approximates in the external realm the a priori normative idea of the general will. In this manner the Kantian principle that the general will is the ultimate foundation for sovereignty can be made good. In this manner the model approximates in the external sphere a kingdom of ends. Kant (1964) writes, "The ends of a subject who is an end in himself must, if this conception is to have its *full* effect on me, be also, as far as possible, *my* ends" (98). The back-and-forth planning procedure outlined above leads to an approximation of this ideal.

(d) Council democracy is not based upon the assumption that those within councils are motivated by a duty to attain the general will. It does not depend upon supposing that the pathological self-love Kant saw as part of human nature is suddenly overcome. In his political philosophy Kant (1970) sets himself the following task:

> In order to organize a group of rational beings who together require universal laws for their survival, but of whom each separate individual is secretly inclined to exempt himself from them, the constitution must be so designed that, although the citizens are opposed to one another in their private attitudes, these opposing views may inhibit one another in such a way that the public conduct of the citizens will be the same as if they did not have such evil attitudes. ("Perpetual Peace," 112–13).

This problem is *not* solved in Kant's own model of institutions; as capital is accumulated those who own or control large-enough units of capital generally are not significantly "inhibited" by others in the pursuit of their self-interest. In council democracy, however, the reciprocal coercion which Kant saw as necessary to freedom is built in.

Suppose that some individual within a worker or consumer council proposes that she perform significantly less labor or receive significantly more consumption goods than the other members of the council. Short of some extenuating circumstance, it is most unlikely that those who are required to do more or receive less would agree to this proposal. The proposal would be voted down. In this manner anyone who exercises a freedom not compatible with the freedom of others will be subject to coercion. This, for Kant (1970) is "the basis not only of the first outline of a political constitution but of all laws as well" (from *The Critique of Pure Reason*, 191)

Second, are there any basic Kantian principles with which the model of council democracy is incompatible? Two possibilities must be considered here: (a) Kant's defense of private property rights; and

(b) Kant's explicit rejection of direct democracy and defense of representational political mechanisms.

(a) It might be objected that the right to private property is so central to Kant that any model of institutions that does not recognize this right is fundamentally incompatible with his position. On closer examination, however, this is not the case. Kant argued that the individual's property is an extension of the self. Without a person being able to say "that is mine" and "that is yours" safely, there can be no settled society. This entails, for Kant, that the concept of intelligible possession (*possessio noumenon*) must be a reality, as opposed to mere possession in appearance (*possessio phaenomenon*). Council democracy is fully compatible with this. The goods and services distributed to individuals within consumer councils are their private property. No one has a right to infringe on their enjoyment of those goods and services. Thus there is no problem regarding two or more persons claiming a right to the same object, with each being equally right/equally wrong in making this claim. This was the problem which Kant sought to resolve in his doctrine of property (See H. Williams, 79).

It is true that in council democracy private property rights do not extend beyond items of personal consumption. Specifically, they do not extend to private ownership of the means necessary for production and distribution. It is true that this is quite different from the model that Kant defended. However, this is not contrary to Kant's fundamental principles. In the first part of the doctrine of right, "private right," Kant attempted to deduce property rights from the idea of the original communal possession of the soil. Surely unlimited *private* property rights to society's productive capacity cannot be directly derived from an original *common* possession. From that idea one could only derive directly a notion of *social* ownership and control of productive capacity. Kant's justification of this form of private property, therefore, was indirect: given the original communal possession, private property rights to productive resources follow only if there exists a public consensus that this arrangement is best suited to furthering the general will. If this consensus breaks down, the foundation of this sort of property right is removed.

There are a number of passages in Kant that support this reading. In the section "Public Law," Kant (1965) states that a "universal public owner" has priority over "private property," and that particular private ownership is based on a distribution of a prior whole (i.e., social wealth) rather than a mere aggregate of what is basically separate and private by nature (90). Kant (1965) went on to assert that the private property rights of the nobility and clergy are not ultimate. They rest instead upon the consent of the community as a whole. When that consent is revoked, their property rights dissolve:

> From this it follows that there can be no corporation, class or order in the state that as owners can under certain statutes transmit lands to succeeding generations for their sole and exclusive use (for all time). The state can at all times rescind such statutes. . . . Those who are affected by such reforms cannot complain that their property has been taken from them, inasmuch as the only ground for their previous possession was the opinion of the people, which, as long as it remains unchanged, makes the possession necessarily valid. As soon as public opinion changes, however . . . then the presumptive ownership must cease. (91)

If the community today were to decide that granting private property rights to unlimited accumulation of capital is not in the public interest, there are ample grounds in Kant to regard an appropriation of that capital as just.

(b) One final difficulty remains. Council democracy is based on the principle that all exercises of public power should be democratized. Kant, however, rejected democracy vehemently. He not only argued that a representational system is far superior, he went on to term the democratic form of exercising power "despotic." He (1970) wrote,

> Despotism prevails in a state if the laws are made and arbitrarily executed by one and the same power. . . . *Democracy*, in the truest sense of the word, is necessarily a *despotism*, because it establishes an executive power through which all the citizens may make decisions about (and indeed against) the single individual without his consent, so that decisions are made by all the people and yet not by all the people; and this means that the general will is in contradiction with itself, and thus also with freedom. ("Perpetual Peace," 101)

How can it be maintained that a defense of council democracy follows from Kantian principles in light of this?

In reply it is not sufficient to point out that in council democracy representational decision-making is far from abolished. That is certainly true. All nonlocal-level councils will be representational bodies. Even within local worker and consumer councils, many tasks concerning the day-to-day management of factories and neighborhoods will be delegated to elected representatives. Nonetheless, within council democracy direct democratic participation in the running of factories and neighborhoods is given an emphasis that appears to be quite un-Kantian in light of the above argument. Before drawing this conclusion, however, we should consider a number of points.

First, Kant committed a category mistake in the above argument. Kant's notion of the general will is a normative concept, defined in terms of policies that maximize the freedom of each consistent with the freedom of all others. The general will can *never* be in contradiction with itself; the will of each citizen is here by definition harmonized with the will of every other citizen. If on the empirical level the will of an individual is not so harmonized, this does not reveal any contradiction in the general will. When an individual dissents from the consensus attained by a majority, it simply reveals a gulf between the real (the empirical consensus) and the ideal (the general will). But since for Kant *no* system of institutions can fully overcome this gulf, it is not in itself an objection to democratic decision procedures.

Second, Kant failed to distinguish what we can term first- and second-order consent. First-order consent regards the content of a decision, while second-order consent refers to the procedures to be followed in making the decision. A person's fellow-workers and neighbors may make a decision with which she does not agree. Yet that same person may accept the principle that in cases where a consensus cannot be attained and time constraints make a decision imperative, the principle of majority rule should hold.[24] In such a case, the decision is made in one sense without the consent of the individual. But in a deeper sense it is made with her consent.

Third, an individual may refuse to consent to democratic decision procedures as well as to the content of specific decisions. There are two possible cases of this. The person may not wish to submit his proposals to the test of whether they are compatible with a general will. Kant, of course, would have no sympathy with this. Or the individual may believe that some other decision procedure can better perform this test than democratic mechanisms. This is Kant's own view (1970): "We can say that the smaller the number of ruling persons in a state and the greater their powers of representation, the more the constitution will approximate to its republican potentiality ("Perpetual Peace," 101). This position is not plausible. Let us forget for the moment the restrictions on public discourse that would actually emerge in Kant's model. In Kant's system we have a supposedly unrestricted public discussion arriving at a public consensus that approximates the general will, which is then to be instituted by representatives of the public (the fewer the better). In council democracy we have unrestricted public discussion arriving at a public consensus that approximates the general will, which is then instituted directly by the public itself. One case is based on the hope that representatives will follow the public will. The other case is based on mechanisms that directly institute the articulated public will. Given Kant's own insistence that in the realm of external action we cannot suppose that people are motivated by a duty to do what is right, it is clearly the latter which is a superior arrangement on Kant's own reasoning. He admits as much in the following passage:

> Now, when someone prescribes for another, it is always possible that he thereby does the other an injustice, but this is never possible with respect to what he decides for himself (for *volenti non fit injuria*). Hence, only the united and consenting Will of all—that is, a general united Will of the people by which each decides the same for all and all decide the same for each—can legislate. (1965, 78)

This leaves Kant's claim that democracy is always despotic, in that the same entity both legislates and executes the law. It is true that in all cases of despotism legislative and executive functions are combined in the despot. But it does not follow from this that all such combinations are despotic. All cases of evil in Kant's view stem from the free will, but Kant did not conclude from this that all exercises of free will are evil! Just as the proper use of freedom allows us to attain the greatest heights possible for humanity, so too does the proper combining of legislation and execution of law. Indeed for Kant (1964) we are fully autonomous only when we follow ("execute") a law that we ourselves have made (100). In council democracy, as we have seen, despotism (i.e., one person or group demanding significantly more than others while contributing significantly less to society) is structurally ruled out. Instead, resulting decisions will approximate a general will. If under these circumstances a community both legislates and itself executes the laws, it acts autonomously in the external realm to the highest extent possible for finite creatures.

VIII

Rawls and the Structural Limits of the Capitalist State

In the previous chapter I argued that the normative model of institutions Kant proposed as the ultimate end of social policy does not cohere with the principle of universalizability he affirmed. At this point one option would be to retain the model and select a different ethical principle, one that would cohere with it. However if the arguments presented in Chapter II are accepted, the case for the principle of universalizability is compelling. A second option is to retain this normative principle and modify the Kantian model, while retaining many of its basic features. This is the option taken by both Rawls and Habermas in the sections of their work falling within the seventh branch of social theory. My own view is that a third option should be taken. Here the model Kant advocated is abandoned completely in favor of a model of democratic socialist planning, on the grounds that the latter better institutionalizes generalizable interests. In this chapter and in Chapter IX, I hope to make the case for this third option more plausible by considering the difficulties that beset the normative models of institutions advocated by Rawls and Habermas, respectively.

Rawls's Normative Model

Just as Habermas defines universalizable interests in terms of what people would agree to in a discourse anticipating an ideal speech situation, Rawls asks what people in an original position behind a veil of ignorance would accept.[1] Rawls believes that in such circumstances those in the original position would insist upon a principle of equal political liberty and a principle which asserts that socioeconomic inequalities must both benefit the least advantaged (the difference principle) and result from offices and opportunities open to all. If we assume for the sake of argument that these principles do indeed represent generalizable interests, then the ultimate end of social policy would be a normative model of institutions (Rawls refers to a "basic structure") that embodies these principles. What would such a model look like?

Rawls holds that an economic system based on market mechanisms is consistent with these principles.[2] In this, the institutional framework he advocates is similar to the Kantian framework considered in the previous chapter. However Rawls is well aware of some of the empirical tendencies that undermine Kant's position.[3] He sees certain fundamental problems emerging in an unregulated market economy that Kant did not foresee. And so Rawls proposes a modification of Kant's *Rechtsstaat*. He introduces various branches of government,[4] each of which is assigned the task of resolving one of these fundamental problems.

Let us examine Rawls's evaluation of market societies in more detail. Rawls accepts as empirically established the view that this sort of economic system achieves a high level of allocational efficiency and, as a result, a high level of output. Of course it also allows—indeed requires—a certain degree of inequality; those who own and control capital accumulate more than others, have more market power than others, and so on. But according to Rawls this power gives them an incentive to invest, which leads to increasingly higher levels of material output. Rawls assumes that this output will increase to the point where inequality could be in the interest of even the least advantaged in this system. However, when the economic sphere is examined in isolation this is no more than a rather unlikely possibility. The economic sphere by itself provides no mechanism to distribute any of this increased output to the least advantaged, or to meet certain other necessary conditions for a just society. Left to itself the much more probable results are (a) a concentration of market power in the hands of the largest controllers of capital; (b) unemployment and economic stagnation whenever it is in the private interests of the controllers of capital not to hire all the available labor power and not to invest available resources; and (c) the failure of the least advantaged to attain a reasonable minimum of goods and services.

As a result of these tendencies Rawls insists that a laissez-faire market in which the economic sphere functions without interference is not morally justified; that is, it would not be accepted in an original position of the sort Rawls describes. And so in Rawls's model the state, unlike Kant's *Rechtsstaat*, plays a more than minimal role. It must actively intervene in the economic sphere in order to ensure the justice of the model as a whole. Rawls introduces three branches of government (274ff.), each designed to correct one of the difficulties listed in the previous paragraph. These are (a) the *allocation branch*, which "keeps the price system workably competitive and prevent(s) the formation of unreasonable market power"; (b) the *stabilization branch*, which "strives to bring about reasonably full employment"; and (c) the *transfer branch*, which "guarantees a certain level of well-being and honors the claims of need." To regulate the economy in these three areas requires revenues. A fourth branch of government, the *distribution branch*, is therefore needed to formulate and enforce "a scheme of taxation to raise the revenues that justice requires." In doing so it also is "to preserve an approximate justice in distributive shares" by imposing inheritance and gift taxes as well as by setting restrictions on the rights of bequest. (A fifth branch of government, the *exchange branch*, is concerned with the provision of public goods beyond what justice requires (282ff.) This branch will not be discussed in the following.) A state performing such functions would ensure that the described model fulfills both the difference principle and the economic preconditions for the principle of equal liberty. If the state mandates as well that the political liberties familiar to liberal democracies are safeguarded and that the principle of equal opportunity is enforced then, Rawls concludes, the model fulfills the principles of justice he has formulated.

Referring to his model Rawls writes:

> As these institutions presently exist they are riddled with grave injustices. But there presumably are ways of running them compatible

with their basic design and intention so that the difference principle is satisfied consistent with the demands of liberty and fair equality of opportunity. It is this fact which underlies our assurance that these arrangements can be made just.(87)

In the following section this claim will be tested.

Structural Analysis of Rawls's Model

Rawls writes that, "In designing and reforming social arrangements one must, of course, examine the schemes and tactics it allows and the forms of behavior which it tends to encourage"(57). I shall now attempt to do precisely this with Rawls's own proposals. In doing so, I shall show that the model of institutions advocated by Rawls is beset by structural contradictions. By this is meant that the functioning of one part of the model, the economic system, sets structural limitations that prevent another part of the model, the state, from functioning in the manner Rawls envisions. In order to establish this each of the four branches of government introduced by Rawls must be discussed in turn, making reference only to the general facts of social theory.[5]

Allocation Branch

The allocation branch must regulate markets to ensure that they are as competitive as possible "consistent with the requirements of efficiency and the facts of geography and the preferences of households"(276). As a result, "land and capital are widely though not presumably equally held. Society is not divided that one fairly small sector controls the preponderance of productive resources"(280). This presupposes that the formation of noncompetitive market power can be checked by state regulations without impairing the functioning of a market economy. This presupposition is why Rawls can write, "The objection that the difference principle enjoins continuous and capricious interference with private transactions is based on a misunderstanding" (Rawls 1977, 164). But if anything counts as a general fact of economics it is that the process of centralization and concentration of capital is a structural tendency in the logic of market societies. Therefore the state cannot check this process as long as that logic is operating. It is of course not possible here to enumerate all the structural mechanisms behind this tendency. Only two will be mentioned, one that operates during all phases of the business cycle and one that operates especially during periods of economic downswing.

In Rawls's model the spur to profit maximization is the motor of the economic realm. The most obvious way of maximizing profits is by being able to sell your products profitably at a price that undercuts your competitors. In a given market sector the first enterprises that attain economies of scale are able to pursue this strategy successfully. Further, in many sectors of the economy economies of scale demand significant investment in fixed capital. From these "general facts" three conclusions follow: (1) those enterprises that happen to have sufficient capital at their disposal and sufficient skill/luck/ruthlessness will invest significant amounts in fixed capital to attain economies of scale; (2) this will drive many if not most of their competitors out of the particular market in question; (3) given the higher start-up costs now required for production in this sector, few if any new enterprises are likely to arise. In short, a structural tendency towards the concentration of market power in the hands of a few firms exists. This basic tendency is then reinforced by other factors. Investment capital flows from the less profitable to the more profitable firms. With more capital at their disposal these firms will tend to be able to develop research and development programs, to initiate advertising campaigns, and other actions that draw a yet-larger market share, making them yet more profitable, encouraging yet more capital to flow to them.

A second mechanism leading to a concentration of market power operates during periods of economic decline. In periods of downswing the strongest firms are best able to withstand the crisis, while others in the same sector of the economy fail. This allows the former firms to increase their market share, making it more likely that they will be able to withstand the next downswing, which would increase their market power yet more. Which of the firms in the sector are the "strongest" is, of course, a thoroughly contingent matter. What is not contingent is a structural tendency for market power to be concentrated in them.

It is important to stress what this argument does *not* imply.

First, it does not follow that all sectors of the economy are dominated by a handful of firms. For one thing, new markets regularly arise, and while a market is growing, it is likely to allow for a number of competing firms. The tendency to concentration may not appear before the particular market matures. Also, certain sectors of the economy develop in a manner that is labor-intensive rather than capital-intensive. If the wage level is low enough, the result is that start-up costs to enter these sectors will not be high enough to exclude potential competitors from entering. It should be noted, however, that the existence of competitive sectors in the economy in no way offers a counterweight to oligopoly power. Just the opposite is the case. It is in the oligopolies' interest to have their suppliers and distributors competing against each other; this lowers their production and selling costs.

Second, it cannot be argued that no competition exists within the oligopoly sectors. Even if something less than a handful of firms controls most of a given market, the competition among these firms may at times be quite intense, especially during periods of downswing. Also, if at some point the profits made in a concentrated sector rise sufficiently, this may attract new investment capital so that new firms may arise in the sector despite the high start-up costs. Finally, the giant firms within one nation may find themselves facing considerable international competition. None of these factors, however, lessens the fact that there exists a structural tendency for the formation of concentrated market power.

Two moves are open to Rawls at this point. First, he could say that the allocation branch only has the function of keeping markets competitive "consistent with the requirements of efficiency," and that the mechanisms described above simply express the efficient workings of the market. The task of the state, according to this view, is simply to break up market power based on extra-market factors such as collusion. The workings of the market as described above are therefore of no concern to the allocation branch. With this move the principle behind the allocation branch breaks down in incoherence. A branch of government whose avowed purpose was the *limitation* of concentrated market power would actually serve for the *legitimation* of such power. Because this would tend to lead not only to control over specific markets, but also to private control of the development of technology, private appropriation of information, privileged access to financial resources, and disproportionate influence on at least some sectors of the state apparatus, the spirit of Rawls's theory of the state would be considerably undermined.

The second move Rawls could take would be to bite the bullet and accept that if the allocation branch is to limit the concentration of market power the state must intervene greatly. The problem is that this would require taking away the "right" to allocate investment capital from those concerned only with private profit maximization, at least in those sectors of most importance to the economy. This could take place in either a democratic socialist, a bureaucratic socialist, or a fascist direction, depending upon where the power to make investment decisions was then placed. But in any case the liberal market society Rawls defends would be abolished. Here too, then, Rawls's theory of the state breaks down in incoherence. A branch of the government intended to further a liberal market society actually demands its abolition.

Before concluding this section it is worthwhile to stress just how much is involved here. Rawls writes: "There is a maximum gain permitted to the most favored on the assumption that, even if the difference principle would allow it, there would be unjust effects on the political system and the like excluded by the priority of liberty"(81). If the state Rawls describes has no effective check on the formation of concentrated economic power, a Rawlsian justification of that state is undermined in a most fundamental manner.

Stabilization Branch

The task of the stabilization branch is to ensure that "those who want work can find it and the free choice of occupation and the deployment of finance are supported by strong effective demand"(276). There are thus two issues to be discussed here: (a) the goal of full employment and (b) the means both to attain full employment and to avoid economic stagnation, the provision of effective demand by the state.

Ironically, measures providing full employment would have a *destabilizing* impact within a capitalist framework. In periods of expansion full employment is compatible with continued capital accumulation. But as markets begin to mature and growth slows, full employment begins to contradict the needs of capital accumulation; the rising wages that come with full employment begin to squeeze profits at this point (see Broddy and Crotty 1975). Unemployment is now functional for capital accumulation. If despite this the state follows full employment policies, one of three things will happen. Either the squeeze on profits will lead the private holders of capital to not invest their capital, thus throwing the economy into deep crisis; or firms may raise their prices in order to attain the rate of return they desire, setting off an inflationary spiral that will lead to crisis eventually. Or both may occur at once, combining stagnation with inflation. None of these is a "stable" state of affairs. If anything counts as a "general fact" of social theory it is that a capitalist state must regularly tend to pursue policies encouraging *unemployment* for the sake of the stability of the system.

The general proposition just stated is incomplete. In its full formulation it would read, "When in a cycle of slow/stagnant/declining growth and profits squeezed by high wages, the state must regularly tend to pursue policies encouraging unemployment." This suggests that if the condition stated in the first clause were not given, the tendency under discussion would not exist. As a Keynesian, Rawls believes that economic crisis can be avoided through the management of effective demand by the state. This would not only allow the stabilization branch of government to fulfill its function. Avoiding crisis would also eliminate one of the mechanisms leading to the concentration of market power, making it somewhat more plausible that the allocation branch could function in the manner Rawls proposes. The avoidance of crisis would have a similar effect on the prospects of the other branches as well, as will be seen below.

Crises occur when productive capacity and aggregate demand are not in sync.[6] Crisis-management techniques can be employed by the state whereby when a supply is produced that exceeds effective demand (thereby setting off a decline in productive investment), the state steps in to provide the required demand. But if those in the original position had knowledge of the general facts of economics they would know that these crisis-management techniques set off inflationary tendencies. In the medium-to-long run, crisis-managment techniques employed to counteract tendencies to crisis themselves lead to crisis.

The simplest way of explaining the mechanisms at work here is to consider the economic expectations that would predominate in a social system with a stabilization branch functioning as Rawls describes. A government sincerely committed to guaranteeing effective demand and full employment would place a floor under the downward movement of the economy. But it would do so only at the cost of greatly increasing its instability upwards. Were Keynesian countercyclical interventions by the state predictable, this would have effects on the price- and wage-setting process. Corporations would not feel a need to lower prices at the first signs of an economic downswing, nor would households feel impelled to practice thrift, nor would unions be compelled to refrain from asking for aggressive wage settlements. In brief, the structure of government Rawls advocates "gives rise to, and sustains, precisely the kinds of expectations that are necessary for chronic inflation."[7] Faced with spiraling prices, both businesses and consumers take on self-cumulative debt; in response, creditors raise interest rates to protect the value of their loans; in response, financial markets lose confidence in investment, credit, and anticipated consumption, and so on. In short, chronic inflation leads to a threat of financial collapse. Therefore a state committed to ensuring the conditions necessary for stable capital accumulation eventually would have to attempt to end this chronic inflation. It could do so, however, only through a more restrictive budgetary policy. But this means that the state would no longer provide effective demand and jobs. The initial tendency to stagnation would then return, leading to a reduction in investment and to a rise in unemployment. Rawls's stabilization branch would not bring about stability. For structural reasons it would instead lead to a ceaseless to and fro between inflation and recession.

Transfer Branch

The function of the transfer branch is to supplement the wages paid (or not paid) in the labor market. In Rawls's view, "By adjusting the amount of transfers (for example, the size of supplementary income payments), it is possible to increase or decrease the prospects of the more disadvantaged, their index of primary goods (as measured by wages plus transfers), so as to achieve the desired result"(285), the maximization of the long-run expectations of the least advantaged.

In assuming that a transfer branch of government is compatible with a market system, Rawls overlooks a crucial feature of this type of system. One of its distinguishing features is that in it labor power is a commodity. Because market systems do not encourage social motives for engaging in labor, the continued functioning of the system demands that the owners of labor power be forced to sell it to the controllers of capital in order to ensure their survival. Now any transfer payments sufficiently large so as to maximize the long-run expectations of the least advantaged would almost surely be sufficiently large to ease the compulsion exerted on those who own nothing but their labor power to sell that labor power to a member of the capitalist class.

> Just as the recipients of stock dividends often choose not to work, so too might others if welfare benefits, unemployment compensation, etc. were adequate and readily available. After all, capitalist ideology glorifies the pursuit of self-interest and provides little concept of social obligation. Moreover, in a system of alienated labor, individual material rewards (rather than, for example, the social necessity of production or the intrinsic rewards of the job) are the chief motivation to work; if an alternate means of livelihood were provided, large numbers of people might well quit work. "Decent" welfare benefits would thus come into serious competition with low-wage, boring, exhausting, and dangerous wage-labor. (Edwards 1978, 308)

Enticing workers to continue selling their labor power after a payment of transfers significant enough to "increase the prospects of the most disadvantaged" would necessitate a rise in wages, setting off the same squeeze on profits and the same resulting tendencies to crisis as would the full employment to be attained by the stabilization branch. In short, substantive transfer payments of the sort Rawls envisions are likely to be incompatible with the needs of capital accumulation.[8]

Distribution Branch

The task Rawls sets for the distribution branch of government is "to preserve an approximate justice in distributive shares by means of taxation and the necessary adjustments in the rights of property" (277). The particular scheme of taxation Rawls approves, a proportional expenditure tax, is not without its difficulties. By taxing only consumption and not income or wealth the scheme reflects a definite class bias. The wealthiest spend the least percentage of their holdings on consumption, while the poorer classes are forced to spend practically their entire wealth on consumption goods. By choosing to invest rather than consume, the wealthiest are able to attain increased security, status, and, most important of all, increased power over the labor of others. An expenditure tax system would not only allow extreme inequalities in these areas, but would actually encourage it.

No matter what tax scheme is selected, however, the distribution branch faces a fundamental tension. On the one hand, it must raise revenues sufficient to ensure that the government is able to provide the demand necessary to keep the economy going, to provide transfer payments that will maximize the expectations of the least advantaged, etc. On the other hand, Rawls accepts the hypothesis that economic inequalities are required for incentives and growth. Hence the tax system must allow such inequalities to exist (which is at least part of the reason why Rawls suggests a proportional rather than progressive tax system). There is a tension between these two imperatives in that the former can be assumed to require a considerable amount of revenue while the latter would minimize the amount of revenue available to the state by protecting the holdings of the wealthy from incentive-reducing taxation.

In periods of economic upswing this tension could remain latent. But in downturns in economic cycles, not to mention long waves of economic decline,[9] the latent tension would turn into outright contradiction. In crisis periods the holders of private capital demand extra incentives to invest their capital, which means that the required degree of inequality would grow. As more of their wealth is thereby protected from taxation, the state has less of a pool from which to draw its revenues. Further, it is precisely during periods of decline that the need for state expenditures to provide demand and furnish transfer payments is the greatest. Beyond a certain point the available revenues would not be sufficient to fund the required expenditures. At this point the state is forced to do one or more of the following: (a) reduce expenditures providing the needed demand, which would plunge the system into deeper crisis; (b) reduce the expenditures that maximize the expectations of the least advantaged, which would undermine the justice of the society; or (c) engage in deficit spending to make up the difference between revenues and expenditures, which is known to be inflationary and therefore is at best only a short-term solution to the problem of crisis. In short, not only is a capitalist economic order subject to structural tendencies towards economic crisis, but the capitalist state likewise faces a structural tendency towards fiscal crisis (see O'Connor 1973). This structural tendency towards a fiscal crisis of the state makes it most questionable whether the distributive branch of government can fulfill the tasks assigned to it by Rawls.

It has been argued that each of the branches of government proposed by Rawls confronts specific structural limitations that prevent it from functioning in the manner Rawls envisions. But for the sake of argument let us assume that these specific structural limitations would not operate. Even then Rawls's theory of the state is not cogent. For even if the state were to attempt seriously to impose regulations of the sort suggested by Rawls, and even were it possible in principle for these regulations to be effective, that state would still find the range of actions open to it severely restricted. In response to this general structural limitation, either the tasks assigned to the state by Rawls would have to be abandoned or the capitalistic nature of the economy would have to be abandoned. In that Rawls does not abandon either, a further argument is provided for the incoherence of his model of institutions.

To introduce this argument it is necessary to note that it is by no means the case that accumulated capital not going toward the consumption needs of capitalists must be reinvested productively. Within Rawls's model the private controllers of capital have another option: nonproductive expenditure. Under this heading falls things such as simple hoarding, luxury consumption (e.g., overseas trips to resort areas), and speculative investments (e.g., in foreign currencies, commodity futures, gold, real estate, art works). In economic down-swings such forms of expenditure may appeal to the holders of private capital much more than productive investments. When this is so, labor power is not hired and means of production goods (machinery, raw materials) are not purchased. As a result consumer demand weakens (unemployed workers do not good consumers make), firms produc-ing means of production goods go bankrupt, leading to further un-employment, further weakening of consumer demand, further bank-ruptcies, and so forth. In short, a downswing threatens to become an out-and-out crisis.

Branches of government sincerely directed towards regulating the economy so as to attain the objectives Rawls defends would both impose significant costs on business and threaten what the holders of private capital are likely to regard as their prerogatives in a direct and inescapable fashion.[10] The holders of private capital, accustomed to calculating how best to maximize their private advantage, would assuredly attempt to calculate how best to respond to this situation. One very effective response is at hand. The option of a nonpro-ductive employment of accumulated capital does not exist only in periods of downswing. This option can be taken whenever the holders of private capital deem it in their interests to do so. This would almost certainly be the case in the situation under discussion.

The general structural feature of a market society, then, that would tend to undermine the branches of government under con-sideration is the possibility of a *capital strike* (or investment strike). When capitalists refuse to invest their capital the economy is brought to a screeching halt. Unemployment rises, bankruptcies multiply, the tendency towards fiscal crisis in the state is exacerbated. The mere threat of such a capital strike in effect gives the holders of private capital a veto power over those proposed state regulations that funda-mentally affect their perceived interests. Free-market "realism" would dictate that no branch of government provoke an investment strike by significantly threatening those interests. Any state officials who, inspired by Rawls's theory of justice, nonetheless attempted to insti-tute regulations that did threaten those interests significantly would soon find themselves confronting a choice. Either the regulations would have to be rescinded in order to encourage renewed investment, or private capital would have to be appropriated in order to take away from private interests this ability to mandate public policy. But to do either is to abandon Rawls's model.[11]

Conclusion

In Part Four I am assuming that the argument presented in Chapter I established that the case for the ethical principle of universalizability is cogent and compelling. Kant, Rawls, and Habermas have all accepted this principle. Each thinker has constructed a normative model of institutions that is intended both to embody that principle and serve as the ultimate end of social policy. In the previous chapter I argued that Kant's model fails to institutionalize the satisfaction of generalizable interests, due primarily to development tendencies within market societies. The basic structure of institutions Rawls affirms is distinct from Kant's. In Rawls's view that state ought to fulfill certain tasks that go beyond those assigned by Kant to the *Rechtsstaat*. However I hold that general structural tendencies in market societies make it quite unlikely that a state constructed along Rawlsian lines could adequately fulfill the tasks he assigns to it. A consistent Rawlsian, no less than a consistent Kantian, must be open to the possibility that democratic socialism would best institutionalize her normative principles (see Schweickart 1978 and Grcic 1981).

IX

Habermas and History:
The Institutionalization of Discourse
as Historical Project

Chapters VII and VIII followed the same basic pattern. First, it was noted that in the part of their work falling in the fifth branch of social theory both Kant and Rawls accepted the ethical principle of universalizability. Then we examined their contributions to the seventh branch, the normative models they believed would institutionalize that principle. Next these models were assessed in the light of empirical tendencies, that is, in the light of results taken from the first two branches of social theory. Finally some brief comments were made regarding an alternative model that might better allow the institutionalization of generalizable interests.

The present chapter follows this pattern for the most part. However, Habermas presents his model of the ultimate end of social policy within the context of his version of historical materialism (see Chapter IV, this book). From this perspective the normative model Habermas defends is not just the embodiment of an abstract ethical principle. It is also the historical solution to the problem of modernity. I shall begin my examination of his position with a brief account of Habermas's analysis of modernity. The main text of interest here is *The Theory of Communicative Action* (1981b), Habermas's most comprehensive work.

The Analysis of Modernity

For our purposes here we can summarize the position defended in *The Theory of Communicative Action* in five theses.

Thesis 1. Underlying modernity is a rationalization process in which the subsystems of political administration and economic production and distribution have broken off from the life world. These subsystems now provide for the material reproduction of the life world. In doing so, however, they now function independently from the life world. They are fuelled by means of power and money, whereas the life world is bound together by the medium of communication. Habermas takes this view over from systems theory. He differs from systems theorists in concentrating upon the four social roles formed at the intersection of the subsystems and the life world: *wage laborer* (who provides input (labor) into the economic subsystem from the life world); *consumer* (who receives output (goods and services) from the economic subsystem); *citizen* (who provides the political subsystem with inputs (legitimations and taxes) from the life world); and *client* (who receives outputs from the political subsystems provided to the life world in the form of services).[1]

Thesis 2. Economic and political subsystems, functioning independently according to money and power, can set off crises in the life world. These economic and political crises affect primarily the social roles of wage laborer and citizen. Left unattended, these crises would set off struggles, especially class struggles, in the life world. In principle, however, these crises can be defused if compensations are provided to the life world. The "social state" *(Sozialstaat)* of developed industrial societies has the function of providing such compensations.[2] First, the social state offers compensations for the risks inherent in owning nothing besides one's labor power. As a result of these compensations class conflict is "pacified":

> The legal institutionalization of wage conflicts has become the basis of a reformist politics that has brought forth a pacification by the social state of class conflict. Essential to the enterprise are labor laws and social legislation that provide for the basic risks of wage labor and compensates for the disadvantages resulting from structurally weak market positions (laborer, renter, consumer, etc.) Social policy does away

with extreme injury and insecurity without, of course, touching the structurally unequal relations of property, income, and dependency. (510–11)

Second, just as compensations to the consumer smooth over the insecurities of the labor market, so services provided to state clients compensate for the lack of effective participation by citizens of the state: "For the neutralization of the generalized role of state citizen, the social state also pays in the coin of use-values that the state citizens receive as claims on the bureaucracies of the welfare state. . . . [T]he role of clients is the pendant that makes acceptable a political participation damned to abstraction and robbed of its effectiveness" (514–15).

Thesis 3. System complexity tends to increase as networks bound together by money and administrative power expand. As system complexity increases, more social compensations are required to "pacify" social relations.[3] But as more and more compensations are provided, the independently functioning systems now determine not just the *material* reproduction of the life world, but its *social reproduction* as well. Habermas terms this process "the colonization of the life world": "The thesis of the inner colonization states that the subsystems economy and state become ever more complex as a result of capitalist growth, and penetrate ever deeper into the symbolic reproduction of the life world" (539).

Thesis 4. Habermas claims that social reproduction (i.e., the processes of cultural reproduction, social integration, and socialization) *must* take place through the medium of communication in the life world. If it is instead subjected to the imperatives of power and money due to the expansion of political and economic subsystems, then social pathologies will inevitably break out:

> These media break down in the realms of cultural reproduction, social integration, and socialization; in these functions they cannot replace the action-coordinating mechanism of understanding. . . . In distinction from the *material* reproduction of the life world, its *symbolic* reproduction cannot be transformed by monetarization and bureaucratization without pathological consequences in the basis of systematic integration. (476–77)

These pathological consequences are built into the very form in which expanding compensations are provided:

> As the social state expands beyond the pacification of the class conflict that immediately arises in the sphere of production, and extends a net of client relationships over the realm of private lives, the expected pathological consequences of state regulations step forth all the more strongly, representing simultaneously a monetarization and bureau-cratization of core realms of the life world. . . . The guarantees of the social state ought to serve the goal of social integration and yet simul-taneously they lead to the disintegration of those life contexts that are dissolved from the action-coordinating mechanisms of under-standing and transformed by such means as money and power. (534)[4]

Thesis 5. The above presents Habermas with the following di-lemma. Habermas wishes to maintain the increase in technical ef-ficiency resulting from economic and political subsystems function-ing independently from the life world. He now agrees with system theorists that any attempt to reincorporate these subsystems back within the life world would lead to a regression in the level of technical rationality, which must be avoided. Further, Habermas feels that prac-tical rationalization in the life world can be successfully accomplished only when the life world is set free from the necessity of concerning itself with its material reproduction: "The life world unburdened from the task of material reproduction can . . . multiply its symbolic struc-tures and set free the unique development of cultural modernity" (564). On the other hand, it is also the case that Habermas wishes to end the colonization of the life world and the social pathologies that stem from subsystems encroaching upon the life world. The normative model of institutions Habermas defends must resolve this dilemma.

Habermas's Normative Model

Habermas's general answer to the dilemma posed above is to in-sist that practical rationalization in the life world and technical rational-ization in the subsystems must be somehow joined: "After we first differentiate in social action between action-oriented to understand-ing and action-oriented towards success, we can then grasp as *com-*

plementary developments the communicative rationalization of every-day action and subsystem formation for purposive-rational economic and administrative action" (1:457). What does this mean concretely?

Before proceeding we must recall our earlier discussion of the notion of "communicative rationality" in Chapter II. The social life world, for Habermas is constituted by networks of communication. In the course of communication certain types of validity claims are continually being made. Here we shall be concerned exclusively with practical validity claims, that is, claims that the social interactions constituted through speech acts are justified. The communicative rationality of a society is measured by the degree to which practical validity claims are subjected to full testing to see if they are warranted. Practical claims regarding the correctness of a particular policy are to-day necessarily couched in terms of the general interest of the com-munity. Testing these claims therefore means attempting to discover whether the proposals are indeed compatible with the general inter-est. Habermas asserts that this can be done only within a special sort of communication. He terms this a "discourse which anticipates an ideal speech situation." This discourse is characterized by two features: (a) the speech is potentially unrestricted; that is, in principle it may include all who are affected by the proposal; and (b) no coercion is exercised upon any of the participants in the discourse. Only pro-posals that are truly in the general interest would be agreed to in an uncoerced and unrestricted speech situation; a consensus would not be attained regarding all proposals that are not generalizable.

We can now introduce what Habermas considers to be the ultimate goal of social policy: a model within which communicative (practical) rationality and technical rationality are satisfactorily com-bined. Habermas argues that the economic and administrative sub-systems ought to be allowed to function independently according to the media money and power *as long as they are fulfilling the conditions for the material reproduction of the life world.* Past this point they cannot be allowed to go.

And what if subsystems based on money and power do spread past this point? Habermas holds that "counterinstitutions" must then intervene. Counterinsititutions are organizations within the life world, functioning according to the medium of communication, whose task is to protect the life world from infringement. As soon as the subsystems transgress their proper limit and begin to affect the process of *social* reproduction (i.e., as soon as signs of a colonization of the life world appear), the counterinstitutions would intervene and prevent the rise of social pathologies: "The life world develops out of itself counterinstitutions in order to limit the autonomous dynamic of the economic and political-administrative systems" (582). As these counterinstitutions are established, then, "a preview of a posttraditional everyday communication arises, which stands on its own feet, which sets limits to the autonomous dynamic of independent subsystems, . . . which works against the combined danger of reification and devastation" (486). Rather than being organized by the exchange of power or money, the counterinstitutions would function along participatory lines: "Procedures of conflict resolution must arise that are appropriate to the structures of action oriented to understanding: discursive processes of will formation and deliberation and decision procedures oriented towards consensus" (544). In other words, a discourse anticipating an ideal speech situation is to be institutionalized in the counterinstitutions, whose task it is to protect the life world from colonization by the economic and political subsystems.

Habermas's model has strong similarities with those discussed in the previous chapters. Habermas's notion of the institutionalization of discourse is obviously a contemporary formulation of the principle of publicity Kant saw as necessary to enlightenment. Like Kant and Rawls, Habermas too affirms a market society. Habermas, along with Rawls, feels that the Kantian *Rechtsstaat* must be gone beyond if we are to ensure that generalizable interests are met. Rawls stresses the role of the state in ensuring this. Habermas, fearing the bureaucratization of the state, places his hopes more in participatory social movements in civil society ("counterinstitutions"). But this may be no more than a difference in emphasis. Habermas's "social state" is essentially identical to the liberal welfare state advocated by Rawls, while Rawls insists upon the importance of phenomena such as the civil rights movement.

There is one other similarity to be noted. All three thinkers reject essential elements of the Marxist version of the proper long-term goal of social policy. In the Marxist perspective, an economic sphere functioning exclusively according to the medium of money ("generalized commodity production") necessarily undermines social relations in the life world. Marx concludes that the processes of production and distribution must be subjected to the decisions of men and women in the life world. Regarding the subsystem of political administration, Marx insists that the social body must take back all the forces absorbed by "the state parasite" and that all political officials be elected, subject to recall at any moment, and paid only average workers' wages. These proposals are ways of subjecting political administration to the imperatives of the life world.[5] In sharp contrast to the classical tradition of Marxist theory, Habermas insists that the independence of these subsystems from the life world is an intrinsic feature of modern societies.[6] He combines this view with a belief that the integrity of the life world can be maintained if discourse is institutionalized in something along the lines of "counterinstitutions."

Habermas' theory of discourse is one of the most significant contributions to social theory made in the twentieth century. I accept that the task of institutionalizing discourse is the most profound practical challenge facing humanity today. Nonetheless it is my view that Habermas's own working-out of the implications of this perspective is inadequate. My central contention is that counterinstitutions cannot fulfill the tasks Habermas assigns them when subsystems are allowed to continue to function autonomously from the life world. One or the other must be given up. Habermas's insistence that political administration and economic production and distribution should function exclusively according to the media of power and money guarantees, unfortunately, that it will be the institutionalization of discourse that is sacrificed.

Evaluation of Habermas's Model

The root problem here, I believe, is Habermas's rigid separation of the material reproduction of the life world (entrusted to the economic and political subsystems) and its social reproduction. There are three areas where this undialectical separation breaks down in ways Habermas does not take into account: 1) the formation of the capacity to participate in discursive situations, (2) the continued generation of class conflict in the life world, and (3) the dynamics of the new forms of conflict set off by social pathologies in the life world.

1. The functioning of the economic and political subsystems, concerned with material reproduction, directly determines the sorts of communicative interactions possible in the processes of social reproduction, one to the other. A first connection is the direct correlation between one's position in the process of material reproduction and one's ability to take part in a process of social reproduction along the participatory lines Habermas advocates:

> The objective situation of alienation at the workplace has deleterious consequences for other spheres of life. The worker who is denied participation and control over the work situation is unlikely to be able to participate effectively in community or national decision making, even if there are formal opportunities to do so. This is because effective participation in decision making requires certain skills (keeping oneself informed, understanding the issues, presenting one's viewpoint clearly and forcefully) and certain attitudes (a motivation to participate, and the self-confidence to do so) which a worker shut off from decision making at work has little opportunity to develop. In other words, participatory democracy at the workplace appears to be an essential prerequisite for meaningful democracy in community and national affairs.[7]

If this is the case then it may be naive for Habermas to think that participatory counterinstitutions can be established in the life world without transforming along participatory lines the institutions of the economy and the political administration.

A second connection is that the process of *political will formation*, a central part of social reproduction, canot occur along the rationalized lines Habermas proposes – that is, political discourse cannot be oriented towards the attainment of uncoerced consensus – if the public's material interests can be manipulated to prevent this. Political will formation cannot be rational in Habermas's sense if there exists a bureaucratic administration that through its power of allocating services can channel will formation in a particular direction. This means that there must be some sort of check on those who exercise administrative power. It is difficult to see what could attain this besides measures along the lines proposed by Marx, that is, the election and recall of, and lack of bureaucratic privileges for, those who administer ("The Civil War in France," in Marx and Engels

1978). Likewise the formation of a public will cannot be rational in Habermas's sense if economic decisions regarding investment can be used to threaten a community with disinvestment were it to form a political will of a particular sort. There must be some sort of democratic public control over the making of investment decisions. It is difficult to see what this could be besides the socialization of the means of production along the lines Marx recommends. What is common to these proposals is the insistence that material reproduction *not* occur independently from the life world. The economic and political subsystems must be subordinated to the life world if discourse is to be institutionalized in any meaningful sense.

2. Habermas would grant that in the early stages of capitalism setting up economic and political subsystems apart from the life world was ultimately incompatible with institutionalizing discourse in the life world. That is because these subsystems set off class conflicts in the life world. The fundamental antagonism of class conflict is incompatible in the medium to long term with attaining a rational consensus uniting all the interests of the community. This consensus is the goal of discourse. Habermas asserts, however, that the compensations provided by the social state of late capitalism prevent these sorts of conflicts from arising:

> The pacification by the social state of class conflict comes about under the condition of the continuation of a process of accumulation whose capitalistic motor mechanism is protected by state intervention, but in no way changed. . . . Namely, with the institutionalization of class conflict, the social opposition, which is set off by private control over the means of the production of social wealth, increasingly loses its power to form structures for the life world of social groups, although it remains, as before, constitutive of the economic system. . . . The class structure, transferred from the life world to the system, loses its historically graspable form. (512)[8]

This supposed success of the social state is significant to Habermas's belief that retaining economic and political subsystems functioning according to the media money and power can in principle be compatible with institutionalizing discourse.

A great number of points could be made here. First of all, one might question Habermas's restriction of his analysis to countries of the first world. Even if he were correct regarding the accomplishments of developed capitalist countries, setting off an economic subsystem functioning exclusively according to the media money involves a *global* system. If the compensations paid to inhabitants of the First World are directly connected to the superexploitation of workers and peasants in Third World countries, then it can hardly be argued that class struggle has been pacified on the global scale (For an overview of the various arguments for this view, see Brewer 1980). Second, even within developed capitalist countries Habermas may be accused of confusing the buying-off of the most organized sectors of the working class with the pacification of class struggle as a whole. The major beneficiaries of the social state were white males within unions, the most politically powerful sector of the working class. Women, those in unorganized sectors, and people of color have benefited quite less from the social state (see Gordon et al. 1982). Third, the compensations provided for those not working ultimately must be kept low enough and be provided in a form demeaning enough so that a system based upon the compulsion to sell one's labor power is not threatened.[9] Can speech situations without coercion be institutionalized when such compulsion remains? Further, it is true that along with other superexploited groups the unemployed possess relatively little political power. Although they lack the ability to threaten the equilibrium of the established order, however, it does *not* follow that this order has been successful in resolving distributional conflicts, as Habermas concludes. Finally, Habermas's account is formulated in subjectivist terms. But the category of class struggle has an objective component to it. From the fact that those within the social state may not use the category of class struggle to interpret their social world, it does not follow that that category is inapplicable to that social world objectively.

These replies to Habermas's position raise issues that he does not consider. But I shall concentrate on an internal difficulty within his position. Habermas notes that the compensations provided by the social state to smooth over class conflict require revenues. With any given level of revenues the more that is spent on social compensations, the less that remains for expenditures necessary for the furthering of capital accumulation. Therefore with a fixed amount of revenues, social state policies set off a zero-sum game in which class struggle is not at all pacified, but merely continued on the political level: "Of course the politics directed toward the building of the social state stands before a dilemma that expresses itself on the fiscal level in the zero-sum game of public expenditures for sociopolitical projects on one side, for expenditures for anticyclical and growth-aiding infrastructure policies on the other" (511). The social state cannot increase its revenues by lessening significantly the share of social wealth of working men and women, as this is the group which is to be compensated. Nor can the share appropriated by the wealthy be lessened significantly, since this would provoke an investment strike. The only way out of this impasse is for revenues to increase as a result of growth in the economy. Only if the economic pie is expanding can the social state appropriate revenues for social compensations without provoking class conflicts:

> Interventions in the pattern of distributions [made through] social compensations in general do not set off reactions on the side of privileged groups only when they can be paid for from the growth of the social product and do not touch property already held; otherwise they cannot fulfill the function of limiting and putting to rest class conflicts. (511).

Yet there are good reasons to think that the dream of uninterrupted growth in capitalist economies is just that, a dream. Habermas himself asserts that "crisis tendencies . . . spring from the indigenous breakdown of the accumulation process" (565). In the short run the state may step in to fill the gaps in the market. But in his own discussion Habermas claims that state interventions eventually just shift the form taken by the crisis, from an economic to a political crisis, which in turn eventually leads the state to attempt to shift the burden of the crisis back to the economic sphere: "Economically conditioned crisis tendencies are not only administratively worked on, flattened, and braked, but are also invisibly transported into the administrative system. They can appear in different forms there, for example, as conflicts between its goals in compensation policies and its goals in infrastructure policies; as an excessive claim on the resource time (state debt); as excessive demand upon bureaucratic planning capacity; and so forth. This can in turn call forth unburdening strategies with the goal of transferring the burden of problems back to the economic system" (506). There is thus an internal tension in Habermas's argument. If the social state is to pacify class conflict, it requires continuous capitalist growth, a continuous growth that Habermas's own discussion of crisis suggests is impossible. Instead of attempting to resolve this tension, he simply proceeds as if the difficulties here could be overlooked: "If one abstracts from crisis-laden system disequilibrium, which is given again to the life world in administratively processed form, [then] capitalist growth resolves conflicts within the life world" (516). This is analogous to asserting that if one abstracts from the deadly side effects of a drug, it is quite effective in curing disease. In both cases one is abstracting from what is crucial.

It is astonishing that Habermas could suggest that this sort of abstraction is legitimate today. It is true that rebuilding after the horrible devastation of World War II set off a tremendous period of economic expansion. In his early writings, impressed by this growth, Habermas speculated that perhaps the key to smoothing over economic and political crises had been found (albeit at the cost of setting off cultural crises). But by the time Habermas came to write in *Theorien des kommunikativen Handelns*, in the late 1970s and early 1980s, this period had been over for quite some time (see Castells 1980; Magdoff and Sweezy 1981; and especially Mandel 1978). Today few pretend that the capitalist state can simultaneously provide adequate compensations to those in weak market positions and further capital accumulation. And because it remains a *capitalist* state, it is the latter which is selected when a choice has to be made. In a period of all-out assaults upon the social state, Habermas praises its stability. In a period where throughout the developed capitalist world the state institutes austerity measures, provides tax breaks to the wealthy, encourages wage cutbacks for workers, reduces social services, and oversees a restructuring of the labor process in the interests of capital,[10] Habermas speaks of class conflict as "pacified." Given that economic and political subsystems set off class conflicts in the life world that the social state has failed to pacify, and given that such conflicts are in principle incompatible with institutionalizing discourse in the life world, we have a second reason for concluding that these subsystems must be subordinated to the life world if discourse is to be institutionalized in any meaningful sense.

3. We have just examined Habermas's argument that the specific

conflicts arising from the wage labor/capital realtionship have been "pacified" under the social state of late capitalism. Habermas, however, does not conclude from this that late capitalism is without conflicts. Conflicts remain inherent in this society, but these conflicts are located other than where Marxists root them: "The more the class conflict that is built into the private economy form of accumulation in society can be dammed up and held latent, the more problems press to the foreground that do not injure immediately ascribable class specific interests" (513).

These are the problems of social pathologies that stem from the colonization of the life world.[11] Like class conflicts, the social conflict resulting from social pathologies are also incompatible with institutionalizing unrestricted and uncoerced discourse in the life world. And so, as we have seen, Habermas advocates something along the lines of counterinstitutions to check the rise of these conflicts. Unfortunately, there is no reason to suppose that these counterinstitutions will be any more successful in pacifying conflict arising from social pathologies than the social state has been in pacifying class conflicts.

Habermas points out that the new movements responding to social pathologies all share a common focus in the critique of growth: "The themes of the critique of growth are the sole bonds connecting these heterogeneous groups" (577). But on his own account there is a yet-deeper principle unifying the different conflict forms. He asserts that these are "conflicts that do not arise primarily in class-specific forms, and yet go back to a repressed class structure that is expelled into systematically integrated realms of action" (515). In other words, all the new forms of conflict resemble each other in being at least partially determined by underlying class relations. That there are a number of mediations between the class structure and the conflicts that "do not arise primarily in class-specific forms" does not lessen the fact that by Habermas's own account the causal chain moves from the class structure generated in the economic subsystem, through the social state and its compensations, through the colonization of the life world and social pathologies, to its culmination in the social conflicts that arise in response. This reading is further confirmed in Habermas's closing summary of the new forms of conflict:

The alternative praxis directs itself against the profit-dependent institutionalization of vocational work, against the market-dependent mobilization of labor power, against the extension of the pressures of competition and achievement to grade schools. It also moves against the monetarization of services, relations, and time, against a consumeristic redefinition of private life spaces and personal life-styles. Further, the relationship of clients to public social-service agencies ought to be broken up and made to function in a participatory manner, according to the paradigm of self-help organizations. Finally, these forms of protest negate the definition of the state–citizen role and the routine of the purposive-rational carrying-through of interests. (581–82)

The first sentence of this passage is interesting in that it seems to contradict Habermas's claim that the wage labor–capital relationship has been "pacified." But I stress here that from this perspective the conflicts Habermas discusses are responses to (1) the generalization of the commodity form, and (2) a corresponding lack of participation in the control of one's own destiny, as more and more social relations are submitted to the commodity form (including the services provided by the state to its clients and the spreading of special interest politics, campaign contributions, lobbying, etc.) Neither of these factors is changed if one allows the economic system to continue functioning autonomously according to the medium of money. Habermas himself asserts that the "thesis of the inner colonization states that the subsystems of the economy and state become ever more complex as a result of capitalist growth, and penetrate ever deeper into the symbolic reproduction of the life world" (539). And the search for growth in a money economy by definition involves the extension of the commodity form into more and more realms of life. Habermas's proposal leaves all this intact. His model leaves the counterinstitutions with the task of addressing a problem without being able to address the underlying cause of that problem. They are in the same situation as a doctor who is forced to treat only the symptoms of a disease, not its cause. This is clearly not a very effective way of guaranteeing the institutionalization of discourse. The only effective way of guaranteeing this is, once again, to reincorporate the subsystems within the life world.

The Institutionalization of Discourse: An Alternative Model

From the above, it follows that the institutionalization of discourse must be done thoroughly. Attempts to institute it only in "counterinstitutions" and not in the main institutions of society are ultimately doomed to impotence. Someone convinced by Habermas's arguments regarding the connection of independent subsystems with social pathologies therefore has only one choice: discourse must be institutionalized *throughout* the society.

Habermas himself is sympathetic to instituting worker control, control of investment decisions, and so forth. Regarding worker control of the production process, for example, Habermas writes: "The justification of normative regulations that help this repressed interest obtain its rights follows the logic of practical discourse" (in Thompson and Held 1982, 312). These are the sorts of things we have in mind. Controlling the production process, the community is controlling investment decisions (We may add that those exercising administrative authority are elected, subject to recall, and not granted special material privileges). What then remains of the "independence" of the political and economic subsystems? In certain circumstances democratic political will formation in the life world certainly may approve setting up an administrative apparatus functioning exclusively according to the medium power (e.g., militia forces) and economic institutions functioning exclusively according to the medium of money (perhaps "farmers' markets" for the exchange of food grown locally in small gardens). But in general it is *not* possible to attain rationalization of the life world in its social reproduction without subordinating political administration and economic action (i.e., material reproduction) to the articulated desires of men and women in the life world.

It obviously is impossible to offer a complete blueprint for the adequate institutionalization of discourse. But whatever the details might turn out to be, it is possible to state that the institutionalization of discourse must involve the organizational structure of council democracy defended in the classical Marxist tradition. This model has already been sketched in Chapter VII above, and there is no need to repeat that discussion here. It is sufficient to note that any adequate institutionalization of discourse must fulfill two conditions: the speech leading to decisions must be unrestricted and un-coerced. Council democracy has been shown to allow for uncoerced and unrestricted decision-making. We may therefore conclude that council democracy is based upon institutionalizing an approxima-tion of an ideal speech situation as described by Habermas.

One last point remains to be considered. Ought not council democracy be rejected on the grounds of its technical inefficiency? Council democracy does not imply that eveyone gets to decide about everything all the time. All higher-level councils are respresentational bodies, and even on the local levels many decisions regarding the day-to-day management of worker and consumer councils can be delegated as well whenever that furthers efficiency. Nor does the in-stitutionalization of discourse in this full sense imply that "system" considerations ought never to be considered independently from the life world. For example, under capitalism advanced mathematical techniques have been developed that can be used to calculate input and output requirements for vastly extended series of possible pro-duction processes. These calculations fix what sorts of production outputs are possible with different possible sets of inputs. The set of technically possible combinations of input and outputs is, of course, *completely* independent from social relations in the life world. There is certainly no reason why the rational techniques allowing the cal-culations of the different possible combinations could not be fully appropriated within council democracy.

Finally, there is a good deal of evidence to suggest that subor-dinating the subsystems to the control of the life world would *not* result in increased inefficiency. Limiting our remarks to the eco-nomic sphere, there are two separate questions to consider here: Is an independent economic system functioning exclusively according to the medium of money truly efficient? Are there convincing arguments for the claim that subordinating this aspect of the ma-terial reproduction of the life world to institutionalized discourse would be inefficient? Regarding the former, there are a great number of inefficiencies built into an economic system held together by money transactions. It would take another book to establish this adequately. Here we can only present a partial list of factors that at least suggest this is the case. In the course of economic cycles a good deal of pro-ductive capacity is unused.[12] Those who are unemployed and underemployed are prevented from making productive contributions to society. Many of those who are employed are in jobs that do not allow or do not encourage the further development of their physical and mental potentials. Many resources are wasted and many potential resources are destroyed as those social costs that are not monetary in form are ignored in profit calculations. Items necessary to meet basic human needs are not produced or are wasted if those who need them lack sufficient purchasing power. In an economy functioning according to the medium of money, whenever investors can maximize their return by buying other companies, by speculating, say, on commodities or art or gold, rather than by investing in new productive buildings and equipment, they will do so. None of these factors should lead one to deny the dynamism of money-based economies or the ability of such economies to foster the development of productive capacity. But they at least provide a reason to question Habermas's assumption that this sort of economic arrangement has attained the highest degree of efficiency that humanity can reasonably hope for.

The question of the efficiency of institutionalizing discourse with regard to decisions regarding the production and distribution of goods and services remains to be considered. There is some empirical evidence that the council-democracy model could function in an efficient manner. Many corporations, seeking to increase worker productivity, have experimented with greater worker participation in management decisions, greater variety in workers' tasks, etc. No matter how the experiments were organized, all changes that provided workers with more power in production than they normally enjoy increased worker productivity (for a summary of these studies, see Blumberg 1973, 124–28). These experiments have been kept within strict limits and remain far short of anything approaching council democracy. In all cases management retained ultimate control over production decisions. Nonetheless, the available evidence strongly suggests that a thorough institutionalization of discourse can occur without a loss in productive output. I conclude that on Habermasian grounds institutionalizing discourse along the lines of council democracy ought to be the ultimate goal of our social policy.

PART FIVE

SOME ISSUES OF
STRATEGY AND TACTICS

How can we bring the normative model of institutions to which we are committed closer to realization? "Strategy" is the branch of social theory devoted to formulating medium- to long-term answers to this question. The final branch of social theory is concerned with tactics. The task here is to discover the most effective means in given concrete circumstances to bring our normative model closer to actualization.

One of the most profound issues in these two branches of social policy is the "dirty hands" problem. The effective actualization of ethical ideals in the concrete often seems to require exercises of power that lead us to compromise precisely those ideals. Resolving this tension in specific circumstances requires practical wisdom, phronesis, a quality that defines the best social activists. However, this tension also raises a more general philosophical issue. In practical life are ethical considerations more basic than power considerations, or does the reverse hold? Habermas has presented a number of arguments that defend the former position. In his view the principle of universalizability has one final role in social theory: it is the principle that must orient our strategies and tactics. In Chapter X, I examine and evaluate these arguments.

Chapter XI concerns a more concrete issue. The normative model defended in Part Four of this book aims at the general institutionalization of a discourse anticipating an ideal speech situation. One strategy follows immediately: we must struggle to introduce this sort of discourse in specific institutions crucial to the society as a whole. One such pivotal institution is the university. In Chapter XI, I present the social policy Habermas advocates regarding the university, and I contrast it with alternative perspectives.

X

Ethics and Power
in the Work of Jürgen Habermas

Social policy encompasses more than the construction of normative models. When we turn to the formulation of concrete strategies and tactics to be employed in the course of partisan struggles for power, ethical considerations cannot be the exclusive focus of attention. What, then, is the role of ethics in these branches of social theory?

We can distinguish two fundamental answers to this question. One position, represented by thinkers such as Machiavelli and Nietzsche, regards "power" as the central category underlying strategy and tactics. An ethical category such as "justice" in this view is of secondary importance here, whether it be defined as an appearance to be feigned in order to maintain power (Machiavelli), or as a notion expressing the "slave morality" of those too weak to oppose the will of the powerful directly (Nietzsche). The other view reverses this ordering, granting conceptual priority to ethical notions such as justice even when it comes to questions of strategy and tactics. Social theorists ranging from Aristotle to Hannah Arendt have defended this position. And just as theorists of the first camp incorporated the notion of "justice" within their systems in various ways, so too is it incumbent upon thinkers of this second camp to account for "power" somehow.

Jürgen Habermas is a member of the second camp. In the first section of this chapter I shall review the outline of Habermas's communicative ethic one final time. The second section introduces the way the power considerations that inevitably accompany questions of strategy and tactics pose a problem for Habermas's standpoint. The third section examines two arguments with which Habermas attempts to show that the exercise of power is a derivative phenomenon, dependent upon communicatively established norms. The second of these arguments requires a relatively extensive digression on the topic of legitimation crises in late capitalism. I do not believe that either of Habermas's arguments is compelling. In the conclusion a third argument for granting Habermas's communicative ethic a foundational role in strategy and tactics is sketched and defended.

Habermas's Communicative Ethic

In the realm of strategy and tactics, as in the other branches of social theory, the key to Habermas's position is the same communicative ethic that has been such a central topic of this book. The essence of this position is captured in the following argument:

Premise 1: The anticipation of an ideal speech situation is not based on an arbitrary decision.
Premise 2: The principle of universalizability is built into the communication anticipating an ideal speech situation.
Conclusion: Therefore the acceptance of the principle of universalizability is not arbitrary.

Premise 1 is established by means of the tu quoque argument discussed in Chapter II. Imagine that some philosopher attempts to construct a counterexample in which the ideal speech situation is not presupposed. Habermas, I think, would claim that his thesis that an ideal speech situation is anticipated in all communicative speech can be defended and rationally affirmed *prior* to hearing the results of the ingenuity of philosophers in constructing counterexamples. This can be done simply by considering the process whereby the philosophers who had imagined the counterexample would attempt to convince their colleagues that it indeed constituted a refutation of Habermas's notion of the ideal speech situation.

A refutation can be undertaken only through the presentation of arguments. It is, of course, always possible for a speaker to bring about a change in the attitude of her audience toward a thesis through the threat of force. Ordinary usage, however, quite correctly refuses to term such a process of manipulation a "refutation." An argument that is to count as a refutation brings with it a claim to be rationally compelling. In other words, it is an argument that would be accepted in a situation where the force of the better argument–and not argument by force–prevails. It is precisely this situation that the description of the structure of an ideal speech situation attempts to explicate. Thus *any* attempt at refuting the notion of an anticipation of an ideal speech situation–which, *qua* refutation, must be presented as an argument–itself *presupposes* that anticipation. Of course this does not mean that Habermas's theory of the ideal speech situation cannot be revised in the sense of being open to proposals for clearer formulations, conceptualizations that bring out aspects neglected in Habermas' account, and so forth. It means instead that the general point of Habermas's thesis cannot be revised or refuted because any attempt to do so itself presupposes what it set out to question.

So far, all that has been established through Habermas' tu quoque argument is that rationally presenting an argument involves the presupposition of an anticipated ideal speech situation. Could not one grant that on the level of argumentation the ideal speech situation indeed is anticipated, but that the move to the level of argumentation itself involves a nonrational decision? In other words, a new objection might be formulated which states that *if* one is in the language game of argumentation, *then* the ideal speech situation may indeed be anticipated. In presupposing that we are in this language game, however, Habermas has begged the question; argumentation is surely not the only language game. And so the tu quoque argument has at best a restricted significance: it does not establish the relevance of the ideal speech situation to any other language game besides that of argumentation.

We are already familiar with Habermas' reply to this objection from Chapter II. Any functioning language game–that is, any language game within which an exchange of speech acts takes place such that communication occurs–presupposes a background consensus. That background consensus is not part of an immutable order; for any number of reasons it may break down. When it does break down, if the communication is to be reestablished, that which was taken for granted before must now be made a subject for discussion and argument. Thus *any* functioning language game *always* has an immanent connection to the language game of argumentation. The ideal speech situation—and the "principle" of universalization built into its structure—does not rest upon any arbitrary choice that we make, beyond the "choice" that always has already been made for us to be communicating beings:

> Anyone who does not participate, or is not ready to participate in argumentation stands nevertheless "already" in contexts of communicative action. In doing so, he has already naively recognized the validity claims—however counterfactually raised—that are contained in speech acts and that can be redeemed only discursively. Otherwise he would have had to detach himself from the communicatively established language game of everyday practice. (Habermas 1975, 159)

Premise 2 is much easier to establish. In a discourse without coercion the participants would agree only to proposals and evaluations in their interest. Any consensus reached would be an expression of generalizable interests. If the anticipation of an ideal speech situation is not based upon an arbitrary decision but is rather built into the structure of all communication, and if a "principle" of universalizability is built into the communication which anticipates an ideal speech situation (since in an uncoerced speech situation participants would agree only to what was in their interest, so that any consensus reached would be an expression of generalizable interests), then it follows that the acceptance of a principle of universalizability is no more arbitrary and based on mere decision than is the fact of human communication.

Armed with this principle of universalizability Habermas can procede to develop his social theory in two directions. First, the principle of universalizability provides a standard that allows the theorist to apply the predicate "unjust" to those social systems in which for structural (noncontingent) reasons the generalizable interests of its members are not met. Second, the conditions necessary for a social system to meet the generalizable interests of its members recurrently (i.e., to be "just") can be formulated. In Habermas's view the main condition to be met is that uncoerced public discourse be institutionalized and made politically effective. Neither of these topics will be explored further here. Instead, I shall ask to what extent Habermas's position must be modified when we turn from critical evaluations and normative models to the realm of strategy and tactics.

Habermas on Power

Let us suppose that a representative of the first camp mentioned in the introduction attacks the above and affirms that "power," and not "justice" in the sense of the "universalizable interest," is the more crucial consideration in the formulation of strategies and tactics. In a first move it might be replied that the tu quoque argument established that in a certain sense Habermas's principle of universalizability cannot be rejected or even revised fundamentally. But a reexamination of the tu quoque argument seems to suggest that this defense cannot be made here. *The tu quoque argument only works within the context of communicative action.* Someone who is authentically communicating of necessity makes certain validity claims, the very sense of which is that these claims could be defended in a discourse anticipating an ideal speech situation, were they to be called into question. In an uncoerced discourse the participants would agree only to what was in their interest; any consensus reached therefore would embody generalizable interests. And so a principle of universalizability is presupposed within all communication, even the communication of those whose intention is to reject or revise that principle. But strategies and tactics are *not* oriented towards the attainment of a rational consensus. They are oriented instead to success, to victory. One does not want to convince the other, but to defeat him or her. Rather than implicitly presupposing the principle of generalizable interests, the person or group engaged in power struggles explicitly and consistently negates the interest of the opponents in their victory and avoidance of defeat. Hence the tu quoque argument has no force in this context.

It often is asserted that Habermas is not aware of this difficulty, that he is guilty of a "reduction of 'praxis' to communication" (Connerton 1980, 108). If this were the case his position would not be relevant to the last branches of social theory. This interpretation, however, is quite mistaken. For example, in referring to the institutionalization of discourse that he advocates, Habermas (1976) writes "that such institutionalizations . . . have not been themselves the result of discourses but rather of struggles, normally of class struggles, is trivial" (331. Translations mine). This fact points to the necessity of what Habermas terms *strategic action* in social policy, an action-type oriented towards success rather than mutual understanding. In the formulation of strategies and tactics to attain success the "other" is not one with whom one communicates. Here the "other" is one against whom one struggles with a "declaration . . . of the temporary incapacity for dialogue on the part of the strategic opponent" (Habermas 1973b, 39). In strategic action "the opponent . . . has been excluded by the breaking off of communication" (Habermas 1973b, 38).

From this perspective it appears that the two positions we have distinguished are based on two very different forms of social action, communicative action on the one hand (with its principle of "justice" in terms of "universalizability") and strategic action on the other (with its principle of "power"). Habermas (1973b) seems in places to suggest that groups simply *decide* for one or the other mode of social action: "The groups which look upon themselves as theoretically enlightened must choose, with a view of their opponents, in each instance between enlightenment and struggle, thus between maintaining and breaking off communication" (38). Habermas stresses that no form of reflective knowledge can justify this choice. Does this not suggest that on the philosophical plane no good reasons can be given for aligning oneself with those social theorists who regard "justice" as the more fundamental category in the realm of strategies and tactics?

If Habermas wishes to claim that the choice between the alternative camps rests on more than a mere decision, then an argument is required that somehow establishes some sort of *priority* of communicative action vis-à-vis strategic action. To my knowledge Habermas has presented two such arguments, one on a microsociological plane and one on a macrosociological level. These arguments will be explored in the following section.

Habermas on the Priority of Communicative Action

On a microsociological level Habermas writes that "the family cannot be even pictured as a . . . network of strategic action." This, he concludes, suggests that "[l]ife relations which are built around direct understanding in a certain sense are fundamental."[1] Here we have hints of an argument that might be reconstructed as follows:

1. The formation of the identity of a "self" can ocur only within a context of communicative action (institutions such as the family provide this context).
2. Since to act strategically is to act in one's *self*-interest, strategic action presupposes the formation of the identity of a "self."
3. Therefore, communicative action is in this sense prior to strategic action.

The first proposition is an empirical hypothesis that can be assumed true here. The second proposition is a tautology. Given these premises, the conclusion indeed follows. But what is established by such an argument? The argument provides compelling reasons for parents to treat their children communicatively. But does it provide reasons for these same parents to grant "priority" to communicative action when they themselves act in the world? In a conflict situation among adults in which a choice is required between communication oriented towards consensus with the other and strategies oriented towards success against the other, this argument seems quite irrelevant.

In other writings Habermas (1976) admits as much. He writes that on a microsociological level in contexts outside the private sphere of the family it appears that the "decisionism problematic" remains, that one can simply "*choose* between consensual and strategic action" (340). But in his view "this appearance is an artifact of a manner of consideration that individualistically proceeds from the modes of action of isolated individuals and contractual behavior in small groups." His fundamental argument for the priority of communicative action, then, lies on the macrosociological plane: "that also individuals in situations rich in political consequences cannot arbitrarily choose between the orientation of a consensual or a strategic actor becomes clear as soon as whole social systems are taken as the point of reference for analysis." This is because "[s]ocieties cannot indefinitely replace intersubjectively valid institutions and norms of action obviously in need of legitimation with maxims of purposeful-rational action. . . . This means that on the level of social systems that possibility of choice which to a certain extent we may grant to individuals normally doesn't exist: the possibility of deciding between consensual and nonconsensual forms of conflict regulation" (1976, 340).

With what argument does Habermas attempt to establish this conclusion? His argument can be reconstructed in the following steps.

1. The success sought in strategic action depends upon power. This proposition may be granted at once.[2]

2. On the macro-level power is not *the* fundamental reality, for "the political system cannot dispose of power at will. Power is a good for which political groups compete and with which political leadership disposes, but both in a certain way find this good, they do not produce it. That is the weakness of the powerful – they must borrow their power from the producers" (Habermas 1978, 120).

3. This "production" of power occurs through the bestowing of recognition. "Strategic disputes concerning political power have neither called forth nor continued the institutions in which they are anchored. Political institutions do not live from power, but from recognition" (Habermas 1978, 117).

4. This recognition in turn depends upon an acceptance of certain cultural norms in terms of which the political order can be legitimated. "When binding decisions are legitimate, i.e., when they are made independent of concretely exercised force and manifestly threatened sanctions and likewise regularly can be carried through – even against the interests of those concerned – then they must be able to count as the fulfilling of recognized norms" (Habermas and Luhmann 1972, 244).

5. These cultural norms do not reside in some Platonic realm. "They have concrete significance only for acting subjects who meet one another on the level of intersubjectivity" (Habermas and Luhmann 1972, 251).

6. Finally, to have validity on the level of intersubjectivity the norms must be thought to be capable of being agreed upon in communication. "This normative validity distinct from power rests on the belief that one can justify the norm and defend it against critique in a given case" (Habermas and Luhman 1972, 244).

Habermas thus attempts to establish that communicative action is prior to strategic action through showing that the reality of "power" is not so fundamental as that of "legitimation." His conclusion follows from the above six premises: "Social systems therefore cannot do without taking up normative validity claims (which according to their sense are only redeemable discursively alone) as need demands. They cannot repress the legitimation problems which result from the implicitly rational structure of linguistically mediated interaction without begetting negative consequences" (Habermas 1976, 341). On the practical level, then, the power required for successfully engaging in strategic action is not an ultimate phenomenon. It instead is derived from recognition begotten in communicative interaction. If this argument for the priority of communicative action works, then there are good reasons for insisting that "justice" remains the fundamental principle even in the arena of strategy and tactics.

Habermas's argument, however, is not sufficient as it stands. The point is important enough to warrant a digression. Rather than having established the priority of communicative action over strategic action, all that Habermas has shown is the need for a justification of authority within social systems. He has not yet shown that the principle of universalizability need be especially relevant in this context. To the extent that a normative framework is successfully established that legitimates an asymmetrical division of need satisfaction, *structural power* is instituted and can be made stable as a result of functioning ideologies. Here a principle of universalizability does *not* play any role. As Habermas (1978) writes,

Structural power is embedded in political institutions (and not only in them). Structural power manifests itself not *as power*; much more it unnoticeably blocks those communications in which legitimation-effective convictions form and grow. . . . In systematically restricted communication the participants subjectively form convictions without manifest force, but convictions which are illusionary; thereby they produce communicatively a power which—as soon as it is insti-tutionalized—also can be applied against the participants themselves. (121)

Thus while "legitimation" on the political level may be more fun-damental than "overt power," it itself may be a form of "structural power."

Habermas's first reply to this turn of the argument would be that this achievement is always potentially unstable:

> Were the systematic restrictions on communication loosened, then the participating individuals and groups could come to the consciousness that ersatz satisfactions are bound up with the accepted legitimations, through which repressed needs not licensed by the institutionalized values were virtualized. (Habermas and Luhmann 1972, 259)

But this potential is not enough. And so Habermas points to what he considers structural mechanisms leading to an actual "loosening." This move is found in his theory of legitimation crisis. Briefly, Haber-mas's argument is that while in the past the structural power of ide-ologies might have been effective, in contemporary societies there are reasons to think that this is no longer the case. The attempt to con-struct a political philosophy whose operative principle is universal-izability, therefore, is not based on a merely arbitrary decision; a con-temporary social system based on any other principle is systematically prone to legitimation crisis.

Habermas presents his theory of legitimation crisis within a general theory of structural tendencies to crisis in late capitalism, a theory that distinguishes economic, political, and cultural forms of crisis. Neither of the first two crisis-forms need overcome structural power. Habermas points out that economic crises have had a disci-plining rather than a radicalizing effect on the members of industrial societies such as West Germany and the United States, an effect mani-fested in the conservative tendencies on the part of labor in these countries (cf. Habermas 1979b).

He has come to similar conclusions with respect to political crisis tendencies. Caught between the conflicting demands of indivi-dual capitalist interests, the collective capitalist interest in the continued functioning of the system as a whole, and the need to keep up the appearance that the state functions "for the people," the rationality of state administrative decisions breaks down. Rationality deficits in administrative decisions then lead to a disorganization in the life-spheres of the members of the polity. But

> [b]ankruptcy and unemployment mark unambiguously recognizable thresholds of risk for the nonfulfillment of functions. The disorganization of areas of life moves, in contrast, along a continuum. And it is difficult to say where the thresholds of tolerance lie and to what extent the perception of what is still tolerated–and of what is already experienced as intolerable–can be adapted to an increasingly disorganized environment. (Habermas 1975, 26)

This brings us back to the notion of *structural power.* It is structural power, manifested in "illusionary convictions," which–as soon as it is institutionalized–also can be applied against the participants themselves." It is structural power when workers whose lives suffer from the consequences of economic crisis are disciplined in their wage demands rather than radicalized. It is structural power when those whose lives are increasingly "disorganized" as a result of political decisions made to further capital accumulation react with tolerance.[3]

Habermas's theory of legitimation crisis is intended to establish that structural power does not "have the last word" in contemporary society. He presents a quite elaborate argument in making this case. The presupposition of this argument is that a legitimation crisis will result if the motives of social actors are sufficiently "dysfunctional" for the social system in question. Legitimation crisis is based upon motivation crisis.[4] This presupposition being granted, the steps of the argument are as follows.[5]

1. It must be shown that established forms of motivation which are "functional" (i.e., the "illusionary convictions" in which structural power has been manifested) are losing their force.

2. It must be shown that new forms of motivation are being established that are not only not functional for the social system but are actually dysfunctional.

3. It must be shown that there are no other forms of motivation established that are functional in the sense of maintaining existing structural power, *or* it must be shown that even if "illusionary convictions" remain their motivating force is for structural reasons less than that of the dysfunctional motivations established in step 2.

There is not space here to examine step 1 in detail. An example of Habermas's argumentation is the claim that the "achievement ideology" of early capitalism has broken down in the face of the increasing recognition that social power rather than achievement determines market success, that formal school education has no direct correspondence to vocational success, that "fragmented and monotonous labor processes are increasingly penetrating even those sectors in which an identity could previously be formed through the occupational role," and that welfare measures have "weakened the spurs to competition for status in the lower strata" (Habermas 1975, 82).

Step 2 also will be assumed for the sake of the argument. Habermas takes as established the hypothesis of Piaget (1965) and Kohlberg (1969) that moral development culminates in a "postconventional" stage. This postconventinal stage is characterized by action directed by universalistic principles. Modern natural law, utilitarianism, and Kantian ethics all provide such universalistic principles. For reasons that have been explored above, however, Habermas (1975) asserts that only a "communicative ethic," in which universalizable principles are derived within uncoerced discourse, is fully satisfactory (88ff.). Motivations formed in this manner, he claims, are dysfunctional from the standpoint of the political-economic subsystems of contemporary society because those subsystems are based upon a particularistic (class) distribution of goods, services, power, and so forth; that is, distribution based upon particular and private (class) interests. They therefore lack the generality and autonomy demanded by a communicative ethic. Because such factors as the expanse of the educational system make it less and less probable that adolescent crises do not end in a universalistic morality, Habermas continues,[6] it is warranted to assert the probability of a coming legitimation crisis. He writes that "a legitimation crisis can be avoided in the long run only if the latent class structures of advanced-capitalist societies are transformed or if the pressure for legitimation to which the administrative system is subject can be removed" (1975, 93), and the motivating force of universalistic moralities makes the latter alternative impossible.

Habermas, however, cannot claim that universalistic moralities alone have motivating force in contemporary society. "Nationalism," for instance, continues to motivate the actions of many social agents.[7] Hence it is upon step 3 that the weight of Habermas's claim rests. But the argument that Habermas presents for the predominance of universalistic moralities in motive formation over the particularistic moralities of "nationalism" seems fallacious. In a first move he affirms the proposition that bourgeois formal right, based as it is on universal principles, has a universal scope that transcends the limits of conflicts among particular states:

> *Since morality based on principles* is sanctioned only through the inner authority of conscience, its conflict with the public morality, still tied to the concrete citizen, is embedded in its claim to universality; the conflict is between the cosmopolitanism of the "human being" and the loyalties of the citizen (which cannot be universalistic as long as international relations are subject to the concrete morality of the more powerful). (1975, 87)

From this Habermas's argument procedes to the assention that "resolution of this conflict is *conceivable* only if the dichotomy between the in-group and out-group morally disappears, the opposition between morally and legally regulated areas is relativized, and the validity of *all* norms is tied to discursive will-formation" (1975, 87).

We thus have the following argument:

Premise 1: Since the introduction of modern natural law there has been a conflict between the "human being" and the "loyalties of the citizen."

Premise 2: Only a communicative ethic can overcome this conflict.

Conclusion: Therefore, only a communicative ethic can have motivating force today.

Even if both premises are granted the argument does not hold. There are two reasons for this. First, a third premise is required asserting that it is in some sense demanded that the conflict mentioned in the first premise be overcome. This claim would itself require a rather elaborate argument. A Machiavellian, for example, would insert a quite different premise into the argument instead. A Machiavellian would assert that the tension between "the cosmopolitanism of the 'human being' and the loyalties of the citizen" is irresolvable, and would conclude that therefore universalistic moralities should have *no* motivating force in contemporary societies, precisely because they abstract from this tension. But let us assume that Habermas can present compelling reasons for accepting the required third premise (for example, on the grounds that continuation of the dichotomy between in-group and out-group morality threatens the continued survival of the human species, given the contemporary state of weapons technology). The conclusion still does not follow. Or, rather, it does not follow only if the conclusion is read as an existential statement. Within the immediate context of this argument it seems that this may *not* be the proper reading. Habermas admits that here he has "left the domain of historical example" and moved to what is "at present a mere construct." If this is the case, then no fallacy has been committed. But within the wider argumentative context it is clear that Habermas must make an existential claim here. It is not enough for him merely to assert the *logical* possibility of a motivation crisis. Habermas uses this argument in support of the *empirical* claim that there is a tendency to motivation crisis in late capitalism. From this point of view, however, he has committed a fallacy in deriving an empirical conclusion (regarding the actual motives of social actors) from a nonempirical thought construct (regarding what would have to be the case *if* the duality of human being and citizen were to be overcome). If Habermas's argument on motivation crisis is not to beg the question he must supplement it with a proof that on the empirical level motivations in terms of the "loyalties of the citizen" are for structural reasons systematically unable to compensate for the dysfunctional motivations that result from an orientation to universalistic moralities. Assuming that the human being/citizen split ought to be overcome, and then working out a construct within which it is overcome, does not constitute such a proof. Habermas's argument for a motivation crisis therefore breaks down, and with it his argument for a legitimate crisis as well.

Summarizing the results of this digression, Habermas has not established a *structural* tendency to legitimation crisis in late capitalism, upon which his claim for the priority of communicative action over strategic action (and, ultimately, for the foundational role of the universalizability principle in the formulation of strategy and tactics) depended. He may claim with complete justification that a legitimation crisis is still possible. It does not depend upon structural factors, however, but upon the thoroughly contingent ability of radical critics to present plausible interpretations of contemporary social processes:

> There is the problem of interpreting the experiences articulated by these movements[8] in a manner such that our reading can be accepted by those immediately mobilized; how to make credible our hypothesis according to which these movements are phenomena caused by a politically uncontrolled capitalist development? (Habermas 1979b, 165–66)

Even if these interpretations are fully "credible" in themselves, however, power considerations once again intrude. Power can be maintained through preparing and presenting expressive symbols to the populace, symbols that create an unspecific preparedness to follow that can be called upon at need, to discredit even fully "credible" interpretations.

> Familiar strategies of this kind are the personalization of substantive issues, the symbolic use of hearings, expert judgments, juridicial incantations, and also the advertising techniques (copied from oligopolistic competition) that at once confirm and exploit existing structures of prejudice and that garnish certain contents positively, others negatively, through appeals to feeling, stimulation of unconscious motives, etc. (Habermas 1975, 70)

These strategies have "above all the function of directing attention to topical areas—that is, of pushing *other* themes, problems, and arguments below the threshold of attention and, thereby, of withholding them from opinion-formation" (Habermas 1975, 70). To the extent that such strategies are successful, a legitimation crisis can be avoided indefinitely.[9]

Conclusion

The conclusion of this investigation must be that power ultimately cannot be reduced to, and is not derived from, the demands of a communicative ethic (or of any other notion of "justice" for that matter). It may be true that the overt power required for successful strategic action ultimately is based upon acknowledgement derived from a view of justice fixed in communicatively established and maintained legitimating world-views. But these legitimating world views may themselves be manifestations of structural power strategically employed by those who benefit from such power. If "legitimation" cannot be shown to be a more fundamental category than "power," then Habermas's argument on the macrosociological level does not show that communicative action is "prior" to strategic action. It seems as if no good reason for making "justice" the foundational category in strategy and tactics can be given from the Habermasian position. It seems as if social theorists are as free to make "power interests" the ultimate principle here as to choose "universalizability" or any other principle of justice.

Before drawing this conclusion, however, one last point must be examined. One indeed may construct coherent strategies and tactics based upon an option for "power" as the fundamental category. Normative considerations of justice thereby would be essentially excluded from consideration. Alternatively, one could construct policies based upon a notion of justice that abstracted from questions of power. An example might be the pacifism of a Tolstoy. It is premature, however, to think that these are the only alternatives.

What the above analysis has shown is that there are two distinct modes of social action, each with its own practical logic irreducible to that of the other. The complexity—and the tragedy—of human existence appears to stem from the tension between the demands of normative justification in a communicative context and the demands of power in a context of struggle. This tension could be discussed in terms of an exclusive choice. One opts for the path of Tolstoy or for that of Machiavelli; there is no middle ground. If one chooses the former, consistency would demand that one's strategies and tactics take an apolitical route such as pacifism. If one chooses the latter, consistency would demand that one give up all concern for the "salvation" of one's "soul." Both options, that of an amoral politics and that of an apolitical ethics, resolve the tension. But is there not something artificial about both of these one-sided alternatives? Does not each in its own way attempt to oversimplify the complexities that arise when one engages in concrete social struggles?

Habermas presents us with a third choice in that the normative principle of universalizability does *not* exclude considerations of power. It is my judgment that this provides a nonarbitrary reason for making "justice" in the sense of "universalizability" rather than "power" the first principle of social policy.

Imagine a group engaged in a power struggle with certain opponents, and that this group makes "universalizability" the principle of the policies they formulate. Within this group decisions will have to be made that take into account all the risks involved in any power struggle. How can such decisions be justified?

> The sole possible justification at this level is consensus, aimed at in a practical discourse, among the participants who, in the consciousness of their common interests and their knowledge of the circumstances, of the predictable consequences and secondary consequences, are the only ones who can know what risks they are willing to undergo and with what expectations. (Habermas 1973b, 33)

Further, it is possible to engage in a power struggle against opponents while interpreting

> hypothetically the constellations of the struggle, from the viewpoint that every victory sought would not merely (as is usual) lead to the assertion of one particular interest against another, but instead would be a step toward the intended goal, which would make universal enlightenment, and by virtue of it, the uninhibited discursive formation of will, possible for all participants (and thus no longer merely those affected).[10]

In this manner the members of the group are led to live and to act *within* the tension between "justice" and "power" rather than dissolving that tension in an exclusive orientation to one or the other of the two poles.

From this perspective Habermas's position rests upon the following claims:

1. The tension between "justice" and "power" (between communicative action and strategic) is an essential characteristic of social policy.

2. Given step 1, it follows that social agents should orient their theoretical and practical activities to a principle that allows them to respect this tension.

3. The principle of "power" does not allow those who follow it to respect this tension. It attempts to resolve the tension in as one-sided a fashion as does an apolitical ethic.

4. The principle of universalizability does allow those who orient their actions to it to respect this tension. Therefore to make it the foundational principle of a social policy is not to make an ultimately arbitrary decision. Good reasons can be provided for this decision.

Of course this does not tell us how to balance the tension in a given concrete situation. That is a matter to be decided by those engaged in formulating strategies and tactics in specific historical contexts.

XI

Habermas on the University: *Bildung* in the Age of Technology

In Chapter III, I presented a critical analysis of scientific research regarding the agricultural sector. Much of this research is performed in university settings.[1] In this final chapter I would like to return to the question of the university. Given the Habermasian project of institutionalizing discourse as the ultimate end of social policy, what strategic goals should be set vis-à-vis the university?

Habermas's policy proposals regarding the university emerged in the course of an attempt to come to grips with both the historical transformation the university has undergone in the twentieth century, and the beliefs of other contemporary German social theorists. I shall first examine the move from early capitalism to contemporary capitalism in terms of the effects this transition has had on the university. Two responses to the new role of the university made by German theorists in the post–World War II period will be presented next. One will be dismissed as anachronistic. The other will be shown to be inadequate. Then Habermas's own response will be discussed. This response seeks to retain the classical German notion of *Bildung* in today's scientific-technical university.

The Changing Function of the University

Early capitalist society introduced what we may term the *princi-*

193

ple of liberalism. In Western Europe the monarchy had actively fostered the development of capitalism through granting charters, protecting trade routes, and so forth. The monarchy, however, also threatened capitalist interests by remaining tied to the old feudal nobility and by intervening in economic activity at the monarch's whim. The principle of liberalism was developed by the rising bourgeoisie in order to protect itself from arbitrary interference by the monarch. This principle strictly delimited a sphere of economic activity apart from the political realm. It asserted that decision-making in the former must be left to private individuals. This would, it was thought, lead to individual initiative and thereby to economic progress. The political realm too was to be transformed, as more and more administration passed from the king's favorites to trained state officials.

The principle of liberalism was not only applied to economic activity and the state. If early capitalism was to stabilize itself other institutions would have to function in a manner consistent with the functioning of economic and political institutions, and so the principle of liberalism was applied to the university as well. As a result the university had two defining characteristics in the period of early capitalism. First, the relationship between the university and the other spheres of society was fixed by what Habermas terms the *quarantine model* of the university. Just as the liberal principle delimited a realm of economic activity separate from the state, so too the university was conceived as possessing an institutional autonomy that must be preserved at all costs from external interference: "In the period of early liberalism, of the self-sufficient entrepreneur, the university with its claim to autonomy and with the institutional form of a self-administered body tied itself to the laws of its time" (Habermas 1981a, 19. All translation mine.).

The second impact of the principle of liberalism on the university concerned its educational ideal. If liberalism asserted that economic decisions were to be made by autonomous individuals, and that officials of the state were to act in a responsible manner, then it must be the task of the university to produce autonomous and responsible invididuals. This is the sociological framework for the development of the classical German humanist notion of *Bildung*, self-formation. This notion is central to the works of German philosophers of the period of early capitalism, and was the central concept of the philosophy of education worked out by thinkers such as Schleiermacher and Humboldt. In this view the mission of the universities was to provide a solid grounding in the traditional faculties. Philosophy was looked upon as the centerpiece, integrating the content of the other faculties into one coherent view. An individual having undergone training in this *Universitas litterarum* would possess the moral and aesthetic sensibility and wide-ranging learning required for enlightened autonomy. In the concept of *Bildung*, theory thus was directly connected to praxis. The theoretical knowledge one acquired in the university served to orient one's practical activity.

It is important to note that training in the techniques of production was *not* part of the role of the university. Scientists in the universities engaged in what was called "natural philosophy," the goal of which was the discovery of ultimate metaphysical truths regarding the universe. These men had no concern whatsoever for the practical application of their theories. Conversely, the practical men in the shop had little use for theory. They regarded traditional lore and the lessons of experience as sufficient in their search for profit. These techniques of production were rules of thumb passed from generation to generation without formal instruction.

Around the turn of the twentieth century all this changed. The centuries-long split between science and the useful arts was overcome. Science became a direct means of capital accumulation through the application of discoveries in physics and chemistry to the processes of commodity production. Noble (1977, 5) describes this transformation as follows:

> Modern science-based industry—that is, industrial enterprise in which ongoing scientific investigation and the systematic application of scientific knowledge to the process of commodity production have become routine parts of the operation—emerged very late in the nineteenth century. It was the product of significant advances in chemistry and physics and also of the growing willingness of the capitalist to embark upon the costly, time-consuming, and uncertain path of research and development. This willingness reflected both the intensifying demand to outproduce competitors at home and abroad and the unprecedented accumulation of sufficient surplus capital—the product of traditional manufactures, financial speculation, and industrial consolidation—with which to underwrite a revolution in social production.[2]

This transition to science-based industries required both the employment and training of scientific personnel and the operation of large-scale industrial research and development. For example, in the United States, research and development expenditures rose from under $100 million in 1928 to $5 billion in 1953–54, $12 billion in 1959, $14 billion in 1965 and $20.17 billion in 1970 (Mandel 1978, 257). The figures for Germany are analogous. There was, in short, a tremendous demand for scientific-technical education. State administration also became rationalized during this period, which created a further demand for scientific-technical research and personnel. In response to this demand the university itself was transformed.[3] Its new role was to provide for the needs of scientific-technical research and expertise.

As a result of this new function both of the characteristics that defined the university in the age of early capitalism changed. While certain features of the old university remained (self-government by the faculty, for example), by and large the quarantine model of the university broke down. The university, now funded to a large degree by contracts and grants from corporations and state agencies, became connected with the social life world in a most direct fashion.[4] This breakdown of the quarantine model was closely connected to a shift in educational ideals away from those advocated in the classical German university. No longer was the goal of a university education the formation of character. Rather than being oriented towards the ideal of *Bildung,* the university now had the goal of producing persons capable of discovering and applying technically employable knowledge. No longer was the ideal the well-rounded humanist of the *Universitas litterarum*. Instead the ideal became the specialist, one who concentrated on a particular area and was able to produce causal knowledge of the regularities of that object realm. With this, philosophy lost its place of priority among the faculties. As specialization increased, philosophy's claim to offer a synthetic perspective uniting all knowledge into a theory capable of providing practical orientation appeared more and more implausible.

Two Alternative Strategies
Regarding the Contemporary University

Different perspectives on this new role of the university have emerged among German philosophers in the last decades. Before presenting Habermas's evaluation I must mention two other positions.

The first response to this new function of the university can be termed *neo-romantic*. This perspective is characterized by a longing for the old ideal of the university and an attempt to make that ideal alive today. Karl Jaspers was very influential in this direction as was also the neo-Thomistic movement in vogue in German universities during the immediate post-World War II period (see "Das chronische Leiden," in Habermas 1981a, 13–40). Both camps called for a return to the *Universitas litterarum* with philosophy once again holding its position of priority, uniting all the other disciplines in a world-view. Creating this world-view, Jaspers said, would require an exercise of *Geist*, spirit. Once created, those educated within it would possess a theoretical system capable of orienting their practical activity, thereby keeping the classical notion of *Bildung* alive in the twentieth century.

Despite initial popularity in postwar Germany the neo-romantic view of the university confronted one ineluctable fact. No matter how much spiritual energy was exerted there remained "That which spirit worked against in vain, in which an objective contradiction – produced by the social life context and not to be removed without removing that context – obviously was fixed and continued" ("Das chronische Leiden," in Habermas 1981a, 17). Increased specialization provides one example of something produced by the social life context and not to be removed by mere spiritual renewal. Faced with such specialization the attempts of Jaspers's *Geist* to work out a synthetic perspective could result only in a dilettantish digest that would itself count as a betrayal of the *Bildung* ideal.[5]

A second perspective on the role of the university in modern society has increasingly held sway among German thinkers: the *technocratic* perspective. This position insists that the increased specialization required to master a particular scientific area and the direct bond between the university and the needs of industry and government have made the classical humanist ideals totally outdated. This stance was taken by thinkers such as Schelsky.[6] He saw the contemporary

197

university as so totally integrated into today's technological society that any return to older ideals was out of the question.

This position on the university was grounded in a general social theory. A key characteristic of this social theory is that it in effect eliminates "the political" as a valid category. According to this view society has increased in complexity to such an extent that it has become a self-regulating system. Technical experts, it is true, must manage this system in order for it to maintain an equilibrium. But the question of the ends of social action does not arise according to this perspective. *All* industrial societies, no matter what their ideologies might be, must fulfill the same technical imperatives. If the question of ends no longer has any relevance given the complexity of contemporary society, then it follows that the university ought to abandon once and for all the ideal of *Bildung*. Rather than training students to select ends, to orient their practical activity, the university must instead provide what is needed by the society: technical specialists who possess the expertise required to attain the "end" already given, the maintenance of the system in an equilibrium state.

If there is one idea that has remained constant throughout Habermas's writings it is that the social theory just described is fundamentally in error. It is, of course, true that in contemporary society technical expertise plays a greater role than ever before. But this is not to assert that the question of ends is now irrelevant. Ends must be selected as before. To assert that a given end is "technically necessitated" is simply to mask the actual situation. The direction in which technology develops, the pace at which it develops, the manner in which it is employed, and so on, involve political decisions that technology in itself does not necessitate: "The scientifically solved problems of technical manipulation are transformed into life problems, for the scientific control of natural and social processes does not absolve humans from action. Now as before conflicts must be decided, interests pierced through, interpretations found. . . . [O]nly these practical questions are today largely determined through the system of our technical achievements."[7] To mask this reality is to mask the exercise of power that occurs when these decisions are made outside of any public control: "The direction of technical progress can be very much influenced by government research policy; however until today it is still dependent to a high degree upon private economic interests, interests which as such are not made objects of discussion of a science oriented to the general interest and beyond that of a formed (*gebildeten*) political public sufficiently knowledgeable of the practical consequences (of technical development)" ("Vom sozialen Wandel," in Habermas 1981a, 115). But, this situation may generate a long-term structural tendency to legitimation crisis. The techno-cratic perspective, then, may not prove stable in the long run.

Habermas's Strategic Orientation

The above account leaves Habermas in the following position. The neo-romantic view of the university is correct in insisting that contemporary industrial society has in no way made irrelevant the need for a theoretical training that would orient practical activity. But its appeal to philosophy as a discipline capable of providing a synthetic theory with practical implications is most questionable. Conversely the conservative technocratic view wrongly rejects the very notion of education as *Bildung*. Yet it correctly insists upon the necessity for specialization and technical training. Is there any way of combining the strengths of both positions while avoiding their weaknesses?

Habermas thinks so. He begins by agreeing with the technocratic view that specialization is a feature of contemporary society that is not about to disappear. The problem, he asserts, is that this specializa-tion is not carried far enough. The implementation of technical knowl-edge involves practical consequences for the social life world, and the study of one's speciality should be pushed until the student is forced to reflect on these social consequences. This sort of theoretical reflec-tion can lead to the orientation of practical activity. It is thus a form of *Bildung*, a form that does not retreat back to the nineteenth-century ideal of the "person of letters" but that is instead compatible with the degree of specialization demanded in the age of technology. "Reflection on the foundation (of the specialized sciences) forces one to a critique of the relations between science and society. And once again this critique must be borne by the single sciences themselves" ("Das chronische Leiden," in Habermas 1981a, 37).

Habermas mentions some measures for structuring the course of university study so as to encourage this sort of reflection among those in the sciences. (For example, he argues against imposing a fixed length of study.) But this is nothing more than the first stage; if university researchers are to connect their activities with the social life world they cannot simply reflect on the social consequences of their research in isolation from this life world. *Bildung* is ultimately a social process, not something that individuals go through alone. The interpretation of the social consequences of research made by those within the university must be mediated with the interpretations of the public at large:

> A double function of teaching corresponds to research: first the transmission of formal and empirical knowledge for training in job techniques and in the research process itself, but then also that retranslation of scientific results in the horizon of the life-world. This would permit the informational content of technical recommendations to be brought into discussions about the practically necessary, the general interest. Today we no longer can leave that to the contingent decisions of individuals or to the pluralism of opinion makers. It is a matter not only of continuing to give a practically effective level of knowledge to the administrative apparatus of technically operating persons, but of also incorporating it back into the language possession of the communicating society. *That* is today the task of an academic *Bildung* which now as before must be taken over by a science capable of self-reflection. If our universities decline to undertake *Bildung* in this sense . . . the enlightenment of a politically mature public also cannot be expected. ("Vom sozialen Wandel," Habermas 1981a, 116–17).

Habermas envisions a model in which public discussions uniting planners from government and industry with scientific-technical experts from universities and research laboratories and with representatives of public interest groups would determine policy through a "dialectic of will and skill." Those with the requisite technical expertise would inform the community of the range of possibilities allowed by the present level of scientific-technical knowledge. The public sphere would be engaged in ongoing discussion (following rules to ensure that the discussion was as free from coercion as possible) to select which of these technical possibilities best satisfies generalizable social needs. Government and production units would have the task of planning the most efficient means of carrying out these public mandates.[8] This policy would ensure the satisfaction of universalizable interests, and thereby overcome the tendency to legitimation crisis. The university's tasks in this model include (a) the scientific-technical training needed by scientists and engineers in order to fix what is technically possible, (b) the training in management techniques needed if government and officials in production are to act in an efficient manner, (c) the training in self-reflection needed if scientists and engineers are to consider the social implications of various technologies in an adequate fashion, and (d) the transmission of scientific-technical knowledge to the public sphere, so that choice among the various possibilities will be as informed as possible. In short, the university must combine the transmission of technical knowledge with *Bildung*.

I would like to conclude with a consideration of some objections that could be made against Habermas's proposal. First, it could be objected that public discourse on university research would lead to an illicit politicization of scientific activity, thereby threatening the autonomy of the university. This objection is based upon what was termed the quarantine model of the relationship between the university and society. This model is not applicable when modern society is as permeated by science and technology stemming from the university as it is today. When this is recognized it becomes apparent that the attempt to quarantine scientific research from public input does not so much preserve the university's autonomy as block off conscious reflection on the links between that research and the social life world. Whether scientific research should or should not be politicized is not a true question. A true question is whether the practical consequences of scientific research will be made explicit. A true question is whether scientists are to be conscious of their responsibility for the foreseeable direct and indirect social implications of their research. If one accepts the view that the university's ideals demand that these last questions be answered in the affirmative, then a forum within which different sectors of the public have the opportunity to articulate how a specific research proposal affects their concerns would provide an aid in making these social consequences of research explicit and in helping individual scientists reflect upon their social responsibilities. Indeed, Habermas goes even further. It is, he argues, precisely the *lack* of such institutionalized public discourse that most threatens the autonomy of the university. Without regular public scrutiny the danger is ever-present that private interests will be able to dictate the direction university research takes.

> Discussion over the goals of the courses of study, over criteria for the selection of research projects, over the social context of scientific qualifications and the information begotten in the research process can first place the groups immediately participating in teaching and research in the position of reflecting upon avoidable and unavoidable social dependencies.[9]

Second, it could be objected that any attempt to institutionalize public input interferes with the academic freedom of the individual researchers in the university. This raises profound questions regarding the notion of democracy. In a democracy, certain decisions are left to the individual and his conscience. Should I become a member of this church or that? Should I marry this woman or not? No one has a right to infringe on these sorts of decisions.

But in a democracy not all decisions are categorized as private matters. The decisions made by state officials, for example, are categorized as public. And in a democracy decisions within which public power is exercised are *not* left to the dictates of one's private conscience. They are instead subject to public control. Democracy could even be defined as that system that *restricts* the freedom of those who exercise public power, as the freedom of a democratically elected president is restricted in comparison to an absolute monarch.

It follows that the attempt to institutionalize public input into decisions regarding university research would count as an infringement of freedom *only* if such decisions were private in scope, like the choice of a religion or the choice of a marriage partner. But, as has been argued above, in a scientific civilization such as our own this is not the case. Scientific research conducted in universities regularly has ramifications far beyond the intimate sphere of the researcher's private life, ramifications that may extend throughout the very fabric of society. Given this public nature of scientific research, it follows that public input into decisions regarding that research should be looked upon not as restrictions on freedom but as furthering the process of democratization.

A third and final objection remains. It is most difficult to change a central institution in isolation from other institutions to which it is structurally related. To bring the university to a new notion of *Bildung* as described above requires a democratization of the university that is not likely to occur without a general democratization of society as a whole. One cannot question the "right" of private corporations to dictate the direction of university research without simultaneously questioning their "right" to determine which sections of the economy will be invested in, which geographical areas will be developed, whether investment will be productive or speculative, and so forth. *All* exercises of public power must be subject to public control, if the university is to be transformed. Strategies and tactics aiming at the thorough democratization of society must be formulated and put into practice. I hope that this book may in some small way help persuade philosophers that they should join social activists in this task. We have much to contribute, and even more to learn.

Notes

Preface

1. With the exception of Chapter I and Chapter V, the essays that make up this book have been published previously. I have, however, extensively modified these essays in places for the sake of continuity and to avoid excessive repetition. Chapter II appeared in *Philosophy and Social Criticism*, 8, no. 1 (1981):68–83. Chapter III was published in *Is There a Moral Obligation to Save the Family Farm?*, ed. G. Comstock (Ames: Iowa State University Press, 1987), 176–86. Chapter IV first appeared in *Theory and Society*, 13, no. 4 (1984):513–40. Chapter VI was published in the *Journal of Peace and Justice Studies*, 1, no. 2 (1989):81–91. The chapter on Kant appeared in *The Review of Politics*, 47, no. 2 (1985):253–80. An abridged version of Chapter VIII can be found in *Ideals of a Good Society: Problems in Social Philosophy Today* (Edwin Mellen Press, 1988: 19–31), Chapter IX reprinted by permission of the University of Georgia Press from *At the Nexus of Philosophy and History*, edited by Bernard Dauenhauer, copyright 1987 by the University of Georgia Press. Chapter X was published originally in *Interpretations: A Journal of Political Philosophy*, 11, no. 3 (1983):333–51. Chapter XI is taken from *Descriptions: Journal of the Society for Phenomenology and Existentialism*, 11 (1985): 274–85. I would like to thank all the publishers of these papers for their kind permission to make use of this material here.

2. The idea of distinguishing the different activities making up social theory according to their "functional specialization" rather than their subject matter initially came from my reading of Bernard Lonergan, whose *Method in Theology* (1972) accomplishes this task for the discipline of theology.

3. The secondary literature on Habermas has grown immensely in the last years. The two most important studies are McCarthy (1984) and David Ingram (1987).

Part One: The Framework

1. In my previous study, *The Logic of Marx's Capital* (Smith 1990) I presented a philosophical defense of the fundamental categories employed in Marx's social science. I then went on to examine some of the normative and policy implications of accepting these categories.

Chapter I

1. The term "social" is not to be taken here in the narrow sense in which it is opposed to the "economic," "political," "legal," "cultural," and so on. It is to be taken instead in a broad sense in which all the latter terms are included.

2. Consider the following passage: "The formal right of a worker to enter into any contract whatsoever with any employer whatsoever does not in practice represent for the employment seeker even the slightest freedom in the determination of his own conditions of work, and it does not guarantee him any influence on this process. It rather means, at least primarily, that the more powerful party in the market, i.e., normally the employer, has the possibility to set the terms, to offer the job 'take it or leave it,' and, given the normally more pressing economic need of the worker, to impose his terms upon him. . . . Coercion is exercised to a considerable extent by the private owners of the means of production and acquisition, to whom the law guarantees their property and whose power can thus manifest itself in the competitive struggle of the market" Weber (1968), 2:729–30.

3. Many argue that a capitalist economy can function only if a state provides those necessary preconditions for profitable private investment which it is not profitable for any individual capitalist firm to provide (see Polanyi [1957] for an example of this claim.) If this is accurate, then it would follow that Nozick's model of a laissez-faire capitalist economy combined with a minimal state could not function, for the functioning of the former would require a more than minimal state. If this were true we ought not to accept this model in branch seven, even if we assert in branch six that this model is to be affirmatively evaluated.

Part Two: Some Ethical Issues in the Social Sciences

1. Weber, of course, has not been the only social theorist to defend a decisionistic position. More recently a version of this viewpoint has been ex-

pressed by Richard Rorty. See the contributions made by Rorty and Habermas to the collection *Habermas and Modernity* (Bernstein 1985). Also see Martin Matustik (1989) for an overview of the Rorty–Habermas debate.

Chapter II

1. Thus, Habermas clearly distinguishes the logic of theoretical discourse from that of practical discourse. See his article "Wahrheitstheorien" in Fahrenback (1973).

2. This was the basis for his critique of Schmoller's practice of issuing value judgments in university settings where they are "neither controlled, checked by discussion, nor subject to contradiction" (Weber 1949, 4).

3. For example, the selection of that which is to be investigated in social science involves the cultural values of social scientists in Weber's view.

4. Not all "social action" is a case of "communicative action," a fact that complicates Habermas's argument somewhat. See Chapter X, this book.

5. "Vorbereitende Bermerkungen zu einer Theorie der Kommunikativen Kompetenz," in Habermas and Luhmann (1972, 141). See also "Diskursethik-Notizen zu einer Begrundungsprogramm," in Habermas (1983, 53–126).

6. The tu quoque form of argumentation to my knowledge was first used in explicit form by Aristotle in his defense of the principle of noncontradiction.

7. Habermas recognizes, of course, that a true consensus may not be reached even if an ideal speech situation is fully anticipated. Hence he has sketched an outline of a theory of justified compromise to complement his theory of rational consensus. See Habermas (1975, 112).

8. "Marx had to make these or equivalent assumptions in the analysis of class struggles. He had: (a) to draw a general distinction between particular and general interests; (b) to understand the consciousness of justified and, at the same time, suppressed interests as a sufficient motive for conflict; and (c) to attribute, with reason, interest positions to social groups." Ibid. p. 114.

9. The specifically linguistic pragmatic function of a speech act, opening us to the realm of language itself and involving the validity claim of linguistic intelligibility, can be neglected here.

10. There is a difficulty in applying this methodology to premodern societies. Habermas is well aware of this difficulty: "every general theory of justification remains specifically abstract vis-à-vis the historical manifestations

of legitimate authority. When one imposes standards of discursive justification on traditional societies one is acting historically 'unjustly.'" With regards to this problem, Habermas writes, "Is there an alternative to this historical injustice of general theories on the one side and the lack of a standard in mere historical *Verstehen* on the other side? The single promising program which I see is a theory which structurally clarifies the observable historical seriation of different grades of justification and reconstructs it as a continuity with a developmental logic" (1976, 299). With this Habermas announces the project of constructing a theory of social evolution as a necessary compliment to the theory of practical discourse. I discuss this theory in Chapter IV.

Chapter III

1. The shift to export production sets off another dynamic that is also often overlooked. As more of the best land is devoted to export crops, greater and greater numbers of the population are forced to turn to land with fragile soil for their subsistence, thus depleting the soil. When a drought occurs, the depleted soil can then turn into desert, triggering a famine. The important point to stress is that the drought is the *trigger* of the famine, not its underlying *cause*. The cause is the social process that pushed so much of the population onto lands with fragile soil. See Tinker (1984). Of course military conflicts can exacerbate this situation greatly.

Chapter IV

1. Both thinkers make original contributions to a discussion that goes back to Vico and the *Natur*-versus *Geisteswissenschaften* debates of the nineteenth century. An adequate discussion of these contributions, however, would require an article of its own.

2. It is revealing that next to Marx and Engels themselves, no other thinker is referred to by Cohen more often that Plekhanov. See Plekhanov (1956).

3. Cohen (1978) limits his discussion to an analysis of the relationship between the de jure legal rights that fix property relations and the de facto powers that fix production relations in the economic structure. Whenever the two are in conflict, he asserts, "The solution is either a change in production relations in violation of the law, with the law later falling into line, or a change in law which facilitates a change in production relations" (234). In either case the production relations have the explanatory primacy. Histori-

cal changes in the law are explained by the functionality of such change for consolidating production relations, even when the former causally influences ("facilitates change in") the latter.

4. See Max Weber's "Critical Studies in the Logic of the Cultural Sciences" (in Weber 1949, 171ff.).

5. Miller (1981) reads Cohen differently. He writes that, "Cohen . . . allows that a society might change before it has yielded every possible increase in productivity" (93). But the text to which Miller refers is a defense of the position Miller says Cohen rejects, i.e., that "No social formation ever perishes before all the productive forces for which there is room in it have developed," (Cohen 1978, 136). In his discussion, Cohen constructs a supposed counterexample to this claim. He imagines that in feudal France a grain yield of six times the amount of seed sown was normal, while in some other possible form of feudalism an input-output ratio of 1:10 was possible. If this were the case it would seem that the transition from feudalism in France falsifies the above claim. Cohen, however, states that in the most plausible construal of the claim, "French fedual society's maximum possible productivity would be set not by the fuedal form as such but by the feudal form in its specific French variation . . . not the dominant production relation alone, which is common to all feudalisms, but more specific features of its economic structure, would figure in determining a particular feudal society's potential maximum. Then the fact that other feudalisms had outclassed the French would not falsify the claim stated above," (Cohen 1978, 140). Hence what Miller regards as a rejection of the position is in reality Cohen's attempt to formulate explicitly a defensible reading of it.

6. On the heightened demand for increased development of the productive forces in times of downswing, see the following comment from *Business Week*: "Five years of inflation, recession, and uncertain recovery have forced the men who manage U.S. business and the men who make U.S. economic policy to a painful conclusion: Somehow the nation must make a quantum jump in efficiency. It must get more output from its men and machines," (September 9, 1982, 71). Also, periodical underinvestment creates a "reserve fund of capital, from which can be drawn the means for additional accumulation . . . to allow a fundamental renewal of productive technology" (Mandel 1978, 114). This is a central part of Mandel's explanation of the three technological revolutions that have occurred since the original industrial revolution.

7. David-Hillel Rubin has pointed out that in Cohen's own discussion of the "distinctive contradiction" in advanced capitalism, he doesn't mention stagnation of the productive forces. He instead points to an "overemployment (of resources)" (Cohen 1978, 307). By this Cohen refers to an irra-

tional tendency to increase output rather than reduce toil and extend leisure. Rather than see this point as fatal to Cohen's theory, however, Ruben (1981) feels Cohen could still maintain that production relations restrict productive forces in capitalism if he accepted the labor theory of value and its implications (234). I do not find this plausible. Mandel, for example, is able to hold with full consistency both the labor theory of value and to deny that the productive forces are ultimately "fettered" in capitalism.

8. This has been central to Habermas's thought from his earliest essays such as "Labor and Interaction: Remarks on Hegel's Jena *Philosophy of Mind*" (in Habermas 1973b, 142–69).

9. Cf. Habermas (1981b, 1:123). All translations from this work are my own.

10. Habermas (1981b, 1:142–49). In the early stages of social evolution these three realms are not distinguished. World-views must be "decentralized" for these differences to become explicit. This is not a problem here, as Cohen's stress upon technical rationality, no less than Habermas's correction, presupposes such decentralization. See Habermas (1981b, 1:254; 1981b, 2:280–92).

11. Thus the distinction does not simply reflect how labor is structured in contemporary society, as Heller (1982, 35) suggests.

12. The following is loosely based upon "Towards a Reconstruction of Historical Materialism" (in Habermas 1979a, 154ff; 1981b, 2:259ff.).

13. Habermas stresses the increase in communicative competence that is required here. Speech must become propositionally differentiated; speakers must be able to separate speech from action if they are to connect the performative attitude of the participant with the propositional attitude of an observer.

14. This too requires a growth in communicative competence. Now the speakers must be capable of engaging in argumentative speech within which the validity claims connected with speech acts are made thematic.

15. Piaget (1965) and Kohlbert (1971) introduced the terminology Habermas employs here.

16. Thus Heller writes that Habermas views the past as being made up of "progress without contradictions," a progress that ignores Auschwitz, Hiroshima, and the Gulag. (Thompson and Held 1982, 40). To reconstruct a thread of advance in history in no way denies the horrible tragedies in history as it is concretely lived.

17. Habermas (1981b, 2:chapter 5) synthesizes the work of Durkheim and Mead in order to reconstruct the process from instinct-directed, gesture-mediated interaction through interaction symbolically mediated by a single

language to interactions mediated by speech, in order to account for the move from natural evolution to social evolution.

18. "The learning capacity at first won by single members of society or marginal groups finds entrance into the interpretive system of the society through exemplary learning processes" (1981b, 2:463).

19. Habermas thus distinguishes the social integration accomplished in the life world by the transmission of cultural traditions, the participation in society, and the socialization of the individual person, from system integration. See Habermas (1981b, 2:230) on the distinction between a life world and a systems perspective.

20. "Societies learn by resolving system problems which present evolutionary challenges. By this I understand problems which overload the steering capacity accessible at the limit of a given social formation. Societies can attain evolutionary learning when they use the moral and legal ideas contained in world views for a transformation of action systems and build up a new form of social integration. This process can be represented as the institutional embodiment of rationality structures which are already worked out on the cultural level" (1981b, 2:464).

21. "The establishment of a new form of social integration allows the implementation of already present (or the production of new) technical-organizational knowledge, i.e., a development of the productive forces and an extension of system complexity" (1981b, 2:4).

22. "Historical Materialism and the Development of Normative Structures" (in Habermas 1979a, 97–98). After presenting his own theory, Cohen (1978) writes, "Perhaps the most promising line of resistance to it would be to propose a development thesis for production relations, a claim, that is, that production relations tend to change in some particular direction throughout history, and not because of the growth of the productive forces within them. We submit, however, that it would be extremely difficult to substantiate any such claim" (159). Habermas's theory of practical rationalization, that is the theory of "the systematically reconstructible patterns of development of normative structures," can be read as an answer to that challenge.

23. "Towards a Reconstruction" (in Habermas 1979a, 152). Klaus Eder (1976) has worked out this theory in detail. (Cf. Habermas 1981b, 2:232ff., 247, 264ff.).

24. "For the motivational anchoring of purposive-rational action orientations, which are so stable and comprehensive that they can constitute a vocational role, the systematizing power of a principle-directed moral consciousness is necessary" (Habermas 1981b, 2:466). (See also Habermas 1981b, 1:238, 345, 348, 353; and 2:468).

25. "Economically conditioned crisis tendencies are not only administratively worked on, flattened and braked, but also are invisibly transported into the administrative system. They can appear in different forms there, e.g., as conflicts between its goals of compensation policies and infrastructure policies, as an excessive claim on the resource time (state debt), as excessive demand on bureaucratic planning capacities, etc. This can in turn call forth unburdening strategies with the goal of transporting the burden of problems back to the economic system" (1981b, 2:506).

26. "Developed capitalism swings between the contrary policies of the 'self-healing powers of the market' and state interventionism" (1981b, 2:565). For an earlier discussion of the various crisis forms, cf., Habermas (1975).

27. Habermas (1981b) mentions both programs granting compensations to individuals (e.g., unemployment insurance) and programs designed to compensate for effects of capitalism that are collectively experienced (e.g., regional planning (2:510–11).

28. It must be said that this pacification can be expected to a much lower degree than Habermas supposes. He himself (1981b) writes that the social state faces a profound dilemma: "The dilemma stems from the fact that the social state ought to break both the immediately negative effects of a capitalistically organized occupational system and also the dysfunctional secondary consequences of economic growth led by capital accumulation . . . without being permitted to touch the form of organization, structure and incentive mechanism of economic production" (2:511). Habermas doesn't, however, seem to have appreciated fully the extensive structural limitations this dilemma sets on the range of possible state action. These limitations make it most unlikely that the social state can accomplish what Habermas claims is in its power. (I discuss this topic at length in Chapter XI.) However, even if Habermas is mistaken here, it does not affect his overall argument. The social pathologies he discusses arise from the attempt of the social state to pacify class conflict, and would remain whether or not this attempt is ultimately successful.

29. "The politically propped up internal dynamic of the economic system results in a more or less continuous increase in the system's complexity, which means both the extension and the internal concentration of formally organized realms of action. At first this hold for relations within the subsystems of the economy and public administration and for the interactions of the subsystems between each other. . . . But the growth of the whole complex affects just as greatly the interchange of the subsystems with these spheres of the life world . . . on the one hand, the private households that are transformed by mass consumerism and, on the other hand, coordinated client services that are redefined by bureaucratic concerns" (1981b, 2:515–16).

30. "The thesis of the inner colonization states that the subsystems of the economy and state become ever more complex as a result of capitalist growth, and penetrate ever deeper into the symbolic reproduction of the life world" (1981b, 2:539).

31. "The uncoupling of the media-directed subsystems and their organizational forms from the life world does not lead to a one-sided rationalization or reification of everyday communicative praxis. Rather this is first caused by the penetration of forms of economic and administrative rationality in realms of action which resist transformation by the media money and power because they are specialized for cultural tradition, social integration and education and remain oriented towards understanding as the mechanism for coordinating action" (1981b, 2:488).

32. In other words, the social state sets off unintended consequences that contradict its intended purpose. "The guarantees of the social state ought to serve the goal of social integration and yet simultaneously they lead to the disintegration of those life contexts that are dissolved from the action-coordinating mechanisms of understanding and transformed by such media as power and money" (1981b, 2:534). Habermas (1981b) discusses a number of examples, for instance, social insurance (531); bureaucratically administered therapy programs (533); manipulation of public opinion (507); and a whole set of what he terms "green problems," such as the destruction of the urban environment, the poisoning of the land, etc. (579 ff.).

33. Mandel (1978) writes that "The future typology of socialist revolutions in the highly industrialized countries will probably follow the pattern of the revolutionary crises already experienced in Spain (1931–37), France (1936), Italy (1948), Belgium (1960–61), France (May 1968), Italy (autumn 1969–70), more closely than that of the crises of 'collapse' of the productive forces" (218). These outbreaks can, however, be accounted for within Habermas's framework. Philippe Van Parijs (1980) criticizes Cohen on grounds similar to ours (505). Parijs (1980) reports that in an unpublished lecture from 1981 Cohen himself suggests that economic crises, and not a fettering of the productive forces, generates a pressure for revolutionary change (510). I do not know what to make of this. This would signify that Cohen has abandoned the position defended in his book, whereas in articles appearing well after the lecture (e.g., 1980,; 1981a), he appears not to have modified his views in any significant fashion.

34. "'Crisis tendencies' in bureaucratic socialism arise from the self-blocking mechanism of planning administrations in a manner similar to the indigenous breakdown of the accumulation process in capitalism. . . . [P]olicies oscillate between increased central planning and decentralization, between

investment and consumer oriented economic programs, without a way out" (1981b, 2:565).

35. "In bureaucratic socialist societies too realms of action which are oriented to social integration are transformed by system integrative mechanisms. But in the place of the reified communicative relations of capitalism steps the illusion of communicative relations in the bureaucratically dried up, coercively humanized realms of a pseudopoliticized intercourse. Pseudopoliticalization in bureaucratic socialism in certain respects is symmetrical to the reified privitization of late capitalism" (1981b, 2:567).

36. Cf. Habermas (1981b, 2:430); Wimmer (1980) and Chapters II and XI, this book.

Part Three: Some Ethical Evaluations of Capitalism

1. In Chapters II and III, I argued that when evaluations are combined with specific empirical studies the resulting synthesis is either "critical social science" or "ideology," depending on whether the standards employed in the evaluations are submitted to a discourse anticipating an ideal speech situation, or whether mechanisms are operating that prevent this. What is the difference between critical/ideological social science on the one hand, and the evaluations that make up the sixth branch of social theory? The difference is one of emphasis, not principle. In critical social science and ideological social science, the normative component emerges within the context of empirical investigations; while in the branch of social theory now being considered, reference to empirical studies occurs within the context of normative inquiries. This is why business ethics, and other forms of applied ethics, are considered philosophical pursuits rather than social sciences, despite the fact that they incorporate considerable amounts of empirical material.

Chapter V

1. For an excellent study of this issue see Wolfe (1978).

2. "A small minority claims that the American system is free of immorality, is sufficiently just, and should not be tinkered with. Most people realize that we do not yet have a completely just society, that our structures can be improved. . . . We can and should make the morally necessary changes in American capitalism, improve it, and work toward a yet unattained maximal mix of freedom and justice. The real alternative to our present Ameri-

can system does not consist in holistic change. What is most likely to succeed is piecemeal change, correcting ills where possible, outlawing immoral practices, and implementing structural changes that promote moral conduct. American capitalism can be made more moral than it is; the task before all of us is to make the required changes where and how we can" (126–27). When I refer to "the underlying structure" or "the basic structure" that De George attempts to legitimate I am speaking of what De George calls the "present American system" in the above passage, and not the (nonbasic) structures which De Georges de-legitimates by saying they can be "improved."

3. It is difficult to understand why De George lists this as a defining feature of capitalism. In the West capitalism preceded the industrial revolution by many centuries and until quite recently the typical Third World capitalist country was industrialized to an extremely limited extent.

4. I do not wish to deny that "consensus" is extremely important in moral justification. But not any sort of consensus will do. It must be a consensus attained under certain specific conditions that ensure fairness and rationality (two attempts to specify these conditions are found in Rawls's notion of an "original position" and Habermas's theory of an "ideal speech situation"). De George himself mentions the possibility that such conditions are *not* present in the United States today. He writes: "The society is divided, and the state, laws, courts, police, schools, churches, and the media are all controlled by the ruling class. The ruling class uses all these social institutions to dominate the workers, keep them subservient, and insure the continuation of the institution of private property" (117). For De George's argument to work he would have to show either that this view is not an essentially accurate analysis of U.S. society, or that it may be accurate in many respects but the consensus under discussion is morally justified nonetheless. As neither point is established, De George's reference to this consensus does not help his case.

5. De George doesn't mention any of the profound and obvious difficulties involved in enacting tax legislation of the sort he describes. For one thing, it is difficult to deny that business interests have a disproportional influence on state officials, making significantly progressive tax legislation quite unlikely. But even if reforms significantly favorable to the interest of the working classes were ever seriously instituted by the state, capitalists would at once go out on a "capital strike" and refuse to invest their capital. This would plunge the society into deep crisis, leaving only the choice of giving into the blackmail and rescinding the reforms, or appropriating private capital in order to take away from private interests this ability to mandate public policy. In either case the liberal optimism expressed by De George in the passage quoted in the previous footnote would appear quite naive indeed.

6. It is rather surprising that De George can later write, "Classes are not obvious, and the division of people into proletariat and bourgeoise is not clearly applicable to the people of the United States" (118). For the existence of class divisions follows with necessity from the fact that "not everyone owns the means of production"! Those few who own the means of production are the bourgeoise. The remaining classes in society are divided into two main groups. Some have power delegated to them by the bourgeoise to manage capital in the interests of the bourgeoise. This class is allied with the bourgeoise; while it does not own capital it shares in its control. Most of the remainder of society forms the proletariat which neither owns nor controls capital. There are, of course, divisions within the working classes such as the racial and sexual divisions referred to above. That is why De George is correct when he writes, "It is sometimes difficult for people to know which class they belong to" (118). (Indeed, racism could even be defined as a system which prevents poor whites and poor blacks from attaining a consciousness of their common class interests.) But this is a fact of social psychology and in no way affects the theoretical distinctions among the different classes. Hence when De George writes, "Managers are as truly employees as assembly line workers" (126), his argument degenerates to equivocation and crass apologetics.

7. This state of affairs is not an accident. Legislation such as the Taft-Hartley Act was specifically designed to bring it about.

Chapter VI

1. See Ernest Mandel (1986). The main problem with Arnold's comment is that it does not distinguish between utilizing market mechanisms within the context of a socialist plan, and turning to the market as the major regulator of economic reproduction. While "socialists who think seriously about economics" accept the former, there is no sch consensus regarding the latter.

2. Examples are all around us: depletable but inexpensive natural resources used wastefully, nitrates in the drinking water of agricultural communities, acid raid destroying the forests of Eastern North America and Central Europe, nuclear waste that will remain deadly long after the pyramids have crumbled, avoidable harm inflicted upon consumers by unsafe products, and so on. Arnold implies that the only difference between the pure model of static equilibrium so beloved by mainstream economists and the real world is the pure profits claimed by entrepreneurs as a reward for correcting malallocations through upsetting that equilibrium (388). Unfortunately there

are also a number of less pleasant features of the real world that this model also fails to capture.

3. It is not possible to determine further what this aspect of an approach to an optimal allocation would involve. The level of productivity attained in the given society, the reserve funds that must be set aside in case of future catastrophe, funds for replacing and expanding productive capacity, etc. would all have to be taken into account. Some trade-offs would have to be made. If the reproduction of the society is to take place, not all produced goods and services can be distributed back to those who produced them. The question to be asked here is not whether such trade-offs are necessary, but whether there is a systematic bias in how they are made within many sorts of market societies.

4. The notion of structural power is developed at greater lengths in Lukes (1974).

Part Four: Three Normative Models

1. It should be stressed that this question cannot be answered in an ahistorical fashion. Social policy in general is always formulated within a specific historical context; this holds as well for reflection on what its ultimate end ought to be. The historical nature of normative models discussed by social theorists will be evident in the three chapters that make up this part.

Chapter VII

1. For example, Riley (1983) interprets Kant's political philosophy in terms of a category taken from his theory of judgment: teleology. Shell (1980) in contrast, interprets Kant's system as a whole in terms of a category taken from his political philosophy: property. The clearest exposition of Kant's political views in English is Howard Williams (1983).

2. The emphasis on the "right" or the "just" (the German *Recht* can be translated both ways) was taken over by Kant from Rousseau, as Shell (1980) has stressed.

3. At the turn of the century there was an extensive discussion in German-speaking countries between socialists and Kantians regarding the relationship of the two systems of thought. The major contributions to this debate are now collected in Sandkuhler and de la Vega (1970). This discussion broke off with the start of the First World War. It was renewed with Goldmann

(1971). More recently Howard (1980) has tackled this topic in a number of articles.

4. Indeed it can be seen as the central principle of his system as a whole. See Kaulbach (1978).

5. On the distinction between a doctrine of virtue and a doctrine of right, see Hoffe (1979). (In this chapter I shall discuss under the heading "doctrine of right" not just the work with this title in German (translated into English as "Metaphysical Elements of Justice"), but Kant's other works in political philosophy as well.)

6. Kant, "On the Common Saying: 'This May be True in Theory, but it does not Apply in Practice'" (Kant 1970, 73). (Henceforth "On the Common Saying").

7. "No-one can compel me to be happy in accordance with his conception of the welfare of others, for each may seek his happiness in whatever way he sees fit, so long as he does not infringe upon the freedom of others to pursue a similiar end which can be reconciled with the freedom of everyone else within a workable law—i.e. he must accord to others the same right as he enjoys himself" ("On the Common Saying," in Kant 1970, 74).

8. "External and rightful *equality* within a state is the relationship among the citizens whereby no-one can put anyone else under a legal obligation without submitting simultaneously to a law which requires that he can himself be put under the same kind of obligation by the other person" ("Perpetual Peace," in Kant 1970, 99).

9. These issues are discussed in Kant (1965) under the heading "Private Law."

10. This is discussed in Kant (1965) under the heading "Public Law."

11. This feature of Kant's political philosophy has been stressed by Habermas (1962), "Publizität als Vermittlung von Politik und Moral," 127–44).

12. "An Answer to the Question: 'What is Enlightenment?'" (Kant 1970, 55). (Hereafter "What is Enlightenment?").

13. "Idea for a Universal History with a Cosmopolitan Purpose" (in Kant 1970, 50).

14. This was first pointed out by Hemleben (1943).

15. This process is described in detail in Dobb (1947). The case of the United States is typical. In 1780, just before Kant wrote his major works in political philosophy, only 15 percent of the economically active population worked for a wage or salary. By 1880, after the shift from merchant to industrial capitalism, 63 percent had to work for wages or salaries. In 1970 only 9 percent were self-employed; 91 percent were wage and salary

employees. See Main (1965, 279–71); and Reich (1978, 180). Similiar data for France and Germany are presented in Mandel (1968, 164–65).

16. Recent accounts of this are found in Braverman (1974) and Edwards (1979). In 1977, 91.4 percent of all wage and salary workers in the United States worked under a supervisor or boss; only 8.6 percent worked without direct supervision (Institute for Social Research 1979, 175). For a philosophical discussion of how work under capitalism denies autonomy, see Sankowski (1981). Sankowski's arguments are not at all undercut by the current fad for Quality Circles. These Quality Circles foster not the participation of workers in self mangement, but pseudoparticipation as defined by Pateman (1970).

17. Here too we can take U.S. economic development as typical of a process that has occured throughout the capitalist system since Kant's day. At the time of the American Revolution the least-affluent 90 percent of families in the colonies owned well over half of all personal wealth. By 1870 they controlled only one-third, the wealthiest 10 percent of families controlling the remaining two-thirds, a distribution that has remained roughly constant since despite the growth of transfer programs. See Jones (1977) and Soltow (1975). Inequality is even more extensive when we look at stock control and not just personal wealth. Less than 1 percent of U.S. households control half of all corporate stock (United States Bureau of Census 1981, Table 786). For white males someone from the wealthiest 10 percent of households is more than ten times as likely to end up in the top 20 percent of the income distribution as someone from the poorest 10 percent (Bowles and Gintis 1976, chap. 5). If an average boy from one of the poorest families could choose between acquiring "average intelligence" or joining a family of average affluence, the latter would be a ten times more effective way of "making it" (Bowles and Gintis 1976, Figure 4.2).

18. One does not have to be a Marxist to acknowledge this point. Consider the following passage from Max Weber (1968): "The formal right of a worker to enter into any contract whatsoever with any employer whatsoever does not in practice represent for the employment seeker even the slightest freedom in the determination of his own conditions of work, and it does not guarantee him any influence on this process. It rather means, at least primarily, that the more powerful party in the market, i.e. normally the employer, has the possibility to set the terms, to offer the job 'take it or leave it,' and, given the normally more pressing economic need of the worker, to impose his terms upon him. . . . Coercion is exercised to a considerable extent by the private owners of the means of production and acquisition, to whom the law guarantees their property and whose power can thus manifest itself in the competitive struggle of the market" (2:729–30).

19. See Cirino (1972) and Kellner (1981). Some of the conceptual issues that arise regarding this form of power are discussed in Lukes (1974).

20. See William Appleman Williams (1980) for empirical confirmation of this point.

21. This was pointed out by Howard Williams (1983): "Kant's optimism is misplaced though where he suggests that the growth of international trade and commerce can only lead to co-operation and peace. . . . . [C]ompetition for markets and raw materials has led to great political instability and often war" (17–18).

22. Marx's defense of council democracy is most explicit in his writings on the Paris Commune, especially "The Civil War in France" (in Marx and Engels 1978, 618ff). He argues there, for instance, that the working class should safeguard itself against its own deputies and officials by having all those who exercise authority be elected, subject to recall, and paid only average workperson's wages. The following description of how a council democracy system might function is based on Albert and Hahnel (1981). In the text the discussion is limited to the exercise of economic power. Albert and Hahnel extend the principle of democratic participation to the political, kinship, and community spheres as well.

23. For a summary of these studies see Paul Blumberg (1973, 124–28). Of course under capitalism these experiments have been quite limited in scope. Those who own/control capital generally choose to retain control over production at the cost of a more efficient method of production.

24. Of course measures would have to be taken to ensure the protection of minorities from the "tyranny of the majority." Some of these measures are discussed in Albert and Hahnel (1981, 353–54).

Chapter VIII

1. I shall limit my remarks to the position Rawls defended in his magnum opus, *A Theory of Justice* (1971). All page references in the text are to this work.

2. Rawls writes that "throughout the choice between a private-property economy and socialism is left open; from the standpoint of the theory of justice alone, various basic structures would appear to satisfy its principles" (258). But his references to socialism are fleeting and vague, while his discussion of market-driven economies is relatively extensive and detailed. It is as a defender of welfare-state capitalism that Rawls is best known, and we will only concern ourselves with him as such. Also, the term "market societies" refers to those societies in which markets provide the main mech-

anisms of economic reproduction, *not* those in which markets hold a subordinate place in the reproduction process.

3. People under the veil of ignorance attempting to assess different institutional models are ignorant of the particularities of their own interests. In Rawls's thought experiment, however, "It is taken for granted . . . that they know the general facts about human society. They understand political affairs and the principles of economic theory; they know the basis of social organization and the laws of human psychology" (137).

4. Wolff (1977) states that Rawls "has no theory of the state" (202). Barry (1978) has already pointed out that this claim is not accurate in his review article of Wolff's book. I hope to substantiate Barry's point in detail in the following discussion.

5. If some formulation of the Marxian theory of exploitation (surplus value) and the theses regarding the state deducible from that theory were accepted as "general facts," then the claim under discussion could be established at once. Here, however, the attempt will be made to establish this claim without counting either the labor theory of value or equally controversial (but by no means indefensible) principles as general facts.

6. *Why* do supply and demand get out of sync? One clue is found in Rawls' discussion of "the problem of isolation." He limits the discussion of the problem to questions of providing public goods (269). This limiting is a mistake. He writes that "the problem arises whenever the outcome of the many individuals' decisions made in isolation is worse for everyone than some other course of action, even though, taking the conduct of the others as given, each person's decision is perfectly rational" (269). This problem threatens *all* market transactions. If a new growth area emerges in which one's competitors are investing, it is rational for an individual corporation to invest there too. Otherwise it risks being left behind and ultimately swallowed up by its competitors. But the result of this rational decision, when repeated by other individual corporations, is irrational. Soon there is more productive capacity in this sector than the market can handle, i.e., a crisis of *overproduction*. Similarly, if one's competitors can lower their wage costs, then it is rational for an individual firm to do so as well. Otherwise its competitors, with lower production costs, will be able to underprice it. But the result of this rational decision, when repeated by other individual firms, is irrational. The consumer market weakens and there is not sufficient purchasing power for the available supply of goods, i.e., a crisis of *undercomsumption*. If Rawls had reflected upon the structural tendencies to crisis that result from the problem of isolation in capitalism he perhaps would have been less sanguine regarding the difficulties faced by a stabilization branch of government within a capitalist state.

7. Robert Heilbroner (1979, 192). Keynes (1964) himself came close to grasping this when remarking on the probable effects of countercyclical policies. He writes, "Instead of constant prices in conditions of unemployment, and of prices rising in proportion to the quantity of money in conditions of full employment, we have in fact a condition of prices rising gradually as employment increases" (296). What Keynes missed here was that as the expectation of a "gradual" rise in prices spreads throughout the economy, this itself provides a sufficient condition for a somewhat more than gradual rise in prices. There are, of course, other structural mechanisms leading to inflation in Rawls' model besides the one mentioned here. For example, given the allocation branch's inability to prevent the formation of concentrated market power, there tends to be an upward bias in the general price level. This is because under oligopoly it is easier for firms to avoid price wars. On this issue see *Monopoly Capital*, by Baran and Sweezy 1966, Chapters 3 and 5.

8. It should be noted in passing that this line of reasoning also undercuts Rawls's theory of wages (304ff.). Rawls states that wages reflect a worker's "contribution" to the firm. This presupposes that the two parties to the wage contract negotiate on an equal footing. But the controllers of capital possess both the productive resources of the society and a considerable reserve fund. Their subsistence is not immediately threatened; they can afford to wait. Workers, in contrast, do not possess any reserves to speak of beyond their hands and minds, which they must hire out within a relatively short period of time if they and their families are to survive. Mandel (1968) writes of the working class: "Not being in a position to 'await a more propitious moment of the conjuncture,' it is thus compelled to accept a wage which is not determined by the marginal productivity of labor. . . . The dice are loaded." Mandel notes that for negotiation to be on an equal footing, "workers should likewise possess reserves of foodstuffs, or money, that would enable them to supply their needs and those of their families, for several years," just as capitalists do now. Perhaps then wages would reflect contribution. But, as Mandel concludes, "it is obvious that in a society like this there would neither exist a monopoly of capital in the hands of the bourgeoisie nor a proletariat as a class, so that it would not be a capitalist society" (1:300–301).

9. For a discussion of long waves of decline see Mandel (1978).

10. Rawls states (263) that the system he advocates is "homogeneous" in that "everyone has a similiar sense of justice." Despite this, however, those who have accumulated capital are likely to regard as their rightful prerogative ultimate control over the capital they have accumulated, the labor power

they have hired, etc., even when this goes against the "sense of justice" of the rest of society. After all, incentives are given to them to maximize their profits, and these are simply means that can be employed towards that end.

11. Post–World War II Sweden is often proposed as a historical approximation of a Rawlsian model. Do not forty years of social democratic rule in Sweden prove that a liberal capitalism structured along Rawlsian lines is indeed possible, contrary to the thesis of the present paper? To answer this we must consider whether the Swedish state fulfills the tasks Rawls assigns to the four branches of government.

(1) In Sweden there exists a considerable concentration of economic power, both regarding corporations ("Fifty large private firms employ 47 percent of all industrial workers and produce over one-half of all goods" [Thorburn 1973, 62]), and regarding ownership of these corporations ("Fifteen families together with two corporations have majority control in 200 large Swedish industrial concerns that employ over 450,000 people, almost half of all those employed in private industry. This represents a very high degree of economic concentration" [Tomasson 1970, 224]).

(2) The postwar Swedish economy has been plagued by regional disparities, stagnation, inflation, and unemployment (cf. Thorburn 1973 and Stevenson 1974, 42–44).

(3) Inequality in the distribution of wealth in Sweden is only marginally better than in other capitalist countries, with 2 percent of the people holding 20 percent of the wealth and the bottom 50 percent having only 25 percent of the wealth to divide (Stevenson 1974, 45).

(4) A study of the taxation system in Sweden concludes that, "The effect has been a horizontal rather than a vertical equalization; the income earned by one person during his working lifetime is levelled out, but not the income as between different categories of earners. . . . [M]any of the benefits offered by the public sector . . . have been utilized in greater measure by the already affluent" (Samuelsson 1968, 254). The regressiveness of other taxes all but eliminates the progressiveness of Sweden's federal income tax ("The regressive value-added tax (now 17.65 percent), the rise of the proportional municipal tax (now averaging 24 percent), the abolition of estate tax and the lowering of the corporation tax have all reduced the equalization effect of taxation" (Thorburn 1973, 63). It would appear, then, that the tasks assigned by Rawls to the allocation, stabilization, transfer and distribution branches of government, respectively, are not being fulfilled in Sweden, at least not to the extent required to provide a historical proof of the possibility of Rawls's model.

Chapter IX

1. "The economic system exchanges wages for rendered labor (as an input factor), as well as goods and rendered services (as output of its own production) for the demand from consumers. Public administration exchanges organizational achievements for taxes (as an input factor), and political decisions (as output of its own production) for mass loyalty . . . From the perspective of the life world the social roles of employees and consumers, on the one hand, and clients and state citizens, on the other, crystalize around these exchange relations" (472). All translations from this work are my own. All page references in text are to volume 2 of this work, unless noted otherwise.

2. "When one proceeds from a model of the exchange between formally organized spheres of action in the economy and the polity on the one side, and communicatively structured spheres of action in the private sphere and the public on the other, one must account for the fact that the problems which arise in the work world are transferred out of the private and into the public spheres of life, and are there changed under conditions of competing democratic will formation into mortgages on legitimation. The social, i.e., initially private, consequences of class conflict cannot be kept apart from the political public. Thus the social state becomes the political content of mass democracy. This shows that the political system cannot be emancipated from the use-value orientation of state citizens without effect; it cannot produce mass loyalty to any degree it wishes, but must rather also make testable offers of legitimation by means of social state programs" (510).

3. "The politically propped-up internal dynamic of the economic system results in a more or less continuous increase in the system's complexity, which means both the extension and the internal concentration of formally organized realms of action. At first this holds for relations within the subsystems of the economy and public administration and for the interactions of the subsystems between each other. . . . But the growth of the whole complex affects just as greatly the interchange of the subsystems with these spheres of the life world that have been redefined in the system-world. Chief among these redefined spheres are, on the one hand, the private households that are redefined by mass consumerism and, on the other hand, coordinated client services that are redefined by bureaucratic concerns" (515–16).

4. Habermas discusses the pathological consequences of state legislation regarding the family and schools (41ff.), social insurance (531), bureaucratically administered therapy programs (533), manipulation of public opinion (507), etc.

5. For Marx's proposal for the life world to reincorporate the economic subsystem, see his "Critique of the Gotha Program" (in Marx and Engels 1978, 525–41). His most explicit remarks regarding the reincorporation of the subsystem of political administration are to be found in "The Civil War in France" (in Marx and Engels 1978, 618–52). Regarding the former, Habermas correctly writes that the goal of the praxis Marx advocates is "to destroy the institutional foundation of the media through which the capitalist economy is differentiated (from the life world) together with private ownership of the means of production, and to incorporate the systematically independent process of economic growth back within the horizon of the new life world" (500). This goal is common to the classical tradition of Marxist theory, including Lenin, Luxemburg, Trotsky, Gramsci, and Mandel.

6. "Thus Marx's starting point of interpretation does not let the question arise whether the systematic connection of the capitalist economy and the modern state does not *also* present a higher and evolutionary privileged integration level. . . . Marx grasps capitalist society as a totality to such an extent that he misses the unique evolutionary *value* that subsystems directed by media, i.e. money and power, possess. Marx doesn't see that the differentiation of state apparatus and economy *also* presents a higher level of systems differentiation, which simultaneously opens up new steering capacities *and* demands a reorganization of the old, feudal, class relations. . . . [He] deceived himself over the fact that *every* modern society, no matter how its class structure is constituted, must show a high degree of structural differentiation (499–500). Also note Habermas's comment, "Bureaucratization must count as a normal component of the modernization process" (471).

7. Edwards, Reich, and Weiskopf (1978, 267). Pateman (1970) developes this point both theoretically and through a number of empirical studies.

8. Habermas gives this as a further reason to distance himself from Marxism. He writes: "Marxist orthodoxy has difficulty formulating a plausible explanation of state interventionism, mass democracy, and the welfare state. The economistic beginning fails vis-à-vis the pacification of class conflict and the long-term success that reformism has achieved in the European lands since the Second World War, under the banners of a social democratic program in a broader sense" (505). Whether Habermas is correct in his estimate of the achievement of the social state will be discussed in this chapter. But here it should be pointed out that Marx *does* have an explanation for the strategies of class pacification pursued by the social state. Similar strategies were proposed by the "democratic petite bourgeoisie" of his own day, which Marx explained as follows: "As far as the workers are concerned, it is certain above all that they are to remain wage-workers as before; the democratic

petite bourgeoisie only desire better wages and a more secure existence for the workers and hope to achieve this through partial employment by the state and through charity measures; in short, they hope to bribe the workers by more or less concealed alms and to sap their revolutionary vigor by making their position tolerable for the moment" ("Address of the Central Authority to the League," in Marx and Engels, various dates, 10:280).

9. "Just as the recipients of stock dividends often choose not to work, so too might others if welfare benefits, unemployment compensation, etc. were adequate and readily available. After all, capitalist ideology glorifies the pursuit of self-interest and provides little concept of social obligation. Moreover, in a system of alienated labor, individual material rewards (rather than, for example, the social necessity of production or the intrinsic rewards of the job) are the chief motivation to work; if an alternate means of livelihood are provided, large numbers of people might well quit work. 'Decent' welfare benefits would thus come into serious competition with low-wage, boring, exhausting, and dangerous wage-labor" (Edwards 1978, 308).

10. Habermas writes, "In the social state the roles which the occupational system offers are normalized, so to speak": (514). This is certainly news to the corporate community, which is presently instituting a massive restructuring of the labor process with the goal of increasing their profits. *Business Week* (May 16, 1983) lists some of their strategies: "Cutting size of crews; enlarging jobs by adding duties; . . . giving up relief and wash-up periods; . . . working more hours for the same pay," (100).

11. "In the developed societies of the West conflicts have developed in the last one to two decades that in many respects deviate from the social-structure paradigm of institutionalized distributional conflicts. They no longer flare up in the realms of material reproduction, they are not channeled in parties and associations, and they also will not be made to disappear by system-conforming compensations. The conflicts appear much more in the realms of cultural reproduction, social integration, and socialization; they are borne by subinstitutional or at least extraparliamentary forms of protest; and the basic shortcomings they point to mirror a reification of communicatively structured realms of action, which cannot be overcome through the media money and power. It is not primarily a matter of compensations, which the social state can guarantee, but of the defense and restitution of endangered modes of life, or the carrying through of new ones" (576).

12. "All these wasted resources add up. We can compute how much output—measured in terms of goods and services in market—the economy *could* have produced if our resources were used in their fullest potential. During the last completed business cycle from 1973 to 1978, according to the govern-

ment's fairly conservative methods for computing potential output, the economy produced at an average of 13 percent below capacity. This means that production in 1978, a year of peak prosperity during the business cycle, could still have been almost $300 billion more than it was. *The economy wasted nearly one-seventh of its potential output during the mid-70's."* (Institute of Labor Education and Research 1982, 161).

Chapter X

1. These remarks are found in Oelmuller (1978). They were made in response to queries from Thomas McCarthy, who was the first to remark on the importance of showing the priority of communicative action for the coherence of Habermas's position.

2. In strategic situations the balance of power determines the results, for "normally, power is asymmetrically divided; then one side can hinder the other in the (strategically effective) following of their own interests, or the one side can force their own interests on the other" (Habermas and Luhmann 1972, 252).

3. What Habermas terms "structural power" usually is termed "ideological hegemony" in Marxist literature.

4. "Only a rigid sociocultural system, incapable of being randomly functionalized for the needs of the administrative system, could explain a sharpening of legitimation difficulties into a legitimation crisis. A legitimation crisis can be predicted only if expectations that cannot be fulfilled either with the available quantity of value or, generally, with rewards conforming to the system, are systematically produced. A legitimation crisis, then, must be based on a motivational crisis – that is, a discrepancy between the need for motives declared by the state, the educational system and the occupational system on the one hand, and the motivation supplied by the sociocultural system on the other" (Habermas 1975, 74–75). Both legitimation crisis and motivation crisis fit under the general heading of forms of *cultural crisis*.

5. A methodological presupposition should be mentioned as well: "In coordinating motivational patterns with stable traditional cultural patterns, I start with the oversimplified assumption that attitudinal syndromes typical of a society must somehow be represented at the level of socially effective cultural value systems. I also rely on a correspondence of meaning structures at the levels of interpreted needs and cultural tradition" (Habermas 1975, 75–76).

6. Assuming that phenomena of the following sort can be avoided: "the retreatist-sided [of the youth movement] represented by hippies, Jesus-

people, the drug subculture, phenomena of undermotivation in school, etc."
(Habermas 1975, 92). Today we would add the New Age movement and
MTV-style hyperconsumerism to this list.

7. As we shall see in the following chapter, Habermas is also well aware
that in contemporary society motives are formed in a manner that allows
the satisfaction of particular interest to masquerade behind a claim to function as "objective" imperatives demanded on scientific-technical grounds.
However he does not present an argument as to why this form of motive
formation will be less significant than motivations based on universalistic
moralities. He does attempt to do this with respect to motivations based
on nationalism, and so I have limited my discussion to this example.

8. Habermas is referring to movements such as that for women's rights.

9. It is true that Habermas writes that a cultural tradition loses its legitimating force "as soon as it is objectivistically prepared and strategically employed" (Habermas 1975, 70–71). But unfortunately this is merely wishful
thinking. For how many centuries was the cultural tradition embodied in
the phrase "for God and King" "strategically employed" before losing its force?

10. Habermas 1973b, 40. Habermas discusses some of the topics considered
in this chapter in a much more concrete way in his recent article "Recht
und Gewalt—ein deutsches Trauma" (in Habermas 1985a, 100–17).

Chapter XI

1. An analysis of an example of problematic scientific research largely performed in a university setting can be found in Smith (1989).

2. Noble describes how this process occurred first in Germany and only
later came to characterize the United States.

3. Of course, as noted in Chapter IV the mere fact that a certain type of
change would be functional for a social system is no guarantee that such
a change takes place. The struggle to bring about this change must first be
successful. Noble (1977) describes this struggle as follows: "In the early nineteenth century the colleges were firmly in the hands of the classicists and
the clerics, and there was considerable academic disdain for the study of
experimental science and even more for the teaching of the useful arts.
Technical education . . . developed in struggle with the classical colleges,
both inside and outside of them. One form of this development was the
gradual growth of technological studies within the classical colleges, resulting
from the reorientation of natural philosophy toward the empirical, experimental, scientific search for truth and from the pressures of some scien-

tists and powerful industrialists for practical instruction; the other was the rise of technical colleges and institutes outside of the traditional colleges in response to the demands of internal improvement projects like canal-building, railroads, manufactures, and, eventually, science-based industry" (20). Here, too, this occurred in Germany prior to the United States.

4. "In the industrially developed lands the maintenance of the social system has become ever more dependent upon the vocational qualifications and scientific information produced in the universities. . . . In the measure that individual scholarship gives way to organized research and science becomes the foremost productive force, the universities (which today demand considerable investment) become integrated—partly spontaneously and partly according to plan—in a growth-oriented, state interventionist social system". ("Demokratisierung der Hochschule—Politisierung der Wissenschaft?" in (Habermas 1981a, 189–90).

5. "All attempts on the part of academic philosophy to interpret the knowledge of relativity theory, atomic theory, organic chemistry, virus research, morphology, animal psychology, etc., into traditional categories— even attempts which take seriously the undermining of the classical framework and do not resort to a conventional interpretation—have reached for the time being hardly more than the speculations of philosophizing special scientists, speculations not free from naivete" ("Das chronische Leiden," Habermas 1981a, 36).

6. Habermas (1981a) discusses Schelsky's view of the educational system in "Konservativer Geist—und die modernistischen Folgen" (41–57).

7. "Vom sozialen Wandel akademischer Bildung" (in Habermas 1981a, 108–9).

8. See "The Scientization of Politics and Public Opinion" (in Habermas 1970a, 62–80).

9. "Für ein neues Konzept der Hochschulverfassung" (in Habermas 1981a, 175).

Selected Bibliography

Ackerman, Frank, and A. Zimbalist. 1978. "Capitalism and Inequality in the United States." In Edwards et al. (1978), 297–86.

Albert, Michael, and R. Hahnel. 1981. *Socialism Today and Tomorrow*. Boston: South End Press.

Alexy, Robert. 1978. "Eine Theorie des praktischen Diskurs." In Oelmuller (1978).

Arnold, N. Scott. 1987. "Why Profits are Deserved." *Ethics*, 97:387–402.

Baran, Paul, and P. Sweezy. 1966. *Monopoly Capital*. New York: Monthly Review Press.

Barry, Brian. 1978. "Review of *Understanding Rawls*. R. P. Wolff." *Canadian Journal of Philosophy*, 8, (4):753–83.

Baumgarten, E., ed. 1964. *Max Weber: Werk und Person*. Tübingen: Mohr.

Beatty, Joseph. 1979. "Communicative Competence and the Skeptic." *Philosophy and Social Criticism*, 6 (3):267–88.

Bernstein, Richard J., ed., 1985. *Habermas and Modernity*. Cambridge: M.I.T. Press.

Blumberg, Paul. 1973. *Industrial Democracy: The Sociology of Participation*. New York: Schocken Books.

Bowles, Samuel, and H. Gintis. 1976. *Schooling in Capitalist America*. New York: Basic Books.

Brandt, Reinhard. 1974. *Eigentumstheorien von Grotius bis Kant*. Stuttgart.

Braverman, Harry. 1974. *Labor and Monopoly Capital*. New York: Monthly Review Press.

Brewer, Anthony. 1980. *Marxist Theories of Imperialism: A Critical Survey*. Boston: Routledge & Kegan Paul.

Broddy, Raford, and James Crotty, 1975. "Class Conflict and Macro-Policy: The Political Business Cycle." *Review of Radical Political Economics*, 7 (1):1–19.

Castells, Manuel. 1980. *The Economic Crisis and American Society*. Princeton: Princeton University Press.

Cirino, Robert. 1972. *Don't Blame the People*. New York: Vintage.

Cohen, G. A. 1978. *Karl Marx's Theory of History: A Defense*. Princeton: Princeton University Press.

———. 1980. "Funtional Explanation: Reply to Elster." *Political Studies*, 28 (1):129–35.

———. 1982a. "Functional Explanation, Consequence Explanation, and Marxism." *Inquiry*, 25:27–56.

———. 1982b. "Reply to Elster on 'Marxism, Functionalism, and Game Theory'." *Theory and Socity*, 11:483–96.

Connerton, Paul. 1980. *The Tragedy of Enlightenment*. New York: Cambridge University Press.

De George, Richard T. 1982. *Business Ethics*. New York: Macmillan.

Dinham, Barbara, and C. Hines. 1984. *Agribusiness in Africa*. Trenton, N.J.: Africa World Press.

Dobb, Maurice. 1947. *Studies in the Development of Capitalism*. New York: International.

Eder, Klaus. 1976. *Die Entstehung staatlich organisierter Gesellschaften: Ein Beitrag zu einer Theorie sozialer Evolution.* Frankfurt: Suhrkamp.

Edwards, Richard. 1978. "Who Fares Well in the Welfare State?" In Edwards et al. (1978), 307–14.

——. 1979. *Contested Terrain.* New York: Basic Books.

Edwards, Richard, M. Reich, and T. Weisskopf, eds. 1978. *The Capitalist System.* Englewood Cliffs, N.J.: Prentice-Hall.

Fahrenback, E., ed. 1973. *Wirklichkeit und Reflexion.* Pfullingen: Neske.

Federal Trade Commission, 1969. "On the Influence of Market Structure on the Profit Performance of Food Manufacturing Companies."

Foucault, Michel. 1980. *Power/Knowledge.* New York: Pantheon.

Gadamer, Hans-Georg. 1975. *Truth and Method.* New York: Seabury.

George, Susan. 1984. *Ill Fares the Land: Essays on Food, Hunger, and Power.* Washington, D.C.: Institute for Policy Studies.

Goldmann, Lucien. 1971. *Immanuel Kant.* London: New Left Books.

Gordan, David, et al. 1982. *Segmented Work, Divided Workers: The Historical Transformation of Labor in the United States.* New York: Cambridge University Press.

Goslin, David, ed. 1969. *Handbook of Socialization and Research.* Chicago: Rand McNally.

Grcic, Joseph. 1981. "Rawls and Socialism." *Philosophy and Social Criticism,* 8 (1):17–36.

Habermas. Jürgen. 1962. *Strukturwandel der Öffentlichkeit.* Darmstadt: Luchterhand.

——. 1970a. *Toward a Rational Society.* Boston: Beacon.

——. 1970b. *Zur Logik der Sozialwissenschaften.* Frankfurt: Suhrkamp.

————. 1971. *Theorie und Praxis.* Frankfurt: Suhrkamp.

————. 1973a. *Philosophische-politische Profile.* Frankfurt: Suhrkamp.

————. 1973b. *Theory and Practice.* Boston: Beacon.

————. 1973c. "Wahrheitstheorien." In Fahrenback, ed. (1973), 211–65.

————. 1975. *Legitimation Crisis in Late Capitalism.* Boston: Beacon Press.

————. 1976. *Zur Rekonstruktion des historischen Materialismus.* Frankfurt: Suhrkamp.

————. 1978. *Politik, Kunst, Religion.* Stuttgart: Reclam.

————. 1979a. *Communication and the Evolution of Society.* Boston: Beacon.

————. 1979b. "Interview." *Telos,* no. 39:163–71.

————. 1981a. *Kleine Politische Schriften I–IV.* Frankfurt: Suhrkamp.

————. 1981b. *Theorien des kommunikativen Handelns.* 2 volumes. Frankfurt: Suhrkamp.

————. 1982. "A Reply to my Critics." In Thompson and Held (1982):219–83.

————. 1983. *MoralbewuBtsein und kommunikatives Handeln.* Frankfurt: Suhrkamp.

————. 1985a. *Die neue Unübersichtlichkeit.* Frankfurt: Suhrkamp.

————. 1985b. *Der philosophische Diskurs der Moderne.* Frankfurt: Suhrkamp.

Habermas, Jürgen, and N. Luhmann, eds. 1972. *Theorie der Gesellschaft oder Sozialtechnologie?.* Frankfurt: Suhrkamp.

Hegel, G. W. F. 1956. *The Philosophy of History.* New York: Dover.

Heilbroner, Robert. 1979. "Reflections: Inflationary Capitalism." *New Yorker* (October 8):121–41.

Heller, Agnes. 1982. "Habermas and Marxism." In Thompson and Held (1982):21–41.

Hemleben, S. J. 1943. *Plans for Peace through Six Centuries*. Chicago: University of Chicago Press.

Hodgson, Geoff. 1982. *Capitalism, Value, and Exploitation*. Oxford: Martin Robertson.

Hoffe, Otfried. 1977. "Kants Kategorischen Imperativ als Kriterium des Sittlichen." *Zeitschrift für philosophische Forschung*, 31:354–384.

———. 1979. "Recht und Moral; ein kantischen Problemaufriss." *Neue Hefte für Philosophie*, 17:1–36.

Howard, Dick. 1980. "Kant's Political Theory: The Virtues of His Vices." *Review of Metaphysics*, 34:325–50.

Ingram, David. 1987. *Habermas and the Dialectic of Reason*. New Haven: Yale University Press.

Institute for Social Research. 1979. *Quality of Work Survey*. Ann Arbor: Institute for Social Research.

Institute of Labor Education and Research. 1982. *What's Wrong with the U.S. Economy?* Boston: South End.

Jay, Martin. 1973. *The Dialectical Imagination*. Boston: Little, Brown.

Jones, Alice. 1977. *American Colonial Wealth*. New York: Arno.

Kant, Immanuel. 1964. *Groundwork of the Metaphysic of Morals*. New York: Harper & Row.

———. 1965. *The Metaphysical Elements of Justice*. Indianapolis: Bobbs-Merrill.

———. 1970. *Kant's Political Writings*. Edited by Hans Reiss. New York: Cambridge University Press.

Kaulback, Freidrich. 1978. *Das Prinzip Handlung in der Philosophie Kants*. Berlin: Walter de Gruyter.

Kellner, Douglas. 1981. "Network Television and American Society." *Theory and Society*, 10:31–62.

Keynes, John M. 1964. *The General Theory of Employment, Interest and Money.* New York: Harbinger.

Kohlberg, Lawrence. 1969. "Stage and Sequence." In Goslin (1969), 347–80.

————. 1971. "From Is to Ought." In Mischel (1971):151–233.

Lappe, Francis Moore, and J. Collins. 1982. *Food First: Beyond the Myth of Scarcity.* New York: Ballantine.

Lonergan, Bernard. 1972. *Method in Theology.* New York: Herder & Herder.

Lukes, Steven. 1974. *Power.* London: Macmillan.

Magdoff, Harry, and P. Sweezy. 1981. *The Deepening Crisis of U.S. Capitalism.* New York: Monthly Review Press.

Main, Jackson. 1965. *The Social Structure of Revolutionary America.* Princeton: Princeton University Press.

Mandel, Ernest. 1968. *Marxist Economic Theory.* 2 volumes. New York: Monthly Review Press.

————. 1978. *Late Capitalism.* London: Verso.

————. 1986. "A Critique of Market Socialism." *New Left Review,* 159:5–38.

Marx, Karl, and F. Engels. 1978. *The Marx–Engels Reader.* Edited by Robert Tucker. New York: Norton.

————. 1975–90 (various dates). *Collected Works.* New York: International Publishing.

Matustik, Martin. 1989. "Habermas on Communicative Reason and Performative Contradiction." *New German Critique,* no. 47:143–72.

McCarthy, Thomas. 1984. *The Critical Theory of Jürgen Habermas.* Cambridge: Polity.

Merleu-Ponty, Maurice. 1969. *Humanism and Terror.* Boston: Beacon.

Miller, Richard. 1981. "Productive Forces and the Forces of

Change: A Review of Gerald A. Cohen, *Karl Marx's Theory of History: A Defense.*" *Philosophical Review*, 90 (1):91–117.

Mischel, Theodore. 1971. *Cognitive Development and Epistemology.* New York: Academic Press.

Mitchell, Juliet. 1977. *Women's Estate.* New York: Random House.

Nell, Edward. 1987. "On Deserving Profits." *Ethics*, 97:403–10.

Nichols, David. 1974. *Financing Elections: The Politics of an American Ruling Class.* New York: Franklin Watts.

Noble, David. 1977. *America By Design: Science, Technology and the Rise of Corporate Capitalism.* New York: Knopf.

Nozick, Robert. 1974. *Anarchy, State and Utopia.* New York: Basic Books.

O'Connor, James. 1973. *The Fiscal Crisis of the State.* New York: St. Martin's Press.

Oelmüller, Willi. 1978. *Transzendentalphilosophische Normenbegründung.* Paderborn: Schoningh.

Pateman, Carole. 1970. *Participation and Democratic Theory.* London: Cambridge University Press.

Piaget, Jean. 1965. *The Moral Judgement of the Child.* New York: Free Press.

Plekhanov, G. V., 1956. *The Development of the Monist View of History.* Moscow.

Polanyi, Karl. 1957. *The Great Transformation: The Political and Economic Origins of our Time.* Boston: Beacon.

Rawls, John. 1971. *A Theory of Justice.* Cambridge: Harvard University Press.

———. 1977. "The Basic Structure as Subject." *American Philosophical Quarterly*, 14 (2):159–66.

Reich, Michael. 1978. "The Development of the Wage-Labor Force." In Edwards et al. (1978), 179–84.

————. 1981. *Racial Inequality.* Princeton: Princeton University Press.

Ricardo, David. 1953. *On The Principles of Political Economy and Taxation.* In *The Works and Correspondence of David Ricardo, I.* Cambridge: Cambridge University Press.

Riley, Patrick. 1983. *Kant's Political Philosophy.* Totowa, N.J.: Rowman and Littlefield.

Rollin, Bernard. 1976. "There is Only One Categorical Imperative." *Kant Studien,* 67:60–72.

Rubin, David-Hillel. 1981. "Cohen, Marx and the Primacy Thesis." *British Journal of Political Science,* 11:227–34.

Saage, Richard. 1973. *Eigentum, Staat und Gesellschaft bei Immanuel Kant.* Stuttgart: Kohlhemmer.

Samuelsson, Kurt. 1968. *From Great Power to Welfare State.* London: Allen & Unwin.

Sandkuhler, Hans, and R. de la Vega. 1970. *Marxismus und Ethik: Texte zum neukantianischen Sozialismus.* Frankfurt: Suhrkamp.

Sankowski, Edward. 1981. "Freedom, Work, and the Scope of Democracy." *Ethics,* 91:228–42.

Schweickart, David. 1978. "Should Rawls be a Socialist?" *Social Theory and Practice,* 5 (1):1–28.

Sen, A. K. 1981. *Poverty and Famine: An Essay on Entitlement and Deprivation.* Oxford: Clarendon Press.

Shalgi, M. 1976. "Universalized Maxims." *Kant Studien,* 67:172–91.

Shell, Susan. 1980. *The Rights of Reason: A Study of Kant's Philosophy and Politics.* Toronto: University of Toronto Press.

Smith, Tony. 1989. "A Critical Examination of the Arguments for Food Irradiation." *Public Affairs Quarterly: A Journal of Philosophy and Public Policy,* 3 (4):15–25.

————. 1990. *The Logic of Marx's Capital.* Albany: State University of New York Press.

Soltow, Lee. 1975. *Men and Wealth in the United States.* New Haven: Yale University Press.

Stevenson, Paul. 1974. "Monopoly Capital and Inequalities in Swedish Society." *Insurgent Sociologist,* 5 (1):41–58.

Thompson, John, and D. Held. 1982. *Habermas: Critical Debates.* Cambridge: M.I.T. Press.

Thorburn, G. 1973. "The Swedish Road to Capitalism." *Canadian Dimension,* 9 (7–8):61–66.

Tinker, Jon. 1984. "Are Natural Disasters Natural?" *Socialist Review* No. 78:7–26.

Tomasson, R. 1970. *Sweden: Prototype of Modern Society.* New York: Random House.

Trotsky, Leon. 1973. *The Transitional Program for Socialist Revolution (The Agony of Capitalism).* New York: Pathfinder.

United States Bureau of the Census. 1981. *Statistical Abstract of the United States.* Washington, D.C.: U.S. Government Printing Office.

Van Parijs, Philippe. 1980. "Functionalist Marxism Rehabilitated." *Theory and Society,* 11:497–512.

Weber, Max. 1922. *Gesammelte Aufsätze zur Wissenschaftslehre.* Tübingen: Mohr.

———. 1949. *Max Weber on the Methodology of the Social Sciences.* Edited by Edward Shils and Henry Finch. Glencoe, Ill.: Free Press.

———. 1964. *The Theory of Social and Economic Organizations.* Edited by Talcott Parsons. New York: Free Press.

———. 1968. *Economy and Society.* 2 volumes. New York: Bedminster.

———. 1969. *From Max Weber.* Edited by Hans Gerth and C. Wright Mills. New York: Oxford University Press.

Wessel, James. 1983. *Trading the Future: Farm Exports and the Concentration of Economic Power in the Food System.* San Francisco: Institute for Food and Development Policy.

Williams, Howard, 1983. *Kant's Political Philosophy.* Oxford: Basil Blackwell.

Williams, William Appleman. 1980. *Empire as a Way of Life.* New York: Oxford University Press.

Wimmer, R. 1980. *Universalisierung in der Ethik.* Frankfurt: Suhrkamp.

Wolfe, Alan. 1978. *The Limits of Legitimacy.* New York: Free Press.

Wolff, Robert Paul. 1977. *Understanding Rawls.* Princeton: Princeton University Press.

Index